Profit from figures

A manager's guide to statistical methods

Other titles in the McGraw-Hill Management series

Bull The Director's Handbook
Foster & Bull The Director, his Money and his Job
Handley Industrial Safety Handbook
Humble Improving Business Results
Humble Management by Objectives in Action
McKinsey The Arts of Top Management
Reddin Managerial Effectiveness
Tatham The Use of Computers for Profit—a businessman's guide
Tomlin Managing the Introduction of Computer Systems

Profit from figures

A MANAGER'S GUIDE TO STATISTICAL METHODS

Cyril J. Anson

Senior Consultant, Urwick, Orr & Partners Limited

McGraw-Hill · London

New York · St Louis · San Francisco · Dusseldorf · Johannesburg · Kuala Lumpur · Mexico · Montreal · New Delhi · Panama · Rio de Janeiro · Singapore · Sydney · Toronto

Published by
McGRAW-HILL Book Company (UK) Limited
MAIDENHEAD . BERKSHIRE . ENGLAND

---

07 094228 5

PRINTED AND BOUND IN GREAT BRITAIN

Contents

Preface

This is a book for all managers from the chief executives of the largest companies to the most junior managers of the smallest. It is slanted towards the manufacturing and distribution industries but applications in banking, transport and local government have been discussed. The purpose of the book is to help managers to provide themselves with a more objective way of managing a business. Sound management is based on facts, which in many instances are expressed in the form of figures. Unfortunately, the measurements used in management produce figures, which are subject to chance fluctuations, and a special approach, the statistical approach, is needed to extract the meaning from them. Naturally, cost and profit are two of the most important measurements used but this is not a book about accounting techniques. It is not concerned with measuring profit but with making profit.

Some of the ideas contained in it are sufficiently straightforward for any manager to be capable of picking them up and applying them. The remainder, although straightforward and easy to understand, call for the assistance of specialists in their implementation. The book has drawn freely on material prepared for lectures and exercises on courses run at the Urwick Management Centre, particularly the General Management, Marketing and Sales Management, and Production Executive courses. Contact with members of these courses and practical experience on consultancy assignments has brought home the need to keep both a simplified outlook and a careful eye on the profit in the situation. These two characteristics have played a dominant role in the approach of this book.

It is intended that this book should be one to which a manager can refer from time to time. To make this easier a glossary of the terms used in the book has been prepared, and at the end of each chapter, the terms used in that chapter have been listed. If it is important to understand the meaning of a term, it is either defined in the chapter or in a previous chapter, in which case it will also occur in the glossary. If you want to read through an isolated chapter, first check the list of terms used in the chapter and then look up in the glossary the meaning of any unfamiliar term.

I should like to acknowledge the contribution of colleagues in the Urwick Group, distilled from discussions and reports. It would be wrong to single out any one of them from the rest. Their contribution has helped to mould the attitude to working with figures reflected in the book, and several of the applications have been based on their consultancy assignments.

Peter Davies, Hamish Donaldson, and Eddie Lambert read the original typescript and made practical suggestions on how it could be improved. They each said that they enjoyed doing this. Nevertheless, I would like to place on record my gratitude for their valuable help.

Tables 2.6; 2.9; and Figure 2.7 have been condensed and adapted from Tables 20; 39; 1 and 4 respectively of 'The Biometrika Tables for Statisticians, Volume 1' with the permission of the Trustees of 'Biometrika'.

Table 5.10 has been adapted from, and Table 5.11 is based on a nomograph in: Ewan, W. D. and Kemp, K. W. 'Sampling Inspection of Continuous Processes with no Autocorrelation between Successive Results'. Biometrika *47,* 363-380 (1960) by permission of Mr W. D. Ewan, Professor K. W. Kemp, and the Trustees of Biometrika.

Figure 8.3 has been condensed and adapted from Table XV of 'The British Association for the Advancement of Science Mathematical Tables Vol. 1' with permission of The Royal Society.

Cyril J. Anson

1. Management's correct use of figures: to improve profitability

In his search for improvement and control, a manager finds that he needs help from analytical and logical tools. He needs to measure plant efficiency; operator efficiency; daily orders received; costs against standard; and so on. He needs to analyse the figures which he has collected and to make the right conclusions from them. He needs to monitor the results arising from his decisions and indeed the figures on which he based these decisions. This book is designed as a simple guide to the practising manager on how he can make figures talk, how he can use them to make a bigger profit.

So far as possible, the pattern of each chapter of the book is the same

what are the benefits,
what are the principles,
what are the applications,
what are the snags?

There are snags. Perhaps the most difficult task is to change the way people think about figures. But there are considerable benefits.

In chapter 2 the basic tools of the statistical approach are introduced. It is these tools which enable the manager to reveal the pattern in the figures; to identify the true exception and to appreciate that the other fluctuations in the measurements have to be lived with; to measure the amount of variability in the figures; to identify and concentrate on the most important few, the 20 per cent which account for (say) 80 per cent of the sales. There are potential benefits in all areas of management arising from the use of the correct tools—there is an economic angle for the manager to identify and turn into profit.

The payoff from sampling, which is discussed in chapter 3, lies in speed, cost and reliability. The use of samples is well established in such areas as work sampling and quality control but it can be a valuable tool in carrying out special investigations. A key feature is to ensure, through proper planning, that effort and money are not wasted.

Chapter 4 covers the rewards and risks, as well as the techniques, in analysing figures. The objectives are to get a better estimate, and to make a better decision on the basis of that estimate. The rewards lie in more efficient use of machinery and manpower; in better control of excess costs; in reductions in stock levels; in better delivery promises; in better marketing and pricing policies; in improved industrial relations. Three areas of potential profit improvement are:

1. In finding out how to reduce the total variability of a process.
2. In manipulating the factors affecting the effectiveness of a process in order to bring about a significant improvement, and,
3. In determining underlying relationships—to build sound policies or to simplify the task of estimating.

Management's responsibility for controlling the present situation is covered by chapter 5 which deals with the techniques of monitoring. The statistical tools for monitoring performance enable the manager to avoid being misled by random fluctuations in the measurements used for monitoring. Increased efficiency, reduction in losses, increased output and a greater understanding of the business, all follow naturally from improved control. These tools simplify the manager's role in carrying out the holding operation and so free capacity for him to carry out improvement plans. Furthermore, there is a positive motivation provided by target setting and the correct monitoring of performance against target.

Forecasting is an essential function of management. Chapter 6 outlines an analytical approach which can improve the quality of forecasting and at the same time reduce the amount of time which a manager need spend on the inevitable routine. This approach provides invaluable information in addition to the forecast, namely a measure of the uncertainty of the forecasts.

Planning is a further essential function of management which can increase the efficient provisioning and use of the resources of manpower, machinery, finance and materials employed in business. Chapter 7 covers the role of figures in planning, either in deciding the level of buffers needed to accommodate the inherent uncertainty of a business, or in adaptive methods to build on the results of past experience. It also describes the basic techniques of network analysis and their application to project planning, with the objective of avoiding losses such as those which occur:

due to men and machines being idle;
due to lost sales arising from delay in going into production, or
due to the use of overtime or sub-contract labour.

Moreover, if routine responsibilities can be planned and then delegated, a manager can concentrate on exceptions and on the important few areas where the profit is being made.

Chapter 8 concentrates on finding a better way, and examines:

how to balance alternative losses when product outside one tolerance can be rectified much more cheaply than product outside the other;
how to put in the right bid to maximize the company's profit over an extended period of time;
how to calculate the quantity to order, so that the total costs of ordering and holding stock are minimized;
how to cut down the capital tied up in stocks and at the same time avoid the unbalanced stocks which can ruin service to customers;
how to make better use of limited resources, a problem which is particularly difficult to handle when the company is operating in the face of a large number of interwoven limitations.

Chapter 9 is a short chapter on the use of mathematical models and simulation, techniques which make it possible to tackle problems to which it is impossible to apply analytical methods. This is done by building a model of an operating situation in terms of logic and numerical information on which one can experiment without risk. In this way a paper exercise can generate facts on which to make a decision. The costs of building these models are usually high but the payoff in strategic decision making can far and away exceed the costs.

The role which computers play in making a profit from figures is described in chapter 10. The benefits of using a computer in this field are:

it becomes possible to tackle problems, where previously the amount of calculation was prohibitive;
it can be cheaper;
it can be quicker, and in all instances more accurate.

Furthermore, a computer can be used as a means of extending the management science skills in a small company, to bring expertise in such techniques as multiple regression analysis; network analysis; linear programming; sales forecasting; stock control and so on. Perhaps the greatest potential lies in the use of a computer and mathematical models to simulate the many possible alternatives facing a company.

This chapter is intended as an aperitif, perhaps a very light hors d'oeuvre. The nine chapters which follow show the techniques by which the benefits described in this chapter can be won. Making a profit from figures is not a job which staff advisers can do by themselves. Managers are involved—it is their problems to which these techniques are applied, and their responsibility to see that they are applied and improve profitability.

List of terms used

Variability
Sample
Work sampling
Quality control
Random fluctuations
Monitoring
Forecasting
Adaptive methods
Network analysis
Mathematical model
Simulation
Multiple regression analysis
Linear programming
Stock control

Italicized terms are defined in the glossary (page 262) as well as in the text where it is appropriate.

2. Scientific management means measurement

2.1. The growth of measurement in management

The progress in improving management has arisen primarily from the growing use of measurements. The relative worth of jobs is determined numerically by the tools of *job evaluation*; time standards are established by *work measurement*; and now *management by objectives* sets its objectives in a measurable form so that performance against the objectives may be quantified.

Moreover, there are many figures used to identify a company's performance: weekly orders received, invoiced sales, stock levels, vehicle miles travelled, production output in tons, barrels, yards or sterling. The arrival of the computer makes it easier to tabulate more and more figures. If we are not careful management will be swamped with figures, more up to date, analysed in all possible ways, but too much to comprehend. So, before it happens to you, realise that there is a need to make the figures talk.

There are statistical techniques which can help by identifying the pattern in the figures, but the first steps should be to ensure that the correct criterion is being measured. A typical instance occurred in a carpet manufacturing company during a sales forecasting study aimed at production planning. The introduction of new designs distorts the seasonal sales pattern since there is a tendency for these designs to have extremely high sales during their early months. So in order to obtain the seasonal sales pattern on the running lines the sales of new designs and dropped ones were eliminated from the sales figures.

In a company making heating components it was agreed that the sales forecasting for the budget should be based on the forecast of fifteen product groups. Unfortunately, the product groupings had been changed three times during the past five years. So, in order to prepare a forecast based on the past sales pattern for each product group, the available sales figures had to be amended with considerable labour and a degree of inaccuracy.

Even when they truly measure the factors to be controlled, the figures are often subject to considerable fluctuations which make their interpretation difficult. The innate uncertainty of business is reflected in the fluctuations in the figures used to measure performance. To assess the company's success at making money consider, for example, the differences between company invoiced sales and budget sales; between production records and targets; and between actual expenditure and standard expenditure. The company's performance will vary from week to week, and from month to month. How then can the figures be made to talk?

2.2. The statistical approach

When figures vary in this manner, as they inevitably do in industry and commerce, the problem of interpreting them can only be solved by adopting the statistical point of view. The nature of the statistical approach can be understood by considering how to handle the uncertainty in the lengths of the lives of television tubes. The only assurance that the salesman can give is 'I'm afraid I don't know sir, it may last six months or it may last six years'. At the end of the first week, the purchaser, watching his set, can be certain that it has lasted a week. He now knows more about the life of his television tube than the salesman. But consider the impudence of the men who write to him at this point: 'Dear Sir, We understand *you* have recently purchased a television set from Messrs Blank & Co. Ltd. We would be perfectly willing to insure the life of *your* television tube.' They haven't even seen his television set: both he and the salesman are better off, they have seen it and know it works. How do they know how long his television tube will last? In fact the insurance company are not interested in him as an individual, nor in his set as an individual set. They are interested in his tube only as a member of a group. If his tube failed at an early age, then someone else's tube with a long life would more than compensate. Television insurance companies (and life assurance companies also) rely on the basic statistical approach. They ignore the identity of the individual and study them as a group.

The insurance companies have developed extremely successful businesses based on measuring the degree of risk or uncertainty and arranging for the premiums paid by the members of the group to more than cover the expected outgoings. Managers can tackle problems in which the measurements are subject to uncertainty by adopting the same approach. The payoff in the field of stock control (safety or buffer stocks provide an insurance against stock run out) is almost incredible. Stock reductions of 25 per cent to 35 per cent are not unusual, often with a better and more consistent stock availability.

2.3. Patterns in figures—symmetrical patterns

The eye is a very poor device for detecting the pattern in a set of figures. Figures are read serially, one at a time, making it difficult if not almost impossible to merge the individual observations to form the pattern of the group. To paraphrase a well known saying 'One concentrates on the individual trees to such an extent that one often fails to realise that they form a wood'.

Table 2.1. Low stock levels

36	44	36	36	40
37	37	35	38	39
35	40	41	43	37
38	38	37	42	36
40	42	40	37	42
40	42	37	37	40
33	38	39	41	37
41	32	40	43	38
41	37	37	39	38
39	34	37	39	35

A retailer who replenishes his stocks at weekly intervals can note each week on each item the level to which the stock has fallen immediately before the replenishing stock arrives. These levels, the *low stock levels*, on one of his stock items over the last fifty weeks could well be figures such as those shown in Table 2.1.

The statistical approach is to disregard individual instances, not to try to find out why the level was thirty-six on the first week and the next week forty-four. Instead, attention is concentrated on how often, how frequently, each level occurred.

In practice this is done by making a tally diagram (Fig. 2.1). The numbers in the original table are examined in sequence and a tally mark made on the tally diagram opposite the appropriate number on each occasion it occurs. The number of times each low stock level occurred, called the *frequency*, can be readily counted from the tally diagram—especially if every fifth tally mark is used to tie them into bundles of five. The frequency of each low stock level has been recorded on the right hand side of Fig. 2.1.

Level	Tally	Frequency
32	1	1
33	1	1
34	1	1
35	111	3
36	1111	4
37	~~1111~~ ~~1111~~ 1	11
38	~~1111~~ 1	6
39	~~1111~~	5
40	~~1111~~ 11	7
41	1111	4
42	1111	4
43	11	2
44	1	1

Figure 2.1 Tally diagram for low stock levels

Once the frequency of each low stock level has been determined it is then represented in a frequency diagram (Fig. 2.2). This is done by erecting bars of equal width against each low stock level, whose heights are made proportionate to the appropriate frequency.

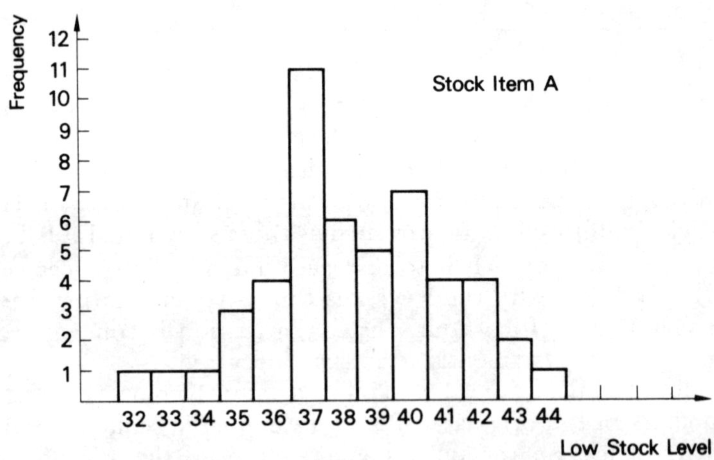

Figure 2.2 Frequency diagram for low stock levels

The visual impact of the frequency diagram is immediate. It is now impossible to see the individual observation: it is lost in the group whose pattern is clearly shown. It looks as though the low stock levels in this company, or this stock item at least, are subject to random fluctuations making them scatter about a central value of about thirty-eight. Moreover the profile of the diagram has a unity which suggests that the same fluctuations were operating during the whole period over which the figures were collected. There are no freaks or abnormalities. As the stock was never less than thirty-two, it also suggests that the stock holding could be reduced by twenty-five or thirty without affecting stock availability.

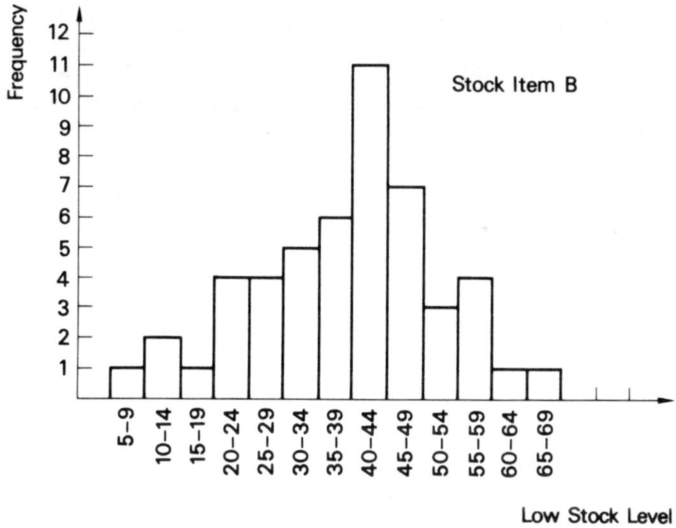

Figure 2.3 Frequency diagram for low stock levels—item with larger and more variable demand

The frequency diagram for the low stock levels on another item, B, is shown in Fig. 2.3. Once again the random fluctuations in demand cause the low stock levels to scatter about a central value of about forty. However in this instance the figures were so variable that in order to give a reasonable representation, the range of the results, from five to seventy, was divided into a number of equal parts. It is suggested that the number of groups is kept between ten and twenty. In this particular case five adjacent numbers were taken in each group, so forming thirteen groups and then the number of occasions on which the low stock level fell into each group (the frequency for that group) was determined. The shape of the resulting frequency diagram again shows a unity indicating an absence of freaks and abnormalities, but it shows that little margin exists for stock reduction on stock item B.

2.4. Measure up the frequency diagram

Sometimes a problem is sufficiently straightforward that drawing a frequency diagram and interpreting it subjectively is sufficient to allow the correct decision to be taken. Nevertheless in such instances, as for example the case of the low stock levels, the following characteristics would be assessed subjectively:

1. The central value of the frequency diagram and,
2. The extent of the variability or scatter of the individual observations which form the frequency diagram.

But instances will arise from time to time when a subjective comparison of two frequency diagrams, perhaps to compare the yields of two so-called identical machines is not sufficient. There then arises a need for objective measurements of the central value and of the variability in order to carry out proper statistical tests. Furthermore, it isn't always possible to collect a sufficiently large number of observations to rely solely on a frequency diagram. A subjective assessment of the central value and the variability would be impractical in such cases.

2.4.1. Central value

(a) *Arithmetic Average.* The most usual measure of the central value of the frequency diagram is the *arithmetic average*, or *mean*. It is simply the sum of the values of the observations divided by their number. The average of the following delivery times, in weeks, for works orders placed within a shoe factory is calculated as shown in Table 2.2.

Table 2.2. Calculation of average

Delivery time (weeks)	
	8
	4
	13
	8
	10
Total	43

$$\text{Average} = \frac{\text{total of all delivery times}}{\text{number of works orders}}$$

$$= \frac{43}{5}$$

$$= 8.6 \text{ weeks}$$

(b) *Median.* An alternative measure of the central value is the *median.* It has the advantage that in small samples it is extremely easy to calculate, and moreover it is only slightly affected by a freak observation should it occur. The median of the five delivery times would be obtained by writing them in order of increasing size:

4 8 *8* 10 13 (Average: 8.6)

and taking the value of the middle observation. In this instance the median is eight weeks.

If there had been a sixth works order with a delivery time of eighteen weeks:

4 8 *8* *10* 13 18 (Average: 10.2)

the median would be taken at the midpoint of the two middle observations. It would be nine weeks.

Of course the median and the average do not always coincide. They are both estimates of the central value of the frequency distribution. It is worth noticing how the introduction of a new and extreme observation increased the average from 8.6 weeks to 10.2 weeks, which is appreciably more than the change in the median, eight weeks to nine weeks.

2.4.2. Variability

(a) *Range.* The simplest measure of the scatter or the variability amongst the individual observations forming the frequency diagram is the *range*, which is the difference between the largest and the smallest of the observations. The range of the following profitability figures for five out of a company's thirty-four shops is calculated in Table 2.3.

Table 2.3. Calculation of range

Net Profit (£)		
2100		
4100	Largest	4100
1300	Smallest	1300
2000	Range	2800
3500		

This method of measuring variability ignores all the values between the two extremes and so it is grossly inefficient when there are a large number of observations. In practice the use of the range should be restricted to cases with less than twelve observations. There is a further restriction on its use since, for example, the range of ten observations is likely to be larger than the range of five observations. This means that if the range is used to measure and compare variability, the same number (preferably less than ten) of observations should be used on each occasion. Once this is done the range has proved to be a simple and efficient measure of variability, for example in day to day control of product quality.

(b) *Mean Deviation.* In order to take all the observations into account when measuring variability it is usual to compare them against the average value. The difference between the observation and the average of all the observations is called the *deviation* and the average of the deviations would appear to be an appropriate measure of variability. Unfortunately, because of the basic definition of the average, the sum of the deviations, taking sign into account is always zero. The simplest way out of this predicament is just to ignore the signs, and the resulting measure, the average of the deviations disregarding sign, is called the *mean deviation.* The analysis of the profitability figures shown in Table 2.4 illustrates the nature of deviations and the mean deviation.

Table 2.4. Calculation of mean deviation

Observation Nett Profit (£ x 100)	Deviation (Obsn. – Ave.)	Disregard sign
21	−5	5
41	15	15
13	−13	13
20	−6	6
35	9	9
Total 130	0	48

Average $= \frac{130}{5} = 26$ Mean deviation $= \frac{48}{5} = 9.6$

The mean deviation is an appropriate measure of variability for simple circumstances but it is difficult to handle mathematically. Consequently the sophisticated techniques for the analysis and measurement of sources of variability and the statistical tests available for comparing averages or variability have been designed to use an alternative measure of variability, the *standard deviation.* However, the arrival of the computer and the need to have simple means of updating the measure of variability has brought the mean deviation out of the cupboard. It is particularly useful for measuring the reliability of sales forecasting especially where the technique of exponential smoothing is employed.

(c) *Standard Deviation.* The other alternative for disregarding sign, more natural to mathematics, is to multiply the offending negative numbers by themselves. Since negative multiplied by negative results in positive, the problem disappears. Consider the weekly mileage returns of a sales representative and the deviations shown in Table 2.5.

Table 2.5. Basis of calculating standard deviation

	Miles	Deviation	Devn. x Devn.
	208	8	64
	200	0	0
	190	−10	100
	196	−4	16
	200	0	0
	206	6	36
Total	1200		216
Average	200	Average of Devn. x Devn. = 36	

The observations have been recorded in miles, and their deviation about the average is in miles, but the average of (deviation x deviation) is in square miles. Consequently, in order to obtain the correct units, namely miles, for measuring the variability in the mileages, the square root of the calculated figure must be found. In fact:

$$\text{standard deviation} = \sqrt{\text{average of (devn. x devn.)}}$$
$$= 6 \text{ miles.}$$

It must be reiterated that the standard deviation is a measure of the variability in the observations. If the mileage had been more variable, the standard deviation would have been larger. Moreover, if a set of figures relating to another representative had a standard deviation of twelve miles it would be reasonable to say that his weekly mileages were twice as variable as those for the representative considered.

The basic method of calculating the standard deviation described above can be tedious and approximate when the average is not a whole number of the measurement units. Consequently, especially when a calculating machine is used, the calculation of the standard deviation can be simplified by using the formula:

$$\text{standard deviation} = \sqrt{\begin{array}{l}\text{(average of the squares of}\\ \text{the observations)}\\ -\text{(square of their average)}\end{array}}$$

Because the calculation of the standard deviation is a formidable task, short cut approximate methods of estimating it have been developed. These are described in the following section (page 17).

2.4.3. Normal distribution

(a) *Its basic properties.* If it were possible to obtain more and more observations on the low stock level of stock item B, the number of groups chosen for the frequency diagram could be increased. The saw teeth of the frequency diagram would become smaller and smaller until the outline of the frequency diagram would turn into a curve. Fig. 2.4 shows a frequency diagram of 1000 low stock levels which could have arisen through daily stock replenishment over a period of three years.

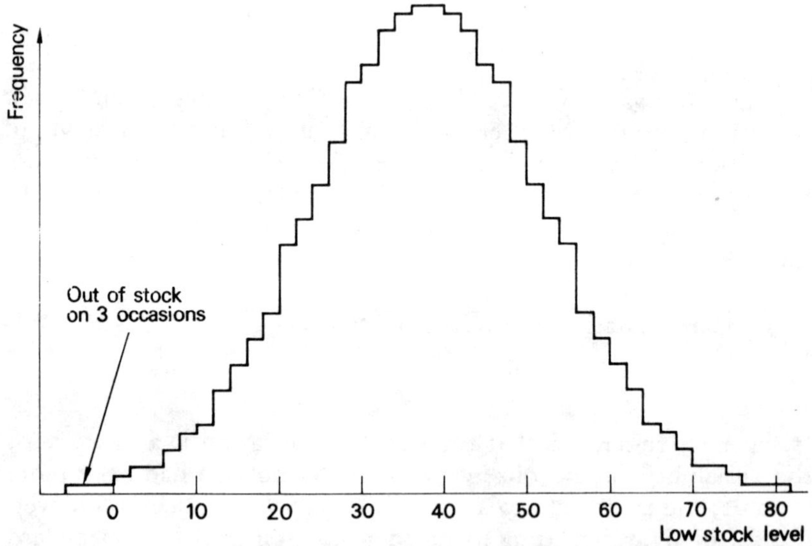

Figure 2.4 Frequency diagram for 1000 low stock levels–item B

In many instances the resulting frequency diagram, as in the above example, will be symmetrically bell-shaped and can be approximated by the *normal frequency distribution,* which is illustrated in Fig. 2.5.

The normal distribution provides a ready means of visualizing the nature of the standard deviation. The majority, about two thirds, of the low stock levels are within one standard deviation (fourteen units) from the average; 95 per cent are within two standard deviations (twenty-eight units) from the average; and almost all of them fall within three standard deviations from the average. These proportions are the same whatever the value of the

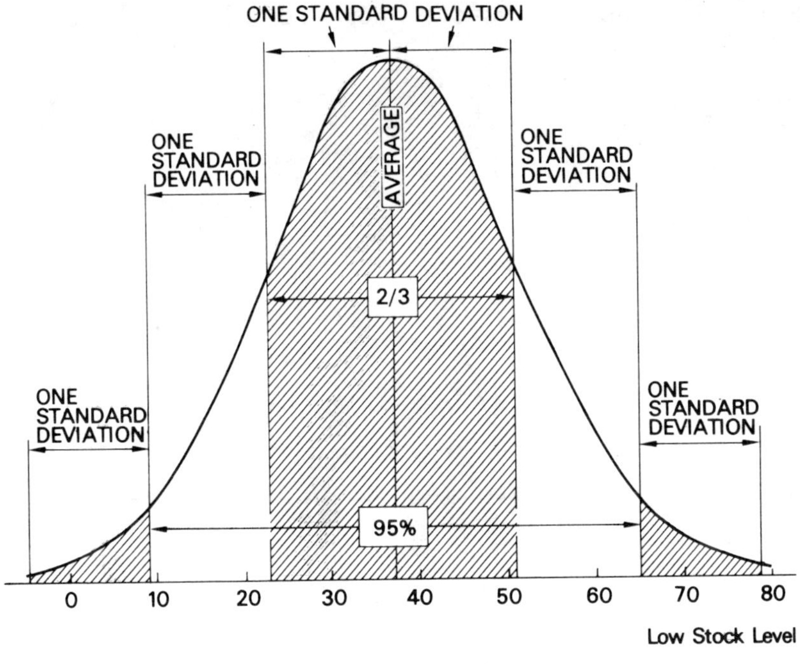

Figure 2.5 Normal frequency distribution

average and the standard deviation since the shape of the normal distribution is completely determined once the average and the standard deviation are known.

Clearly, if a large number of observations had been made it would be possible to count the number falling within chosen limits and so determine the relative frequency of a specific occurrence. For example, Fig. 2.4 shows that stock item B was out of stock on three occasions out of 1000. If the same conditions still apply in the routine of re-ordering, it would be reasonable to judge that the number of instances of out of stock during the next 1000 weeks would be about three. In other words the risk of running out of stock on any week would be three in 1000.

Often it is either impractical or impossible to obtain such a large number of observations. Then the average and the standard deviation of the available observations may be used to estimate the average and the standard deviation of the normal distribution which would arise from a large number of observations. For example, the average and standard deviation of the fifty observations on the low stock levels of stock item A shown in Table 2.1 are 38.4 and 2.6 respectively, and these values would be used to determine the most likely normal distribution.

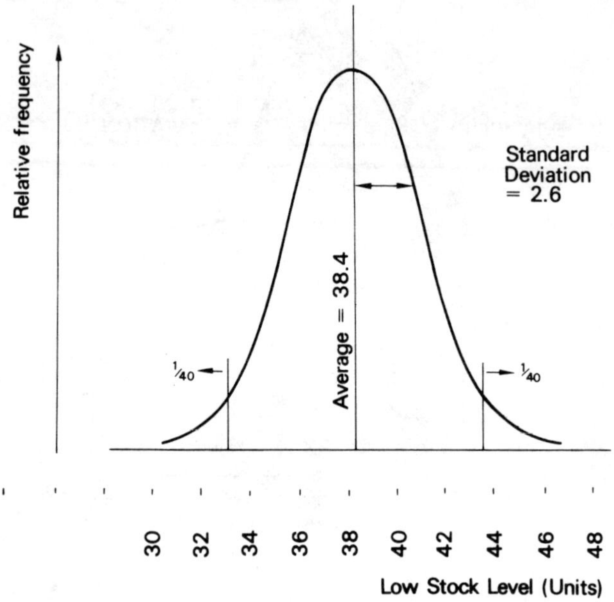

Figure 2.6 Normal distribution estimated from 50 observations on stock item A

Fig. 2.6 shows this distribution indicates that a low stock level of below thirty is most unlikely to occur, that a stock level of below thirty-three would occur about one in forty occasions, and that there is a fifty-fifty chance that the stock level will be thirty-eight or below. Concentrating solely on the average of 38.4, an immediate reaction is to point out that it is excessive and that the ordering routine should be modified to reduce the low stock levels by that amount. This would mean, since the low stock levels scatter about the average, that there would be an 'out-of-stock' situation on 50 per cent of the occasions when new stock is received. Alternatively, concentrating on the variability it could well be suggested that the ordering routine should be adjusted to reduce the low stock level by thirty. If this were done instances of stock out would be very occasional. A further option would be to reduce stocks by between thirty and thirty-eight and accept the possibility of occasional stock shortages. For example, if the low stock levels could be reduced by thirty-three, an out-of-stock would occur on about one in forty ordering occasions.

This example has illustrated how the properties of the normal distribution may be used. It is, of course, desirable to check that the frequency diagram is approximately symmetrical before using the normal distribution. This is likely to be true in situations where measurements are being made, measurements which can fall anywhere on a continuous scale, and a large number of sources of random variability affects the results. If the frequency diagram is not symmetrical it is often possible to change the nature of the measurement being made and so obtain a symmetrical frequency diagram. However, there are a number of important instances where the frequency diagram is far from symmetrical and these are discussed in sections 2.5 and 2.6 of this chapter.

So far only the proportions of the normal distribution beyond 1, 2 and 3 standard deviations have been quoted. It is of course possible to tabulate the proportions beyond any number or fraction of standard deviations, and some useful values are tabulated in Fig. 2.7, on page 18.

(b) *Quick means of estimating standard deviation.* (i) *Use of average range.* It has been mentioned previously that the range grows with the number of observations whose variability is being measured. For instance it has been found both empirically and mathematically that if a large number of pairs of observations is selected from a normal distribution and the range of each pair is determined then the average of these ranges would be 1.13 times the standard deviation of the normal distribution. As a further instance, if on each occasion five observations had been taken instead of two then the average range would be 2.33 times the standard deviation. This relationship can be used to estimate the standard deviation of a process.

One application of this principle occurs in the practice of quality control where a small number of items are selected from the process and a quality characteristic is measured. The range of the measured values is calculated and the same procedure is repeated several times. The average of these ranges can be used to estimate the standard deviation of the process and so determine the closest possible tolerances which can be consistently met by the process.

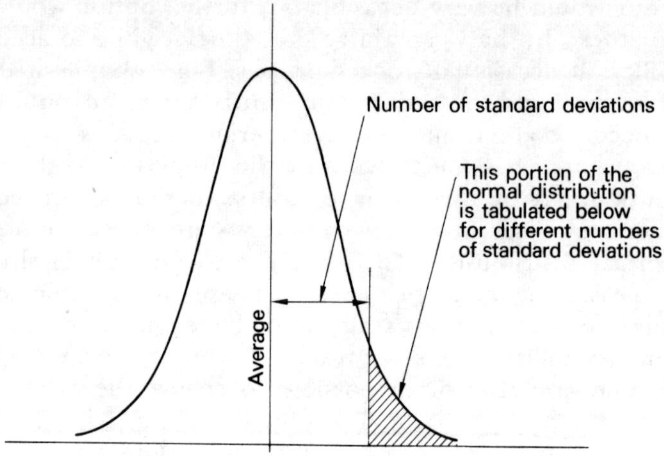

Percentage of normal distribution lying to the right of specified number of standard deviation above the average.

NUMBER OF STANDARD DEVIATIONS	PERCENTAGE	NUMBER OF STANDARD DEVIATIONS	PERCENTAGE
0.0	50.0	0.0	50
0.2	42.1	0.67	25
0.4	34.5	1.28	10
0.6	27.4	1.64	5
0.8	21.2	1.96	2.5
1.0	15.9	2.33	1.0
1.2	11.5	2.58	0.5
1.4	8.1	3.09	0.1
1.6	5.5		
1.8	3.6		
2.0	2.3		
2.2	1.4		
2.4	0.82		
2.6	0.47		
2.8	0.26		
3.0	0.13		

Figure 2.7 Table of normal distribution

The relationship between the average range of a number of observations drawn from the normal distribution depends on the number of observations. The appropriate factor by which to divide the average range to estimate the standard deviation is shown in Table 2.6.

Table 2.6. Factors for estimating standard deviation from average range

Sample Size (Number of observations used to determine range)	Factor
2	1.13
3	1.69
4	2.06
5	2.33
6	2.53
7	2.70
8	2.85
9	2.97
10	3.08
11	3.17
12	3.26

Divide average range by factor corresponding to sample size to estimate standard deviation

Table 2.7 illustrates the method of estimating the standard deviation from the average range for the fifty low stock levels used to develop the first frequency diagram. It was decided, arbitrarily,

Table 2.7. Use of average range to estimate standard deviation

Observations					Range
36	44	36	36	40	8
37	37	35	38	39	4
35	40	41	43	37	8
38	38	37	42	36	6
40	42	40	37	42	5
40	42	37	37	40	5
33	38	39	41	37	8
41	32	40	43	38	11
41	37	37	39	38	4
39	34	37	39	35	5
				Total	64

Average Range $= 6.4$

Standard Deviation $= \dfrac{6.4}{2.33}$

$= 2.75$

to take the range of each row of five observations. The estimate of the standard deviation based on the average of these ranges, 2.75, compares very favourably with the value 2.61 estimated by the standard method.

This example illustrates the point that these short cut methods are sufficiently accurate for decision making. If a further sample of fifty low stock levels was taken the standard deviation of the second sample would probably differ from the first by more than this amount.

(ii) *Use of average successive difference.* If there is no systematic pattern in the observations then the difference between successive observations can be used to estimate the standard deviation of the process. The difference between two adjacent observations determines their range, and the average of the differences between successive observations is the equivalent of the average of ranges of two observations. The standard deviation can be estimated by dividing the average successive difference by the appropriate factor from Table 2.6 namely 1.13.

The average successive difference of the weekly mileage returns previously examined on page 13 is determined in Table 2.8.

Table 2.8. Use of average successive difference

Observation (miles)	Successive difference
208	–
200	8
190	10
196	6
200	4
206	6
	Total = 34

$$\text{Average successive difference} = \frac{34}{5} = 6.8$$

$$\text{Estimate of standard deviation} = \frac{6.8}{1.13} = 6.02$$

In this instance the estimated value of the standard deviation, 6.02, is almost identical to the standard deviation, 6.0 previously calculated.

(c) *Mean deviation.* It has also been found that the mean deviation of a number of observations selected from a normal distribution is related to the standard deviation of the normal distribution. When ten or more observations are selected, the mean deviation approximately equals 0.8 standard deviations. This relationship can of course be used to estimate the standard deviation and consequently all the relevant properties of the normal distribution. However, it has been found in practice that the proportions of the normal distribution determined by the mean deviation are helpful. These are shown in Fig. 2.8.

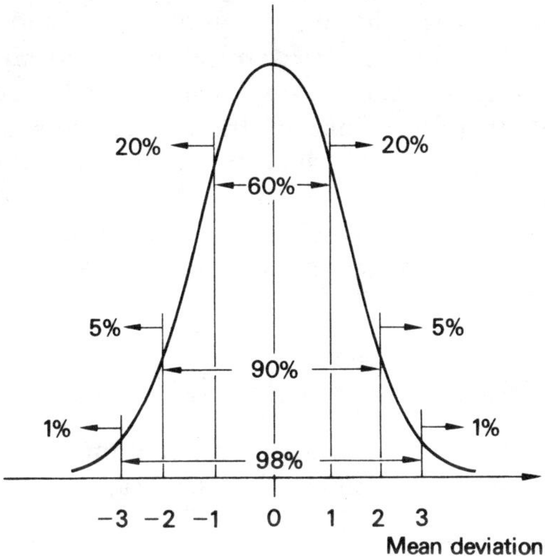

Figure 2.8 Proportions of normal distribution subdivided in units of mean deviation

One application of the use of the mean deviation occurs in sales forecasting. In this instance, calculating the average amount by which sales forecasts differ from actual results (the average size of the forecasting error) is equivalent to calculating the mean deviation. Consequently it would be reasonable to expect 60 per cent of future forecasts to be accurate to within this average amount, 90 per cent to be accurate to within twice and 98 per cent to be accurate to within three times the average amount of the forecasting error. If, for example, the average forecasting error is 79 000 units then we should expect 60 out of 100 future forecasts to be correct to within ± 79 000 units, and 90 out of 100 future forecasts to be correct to within ± 158 000 units.

(d) *When these approximations may be used.* In the majority of applications of the normal distribution to management problems it is highly likely that the decisions to be made will be insensitive to small errors in the estimates of either proportions of the distribution or the width of the band containing a specific percentage.

The ease with which the normal distribution can be applied is an obvious incentive to its use even in situations where the approximation is grossly inaccurate. The accuracy of using the normal distribution depends principally on the symmetry of observations collected. The more symmetrical and bell-shaped they appear to be, the more accurate the approximation. The decision of whether or not to use the normal distribution to estimate the likely proportions of the process considered should be based on an assessment of the likely accuracy and its effect on the consequent management decision. If it is decided to use the normal distribution as an approximation, then the accuracy provided by the quick means of estimating the standard deviation is adequate in all cases.

2.5. The important few—the trivial many

In this and the following section two situations are examined in which the frequency diagrams of observations differ markedly from the bell-shaped normal frequency diagram.

2.5.1. Pareto distribution

The Italian mathematician and engineer, Pareto, noted at the end of the nineteenth century that the bulk of the wealth in Italy was in the hands of 10 per cent of the population. Pareto's Law of the important few and the trivial many is particularly relevant to many management problems. The bulk of your sales value is concentrated on 10-20 per cent of your product list, or on 10-20 per cent of your customers; the bulk of your annual purchase expenditure goes on 10-20 per cent of the items which you buy; the bulk of the faults discovered by quality control can be attributed to 10-20 per cent of the different causes; the bulk of the value in a bill of quantities is in 10-20 per cent of the bill items, and so on.

A typical example which deals with the sales of motor vehicle spare parts at one branch of a distributor is shown in Fig. 2.9. A large number of the stock items, the trivial many, have low total annual sales, whereas only a small number, the important few, have high annual sales. In spite of their large number the trivial many only account for a small percentage of the total sales. This can be most easily seen when the cumulative percentage of the total sales is plotted against the cumulative percentage of the total number of items, taking the items in descending order of their annual turnover.

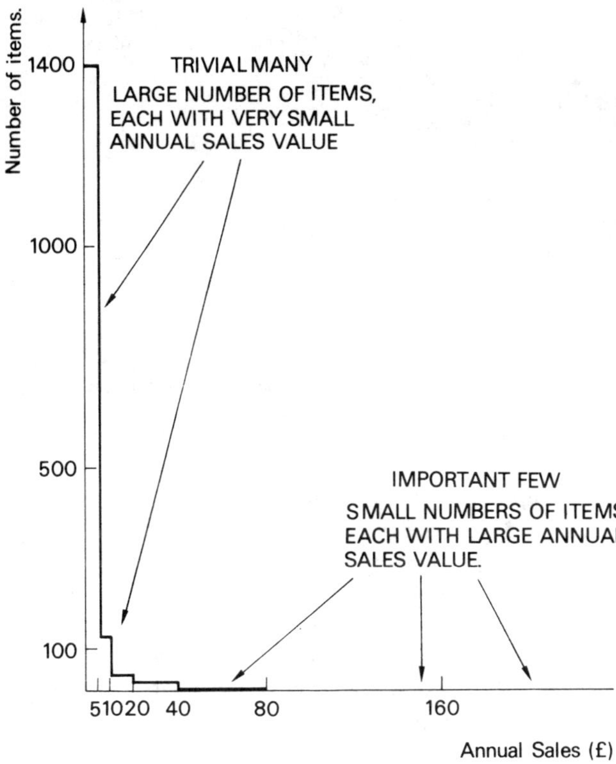

Figure 2.9 Pareto Distribution of Sales of Stock Items

Fig. 2.10 shows that in this particular example the top 10 per cent of the stock items account for about 85 per cent of the total sales. These are the important few for which a high level of aavailability on demand is essential. Many of the slow moving items are selling so slowly that the policy of having sufficient stocks to satisfy a demand from stock is questionable. Certainly a much lower level of availability on demand can be tolerated.

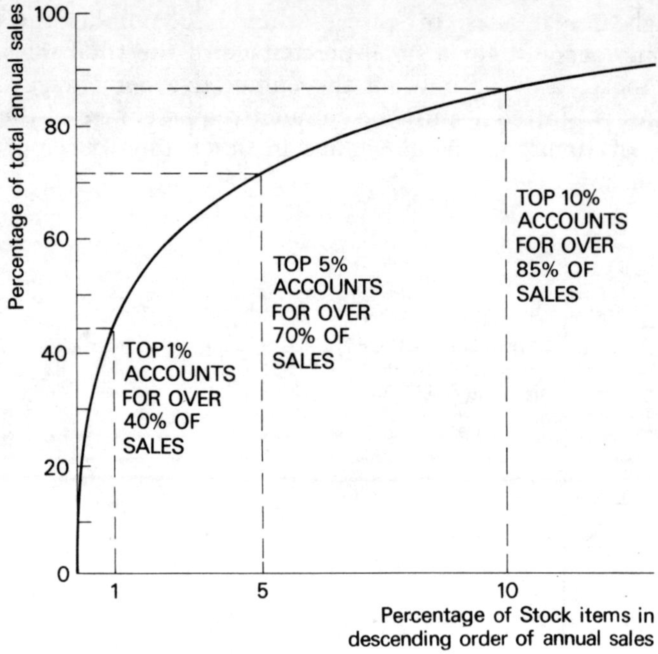

Figure 2.10 Pareto Distribution: top 10% account for bulk of sales

2.5.2. One rule for the rich, another for the poor

Whilst in the law courts all people, whether they be rich or poor, are in theory subject to the same laws, in business the manager should treat the trivial many quite differently from the important few. For instance the sales effort should follow different paths according to the annual value sold to each customer. It may be possible to cover those with very low sales by direct mail or by regular telephone calls; the ones in the middle range would be covered by sales representatives; the important few could well become house accounts handled directly by the sales director; and the key accounts, perhaps one or two only, should be the personal responsibility of the top executive.

In the preparation of tenders, the important few bill items would be the task of a senior estimator; the trivial many would be dealt with by juniors. In the field of quality control, action would be restricted to reducing the frequency or the cost incurred by the important few sources of trouble. However interesting one or other of the many trivial sources of trouble may be, technical skill should be concentrated where it is most likely to yield the greatest benefit.

A further example of the use of different rules for different items is drawn from the procedures established to control the component stocks of a manufacturer making engines for motor vehicles. Here the important few components were each made the responsibility of a member of the purchasing department. Forward schedules were prepared for suppliers who were required at all times to keep a fortnight's stock. The supply situation on these items was checked daily by the appropriate member of the purchasing department. At the other end of the scale, the very trivial many components were re-ordered by a stores clerk without keeping any record of stock levels. Two packets were held and as soon as one packet had been used up a further packet was ordered automatically. The second packet ensured that stock replenishment always arrived before a stock shortage occurred. Stock items in between these two extremes were controlled on the company's computer. The usage of these stock items was recorded on the computer, future usage forecast and orders to replenish stocks to a target level prepared at regular intervals.

Whenever one system is being used to cover all contingencies you should ask yourself if the Pareto Law does not apply. If it does then a saving in time and effort will inevitably result if simplified procedures are adopted for the trivial many. It may be possible simultaneously to tighten the procedures covering the important few.

2.6. What happens when we count

As we have mentioned previously, the normal distribution will usually be a good approximation when data is collected by measurement using a continuous scale. Typical characteristics following the normal distribution would be times, speeds and lengths. However, when data is collected by counting, using a discontinuous scale 0, 1, 2, 3 . . . the frequency distribution may be quite unsymmetrical. Typical data arising from counting would relate to the number of stoppages per day, the number of faults per length of cloth, and so on. The shape of the frequency distribution of data arising from counting depends on the average of the count. The smaller the average, the more unsymmetrical the distribution. Fig. 2.11 illustrates how the degree of symmetry increases with the average count. The diagrams in this figure are based on the mathematical theory for counting rare events devised by a French mathematician, Poisson.

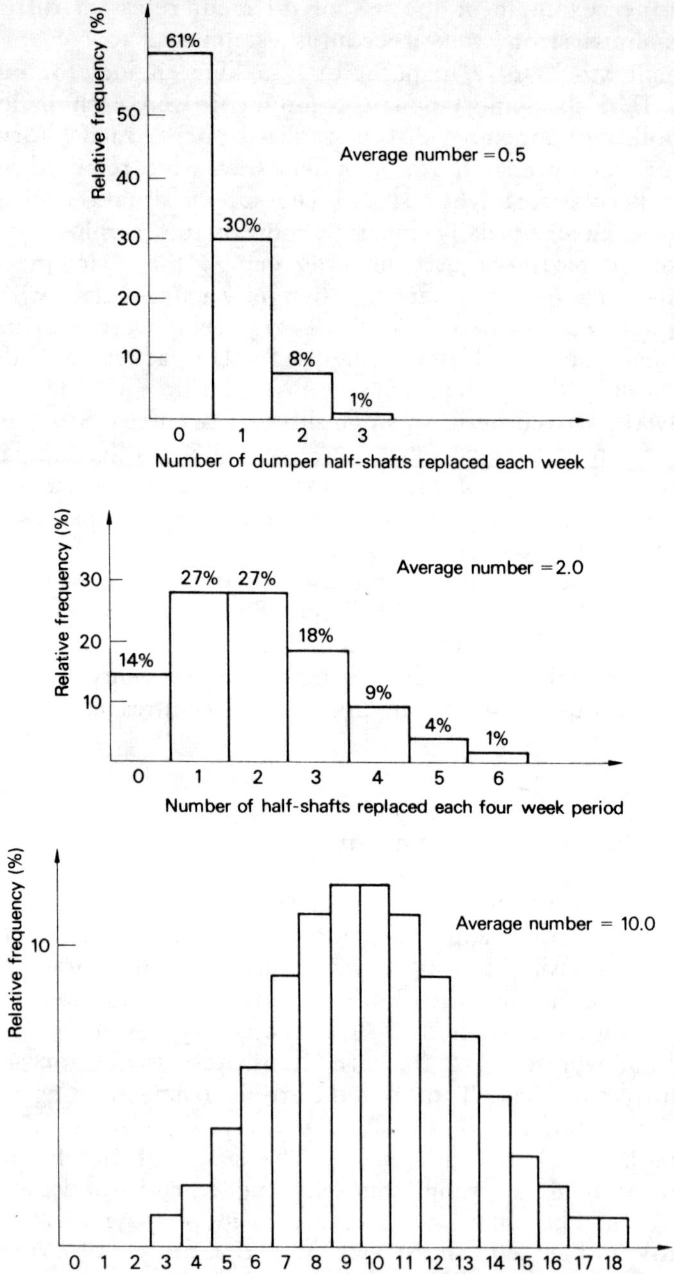

Figure 2.11 Increase in symmetry of frequency diagram for counting

The practical application of the diagrams in Fig. 2.11 would be in deciding to what level the stocks of replacement half shafts could be allowed to fall before ordering further delivery. If half shafts could be delivered in a week, the first diagram shows that hardly ever are more than three half shafts used in one week. It would be reasonable to place the replenishment order when the stock had fallen to three. If the delivery time for half shafts was four weeks, the second diagram shows that hardly ever are more than six half shafts used in this period. In this case the stock should be replenished whenever it had fallen to six. Finally, if the construction site was overseas and in consequence the delivery time went out to twenty weeks, the third diagram shows that the level at which stock should be replenished is seventeen or eighteen.

As previously mentioned, there are many instances where insufficient data exist to be able to construct these frequency diagrams from actual observations. Consequently a small number of observations are used to determine the average count. The mathematical theory developed by Poisson is then used to estimate the frequency diagram which would occur from a large number of observations since the Poisson distribution depends only on the average count. Extensive tables have been prepared to make this possible. Table 2.9 illustrates a typical part of such tables.

Table 2.9. Table of Poisson distribution

		Average number of count = m			
		m = 0.5	m = 1.0	m = 1.5	m = 2.0
Actual	n = 0	.606	.368	.223	.135
Number	1	.303	.368	.335	.271
Observed	2	.076	.184	.251	.271
	3	.013	.061	.126	.180
= n	4	.002	.015	.047	.090
	5		.003	.014	.036
	6			.004	.012
	7			.001	.003
	8				.001

The table shows the relative frequency of occurrence of the actual number n, when the average number of count has the value m.

For example if the average number of accidents each week is 1.5, then we would expect 7 accidents once in 1000 weeks and 2 accidents one week in 4.

These tables which were used to construct the frequency diagrams in Fig. 2.11 show how the frequency diagram for counting becomes more and more symmetrical as the average count increases. As can be seen from Fig. 2.11, the frequency diagram when the average count is ten or more is sufficiently symmetrical to allow the normal distribution to be used as an approximation. When this is done the average is taken as the average count m, and the standard deviation as $\sqrt{m}$. For instance if the average number of faults on a roll of carpet was sixteen, the frequency distribution of the number of faults on a carpet would approximate to a normal distribution whose average was sixteen and whose standard deviation four. Consequently, once in 1000 carpets the number of faults would be expected to exceed three standard deviations above the average, namely twenty-eight; once in forty carpets, twenty-four faults and so on.

2.7. Applications

2.7.1. Principles

This chapter has dealt with the basic tools of handling variability, and these tools are relevant wherever variability occurs in management measurements. Four basic principles stand out. These principles, summarized in this section and then illustrated in four representative applications, are:

1. When variability exists, forget the individual and look for the pattern of the whole.
2. Establish that an exception really is an exception before 'managing by exception'.
3. Measure the variability, and look for an economic angle.
4. Concentrate on the important few.

2.7.2. Quality control—process capability

(a) *Look for the pattern of the whole.* One of the principal steps of quality control is to assess the tolerances which a process can be reasonably expected to meet. The slogan used, 'concentrate on the process and the product will look after itself', is an alternative form of the first principle. Individual measurements are meaningful only if they are pooled with others to form a frequency diagram.

(b) *Make sure the 'exception' really is an exception.* Failure to limit process adjustments to the occasions on which they are really needed will result in the process being more variable still. In many cases too it will result in unnecessary loss of output. The control limits on quality control charts exist to identify exceptional circumstances in the manufacturing process. The fact that they

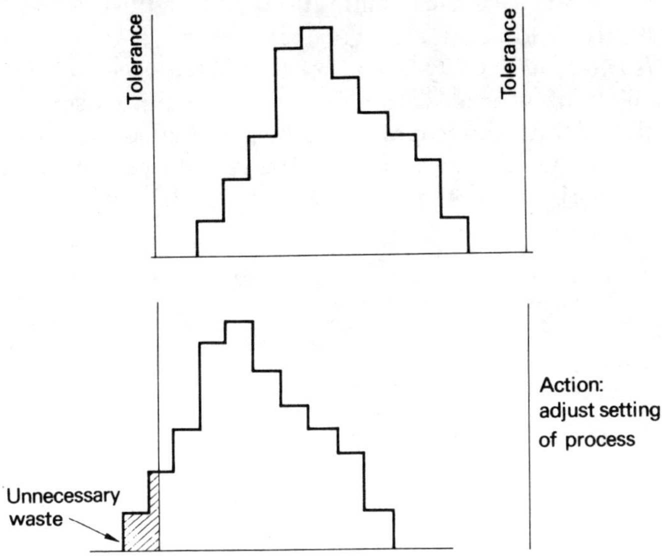

Figure 2.12 Process able to meet tolerances

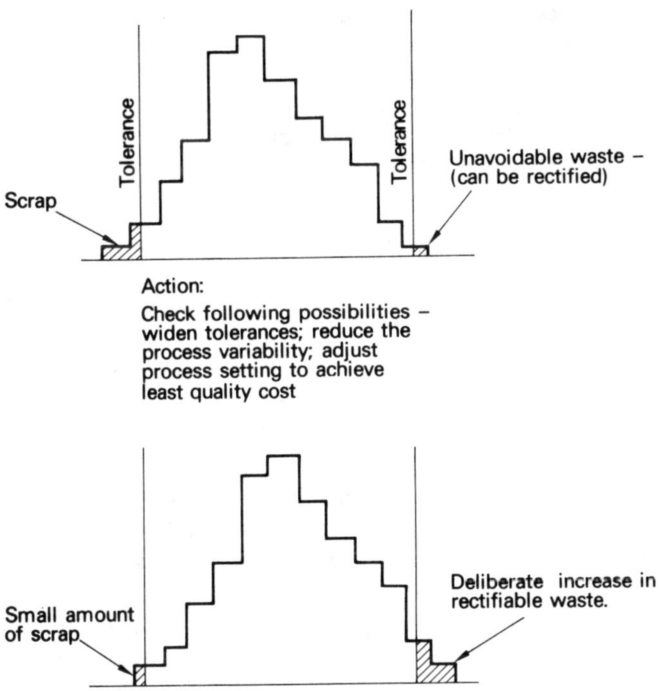

Figure 2.13 Process unable to meet tolerances

eliminate most of the temptations to adjust the process unnecessarily is probably their greatest value.

(c) *Measure variability and look for the economies.* The measurement of process capabilities and the comparison of these capabilities with the appropriate product tolerances is an early and basic step in establishing efficient quality control. The situations which could arise are illustrated in Figs. 2.12, 2.13 and 2.14.

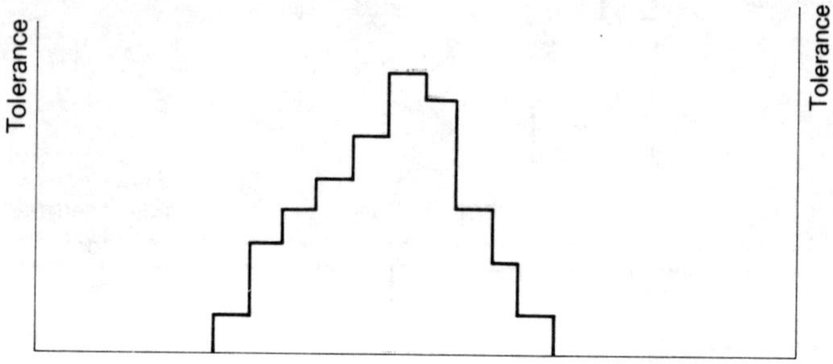

Action:
Check following possibilities–

1. Use less precise (probably cheaper) equipment
2. Speed up the process — can one or more operations be omitted?
3. Work close to the point within the tolerances which minimizes production costs
4. Transfer some of the tolerance to a mating part.

Figure 2.14 Process too precise for tolerances

The processes, shown as frequency diagrams, are compared against the tolerances they have to meet. Wherever there is an imperfect matching, an economic loss occurs and warrants action to remove it. Appropriate steps are outlined in Figs. 2.12, 2.13 and 2.14.

When tolerances are single sided, for example on packet weights, the average of the process must be set well above the minimum permitted value to ensure that all or almost all of the product meets the tolerance. Should it be possible to reduce the process variability, the average of the process can be reduced and the same proportion of the product still meet the tolerance. The potential reduction in 'give-away' is illustrated in Fig. 2.15. This figure also illustrates an instance in which the single sided tolerance is the maximum permitted value of an impurity in a

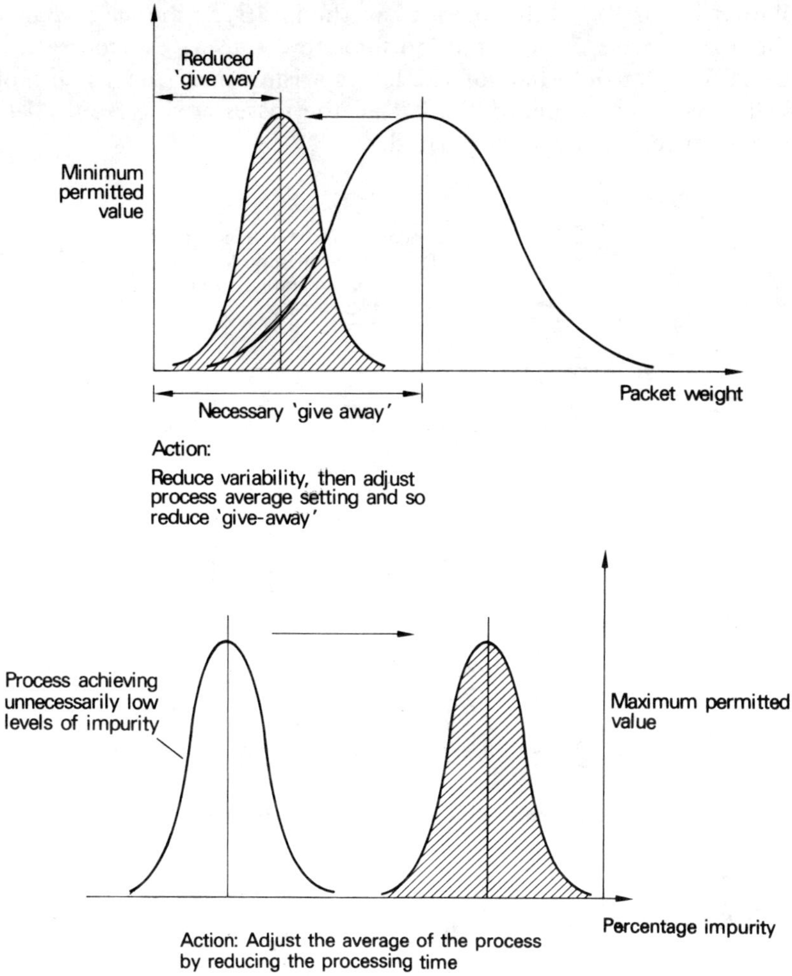

Figure 2.15 Meeting single sided tolerances

product. The current level being achieved was well below the permitted value—at an excess cost on every ton produced. It was possible to cheapen the process and still meet the maximum permitted value on all, or almost all, the batches produced.

(d) *Concentration on the important few.* One of the principal tools for improving quality levels is to concentrate attention on the top two or three causes of faults. The first stage consists of collecting records of faults, and classifying them according to the type of fault or to the source of the fault. A typical picture is shown in Fig. 2.16; the majority of the faults, or the major part of the losses arise from an important few causes. Concentrate on these, remove only half of the losses arising from them and more will have been achieved than if all the losses arising from all the other causes had been eliminated.

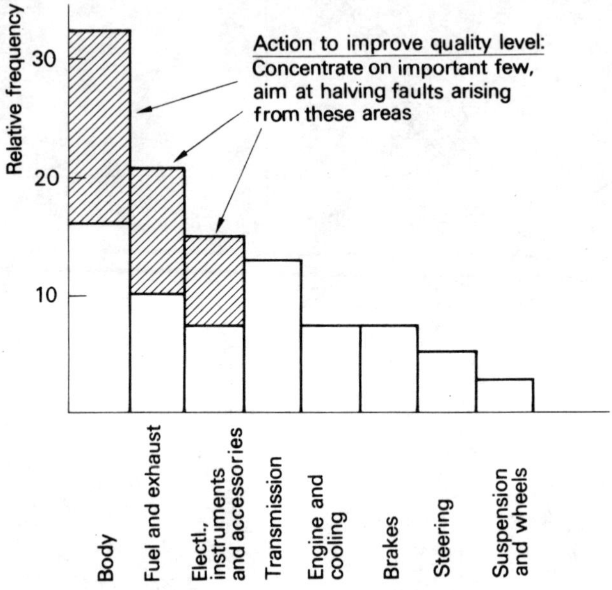

Figure 2.16 Relative frequency of faults during running of motor cars

2.7.3. Sales forecasting

(a) *Look for pattern as a whole.* It is impossible to forecast sales exactly. There will always be some uncertainty associated with the forecast, and this uncertainty will be expressed in the form of a frequency diagram of forecasting errors, as shown in Fig. 2.17.

To achieve this pattern of random variation it is first necessary to eliminate the systematic variation due to seasonality and to trends of growth or decline.

(b) *Identify the exception.* When an actual week's orders differ markedly from the forecast figure it is quite possible that an abnormal situation has arisen. An individual forecasting error more than three times the average forecasting error would warrant a check, firstly of the arithmetic and then of the commercial intelligence associated with the sales figures. Such an anomaly

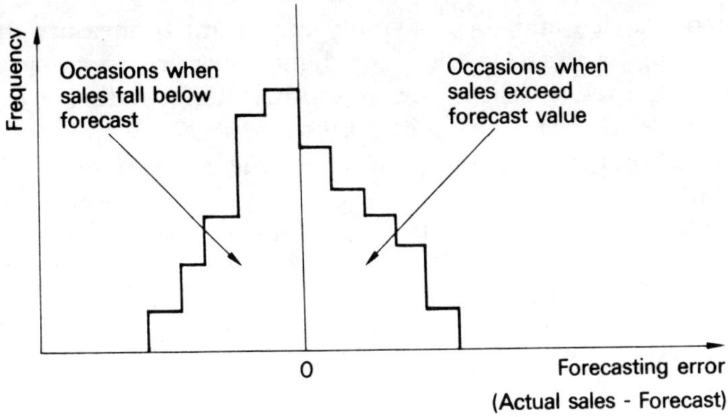

Figure 2.17 Forecasting errors form a frequency diagram

could be due to a change in the buying pattern of the company's principal customers. Sustained under-estimation or over-estimation in the forecasts can also be detected and this could well arise due to a change in the sales trend.

(c) *Economic angle on variability*. When sales forecasts are being made on every stock item as a basis for stock control or production planning the amount of uncertainty in the forecast can be covered by a provision of safety stocks. Fig. 2.18 illustrates how safety stock requirements are determined.

The larger the uncertainty, the larger the safety stocks which

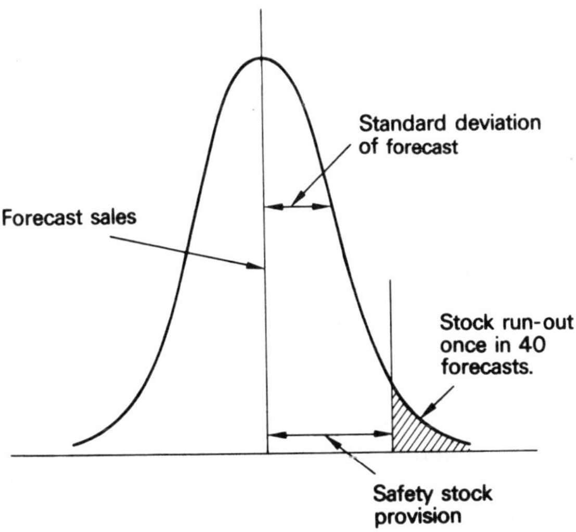

Figure 2.18 Measurement of uncertainty of forecast used to determine safety stock requirements

must be carried and so it is vitally important to measure the sales forecasting errors. On the one hand over-provisioning ties up capital in useless stocks, on the other hand under-provisioning undermines the service provided by the stocks.

When forecasts are made to assess the amount of production capacity needed, the upper and lower limits on the forecasts determine the required flexibility in output. This aspect is illustrated in Fig. 2.19. If flexibility is not met by overtime, or by stock build up and run down, it will show itself in extended delivery delays on those occasions when the demand hits the upper limits of the forecasts.

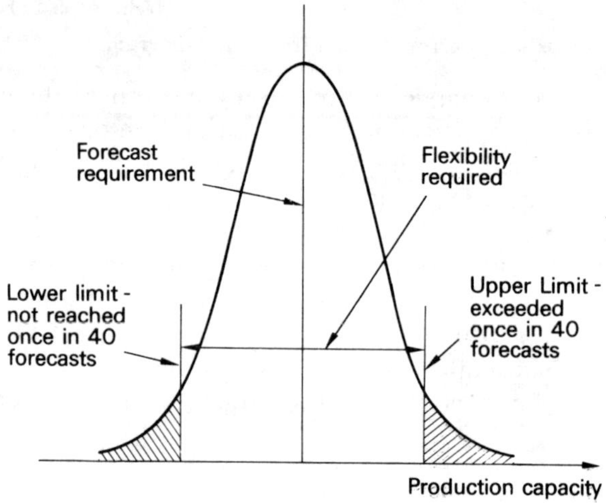

Figure 2.19 Uncertainty of forecast used to determine flexibility requirements

(d) *The important few.* When forecasting for the production planning of a range of stock items, the fast moving items were treated differently from the slow moving items. The production plan had a four week horizon and to marry in with this the sales of the fast moving items were forecast weekly for four weeks ahead. In contrast, the sales of the slow moving items were forecast once every four weeks for a period of eight weeks ahead. The effort involved in making the forecasts was concentrated on the important few at the expense of the larger forecasting errors on the trivial many, where they were unimportant.

2.7.4 Stock control

(a) *Look at pattern as a whole.* We are often told with a shrug of the shoulders that delivery times may be six weeks or six months—the inference being that you cannot hope to use data as uncertain as that. In fact if the delivery times are regarded as a frequency diagram, as in Fig. 2.20, a practical stock control procedure can be devised. We cannot know what will happen in each specific instance, but the instances as a whole will provide the overall pattern on which to base rational and consistent stock holding policies.

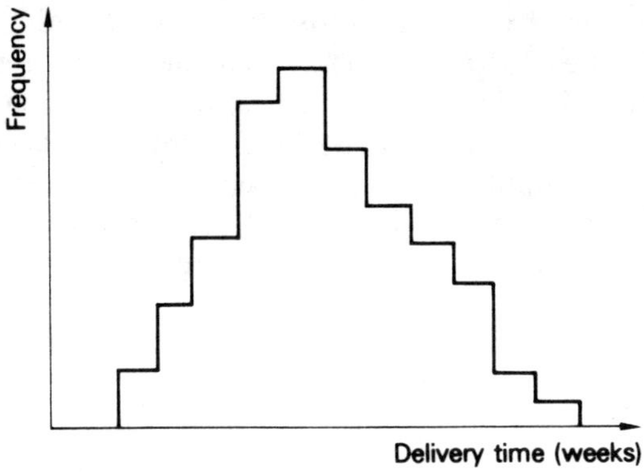

Figure 2.20 However uncertain, delivery times form a frequency diagram

(b) *Detect exceptions which are truly exceptions.* The démand for an item will vary from week to week: this is what causes the weekly demand figures to follow a frequency diagram. There may, however, be figures which are outside the pattern of the frequency diagram as is illustrated in Fig. 2.21.

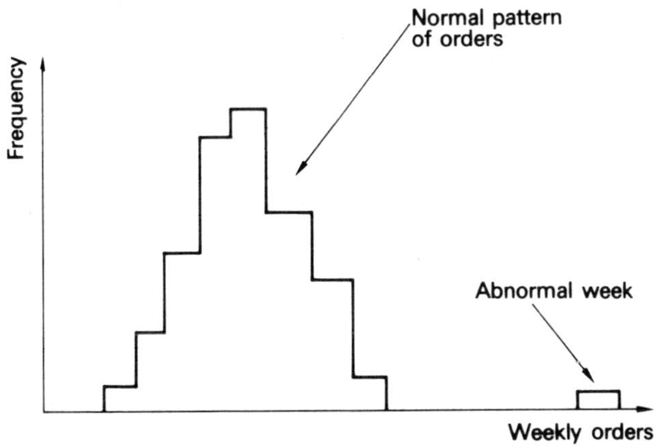

Figure 2.21 An exceptional result does not belong to the pattern of the frequency diagram

These are the exceptions for which an explanation should be sought. In one case an American selling agency was placing orders, very substantial orders, once a year. This anomaly was removed by arranging to spread the order over the months for which the items were needed. As a result of this action the safety stock requirements were considerably reduced.

(c) *Measure variability and look for an economic angle.* Variability in demand and in delivery times will mean that safety or buffer stocks must be kept to insure against running out of stock at the time the stock is being replenished. The amount of this variability is a vital factor in determining how much insurance, at how much cost, must be kept in the form of safety stocks to provide an acceptable level of protection against stock run-out. Fig. 2.22 shows how the safety stock and so the re-order level at which stock should be replenished may be calculated.

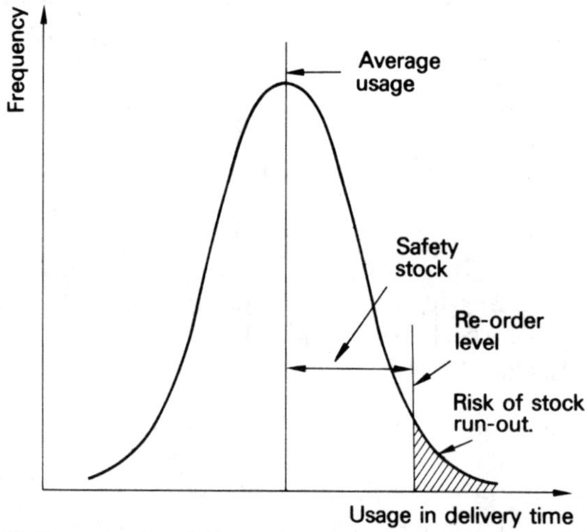

Figure 2.22 Re-order level dependent on average usage, variability and risk of run-out

(d) *Important few.* There is a considerable stock reduction to be had from reducing delivery times to a minimum. However, the cost of improving and monitoring deliveries can absorb the benefits unless only fast moving and expensive items are selected for special attention. In addition, a tight control over the use of these items in production could well be appropriate whereas inexpensive nuts, bolts and washers could be available on free issue.

Again, simple approximate methods of calculating re-order quantities and re-order levels are all that can be justified for the trivial many slow moving items. The fast moving and expensive stock items warrant a more sophisticated approach.

2.7.5. Work study

(a) *Look at the pattern as a whole.* There is variability in the work content of all jobs, there is variability in rating the operator's performance. Work study men are well aware that one reading is not enough and that there is need to look for a frequency diagram of measured times. Even the final figure which is distilled from the frequency diagram is subject to uncertainty. The only real answer is to do it all over again and see just how uncertain it all is.

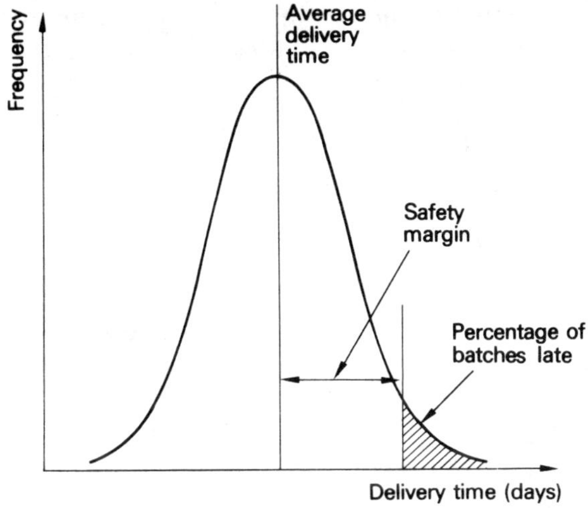

Figure 2.23 Need for a safety margin to ensure that almost all batches are on time

(b) *Identify the true exceptions.* When a measured time does not belong to the frequency diagram it is an exception, a 'wild' reading. The work study man is often faced with the problem of whether or not to discard 'wild' readings. The message of perfection is that there should be a sound technological reason for rejecting an exceptional time. These 'wild' readings could indicate an abnormality in the production operation, in the product, or in the operating conditions which should be corrected before time standards are established.

(c) *Measure variability and look for an economic angle.* In some situations, variability plays a dominant role in determining whether staff and facilities can be fully utilized. A clear example of this occurs in the contrast between the under-utilization of maintenance staff attending random calls for service on machine breakdowns and the high level of utilization achieved on planned maintenance schedules.

Fig. 2.23, on page 37, shows a further example, the planning of inter-factory batch delivery times. It is not sufficient to use the average delivery time for planning, all this does is to ensure that 50 per cent of batches are on time. In the majority of situations, the planner should ensure that a high percentage of batches are delivered on time, and this can only be arranged if the variability of delivery times is measured and taken into account.

(d) *The trivial many and the important few.* Sophisticated work study techniques such as micromotion analysis of cine film should be restricted to the few important jobs which account for a high percentage of man hours. Ideally these are the jobs on the mass production assembly lines.

Simplified techniques such as comparative estimating should be developed and applied to the many jobs which absorb an insignificant number of man hours.

List of terms used

Job evaluation
Work measurement
Management by objectives
Sales *forecasting*
Seasonal pattern
Measurement (continuous scale)
Uncertainty
Stock control
Tally diagram
Frequency diagram
Random fluctuations
Central value
Variability, scatter
Arithmetic average, average, mean
Median
Range
Mean deviation
Standard deviation
Normal distribution
Normal frequency distribution
Risk
Successive difference
Pareto's law
Counting (discontinuous scale)
Poisson distribution
Exception, 'wild'
Process capability
Forecasting error
Safety stock

Italicized terms are defined in the glossary (page 262) as well as in the text where it is appropriate.

3. Use samples more often—it saves time and effort

3.1. Why use samples

A sample to a salesman is an item which he carries with him to show the nature of his company's products. From this sample the buyer is expected to judge the quality and value of the product.

A sample to a market research investigator consists of not one item, but many. The sample could be the people or the companies which he has chosen to interview out of all the many available. From the results of these interviews he could perhaps be expected to judge the national sales of a new product. In industrial applications of sampling the word 'sample' is invariably used in the latter sense, and although it could consist of one item, it usually consists of many more. The salesman must use samples: it would be completely impractical and unnecessary to carry around all his company's output. On the other hand the market research investigator could interview all the appropriate people or companies, but he seldom has either sufficient time or money to do so.

In general, the payoff from sampling lies in speed, cost and reliability. It is almost always quicker and cheaper to use samples than to do a complete 'census'. Speed in collecting and analysing information is important if swift decisions are required, otherwise decisions will be made by resorting to experience. Even experience is a sample. In the worst instances the sample called 'experience' has been either built up in conditions entirely different from the present situation, or distorted by memory and prejudice.

How can samples be chosen which avoid these shortcomings? Samples are not inherently unreliable. On the contrary, because less effort is needed to collect and analyse them, one can afford to use better interviewers than on a census; better measuring equipment than on 100 per cent inspection; better trained staff than could be envisaged on a complete stock check. The weakness of 100 per cent inspection based on visual methods is often illustrated by the ease with which people fail to spot that the word THE is repeated twice in each triangle of Fig. 3.1.

When samples are used, the specific people to be interviewed, the specific electric cookers to be inspected, or the specific stock items to be included in the stock check have to be chosen.

It is unlikely that two independently chosen samples would contain the same items and so the two samples would almost certainly give different results. Many managers are aware of this weakness and consequently are reluctant to use samples unless it is inevitable. However, in a practical situation samples can be so chosen that the difference between the results would usually have little effect on the relevant management decision.

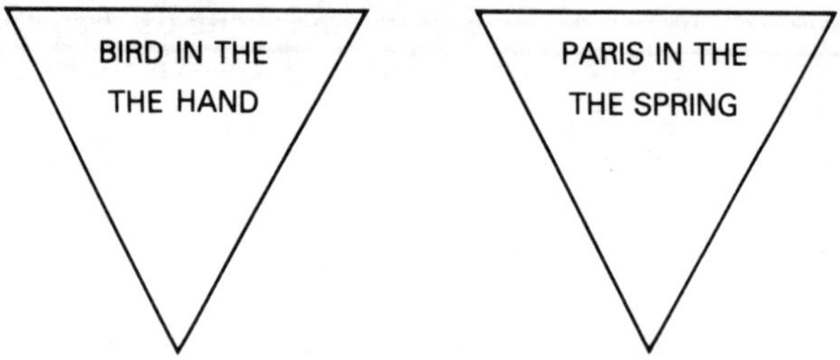

Figure 3.1 The quickness of the eye deceives the reader

3.2. Basic principles of sampling

3.2.1. Samples should mirror the facts without distortion

(a) *Representation in miniature.* Since a sample is used instead of a full 100 per cent evaluation it must be chosen in such a way that it does not distort the picture which would be obtained by the 100 per cent evaluation. One of the older Hollywood films tells the story of an opinion poll where the expert found the perfect sample. His task was to forecast the outcome of the presidential election and he found a small town in which the proportions of the different races; of the different religions; of the different political beliefs at the last election and of the community with specific incomes were in each instance identical to that in the United States as a whole. In fact in this small town he found a perfect miniature of the United States. Consequently, he was able to assess cheaply, informally and at leisure the way in which the small town, and so the United States would vote in the presidential election. So far as we can tell such good fortune only occurs in films, or similar essays into fiction.

However, this story does point out at least two morals. Firstly, it is desirable to know a good deal about the structure of the entirety (textbooks call this entirety, *population*) being sampled. Secondly, the sample should as far as possible represent this structure in miniature. For example, when sampling coal on coal wagons to assess its calorific value, it is important to know that the calorific value of the large pieces at the top differs from that of the smaller pieces at the bottom of the wagon. In this instance, as with a layer cake the representative sample would be obtained by taking a vertical slice through the contents of the wagon.

(b) *Bias in sampling.* Failure to make the correct choice of sample would distort the picture, give the wrong facts and could lead to an incorrect management decision. An incorrectly chosen sample of this kind is said to be *biased,* and one of the main tasks in choosing the items which comprise a sample is to eliminate or at least reduce the effect of *bias.*

The French film *Jour de Fete* contains a magnificent scene which illustrates perfectly the meaning of bias to the sampler. We see a shot of a man holding a tent peg. He has an anxious look in his eyes, and a bead of perspiration trickles down his forehead. We hear the swish of the mallet–followed by a thud on the grass as the mallet hits the ground about a foot from the position of the peg. This inaccuracy of course casts grave doubts on the skill of the man swinging the mallet. Nevertheless, the man in the picture picks up another tent peg and forces it into the ground where the mallet had made its indentation. He then resumes his original position holding the first tent peg, and also his anxious expression. This time the swish of the mallet is followed by a sharp crack as the tent peg standing on its own is driven cleanly into the ground. At this point the camera swings upwards and turns to show that the man holding the mallet is the cross-eyed man who has appeared previously in the film. In fact he is a most skilled mallet swinger, but he has a built-in bias. He can knock a tent peg home with one blow, provided he has another one about a foot away at which to aim.

(c) *Eliminating bias in the choice of samples.* In many situations the person responsible for selecting the items which form a sample has his own personal bias, and he selects items which appear to him to be 'typical'. His sample reflects his personal experience and disposition. It is clearly desirable that the fallible human choice should be eliminated and replaced by an impersonal procedure. In one such procedure, called *random sampling,* each possible item is given an identifying number, and the numbers selected by a random procedure such as drawing them from a hat are used to identify the items which will form the sample. The numbers 0, 1, 2, . . . 9 drawn at random have been called *random numbers.* Special equipment has been built to generate these numbers and the results of this exercise published as tables of random numbers in a form such as that shown in Table 3.1.

Table 3.1. Table of random numbers

07	94	31	40	57	79	06	72	99	23	78	61	12	39	63	76	74	18	69	29
82	08	30	36	82	38	54	81	62	15	59	92	27	29	28	97	30	35	21	39
09	91	37	55	60	19	04	67	47	74	71	99	76	90	64	76	66	14	52	84
70	06	04	46	99	17	77	30	21	23	63	25	81	70	30	98	85	20	18	85
31	15	07	06	02	24	71	13	99	56	04	90	42	23	37	40	42	74	77	53
61	22	64	33	71	83	30	50	23	05	06	00	50	03	97	29	56	29	84	17
01	61	25	35	87	89	53	35	34	65	41	51	04	63	35	94	03	39	52	49
02	09	39	82	74	40	69	03	04	95	33	67	53	43	10	48	03	09	97	42
98	00	23	11	92	99	82	84	35	07	52	83	94	20	33	04	40	98	54	35
03	99	12	29	93	71	58	33	13	22	87	76	09	35	00	45	06	61	14	31

When choosing items to form a sample for goods inwards inspection the random sampling approach is often impractical. In this instance the chances of choosing a biased sample can be considerably reduced by insisting that the sample is split into at least five equal parts and that each part is chosen from a different sector of the batch to be sampled. Both this procedure and random sampling reduce the opportunity for human introduction of bias in selecting the items in the sample. Irrespective of the structure of the *population* (the entirety) being sampled, they should produce a reasonably representative sample.

(d) *Using information on the structure of the population.* When the structure of the population is known, more reliable methods of selecting representative samples can be employed. For instance in a detailed study of the size and nature of the business carried out by an industry there were 120 000 establishments belonging to *four* major associations. Table 3.2 shows how this information can be used to specify a representative sample of 120 establishments.

In this case, sixty establishments belonging to association A would be included in the sample. The precise establishments to be included would be chosen as impersonally as possible, perhaps by taking a random sample from the 60 000 items falling in that category.

(c) *Eliminate bias in measurement.* One of the criticisms hurled at sampling is that the presence of the interviewer or the framing of the questions can distort the situation which the sample is trying to measure. These criticisms apply equally to censuses as well as to samples. The problem to be faced is 'how to measure without distortion'. A typical example is the bias arising when emotive questions are asked—such questions as 'Did you go to church last Sunday?' or 'Do you clean your teeth regularly?' The same problem faces any form of work measurement, where the presence of the observer can influence the operator and result in unrepresentative information. To assess the existence of bias, either in the choice of sample or in the measurement, the results of the sample should be compared against an independent source of the same type of information.

Table 3.2. Specification of representative sample when the structure of the population is known

Association	Number of establishments	Representative sample
A	60 000	60
B	30 000	30
C	20 000	20
D	10 000	10

In the survey on church going, an estimate should be made from the survey results of the size of the congregations and compared either with the capacity of the churches, or records of church attendance. Work study results should be used to assess production output and compared with recorded figures.

3.2.2. Samples should be large enough to be free from sampling fluctuations

(a) *Inevitable uncertainty.* In the first section of this chapter reference was made to the fact that two independently chosen samples would almost certainly give different estimates. This is true whatever the characteristic being estimated, whether it was the demand for ancillary equipment for computers; the value of year end work in progress; the percentage utilization of machine setters; or the percentage of companies in an industry employing less than ten people.

(b) *How exact an answer?* The first question to be answered in such instances is 'How precisely is the answer needed in order to make a decision?' If wide limits of accuracy can be tolerated then a small sample would be adequate. Consider a hypothetical illustration in the field of personnel management. Volunteers in the work force were inoculated against influenza and the number of days lost time due to illness subsequently recorded. In view of the expense and dislocation involved in providing this service the personnel manager judged that unless it resulted in at least a 10 per cent drop in absence due to illness amongst those inoculated, it was not worth continuing officially. If in fact the improvement was in the region of 50 per cent an estimate based on a small sample would be sufficient to demonstrate that it was greater than 10 per cent. However, if the true improvement was between 5 per cent and 15 per cent, larger samples would be needed to decide whether the treatment was justifiable or not.

(c) *How variable is the population?* The second question is 'How much variability is there in the population being studied, particularly in the characteristic being measured?' For instance, if there are two bins, one of which is known to contain only defective items and the other to contain only good items, only one item need be inspected to identify the contents of the two bins. Suppose, however, one bin contained 1 per cent faulty items, a situation deemed acceptable to the company, whereas the second contained 4 per cent faulty items and was deemed wholly unacceptable. In such circumstances a sample of one item would clearly be insufficient to differentiate between the bins.

(d) *What risk can be taken?* When samples are used as a basis for decisions there is an element of risk that the wrong decision will be made. For example, suppose market survey figures are compared for two alternative new products, one with additive WO6 and the other with additive WO7. On the one hand the results of the trials may show that WO6 is appreciably better than WO7, although much larger sized samples would show that there was truly no difference between the effects of the two additives. On the other hand, the results might show no difference between WO6 and WO7 when much larger sized samples would portray the real situation in which WO7 was appreciably better than WO6.

Whatever the decision, there is always a risk that it is the wrong one. If you are prepared to take a large risk of making the wrong decision then you will be able to use smaller samples—but the risk you are willing to take has to be decided.

(e) *Size of sample.* Provided it is possible to answer the first two questions, namely to say how precisely the answer is needed to make a decision and how much variation exists in the characteristics being studied, then it is possible to choose the size of the sample to reduce the risk of making a wrong decision to any specified level.

(i) *Estimating a percentage.* Table 3.3 shows the size of sample needed to estimate a percentage to a specific level of precision and to reduce the risk of making the wrong decision. This table gives the sample size needed to determine an estimate with an error which will exceed a specified level only *once* in twenty samples.

Table 3.3. Factors affecting sample size when estimating a percentage

True percentage in population	Level of precision specified				
	1%	2%	3%	4%	5%
1 or 99	400	100	45	25	15
2 or 98	780	200	90	50	30
3 or 97	1160	290	130	70	50
4 or 96	1540	380	170	100	60
5 or 95	1900	480	210	120	80
10 or 90	3600	900	400	230	150
15 or 85	5100	1300	570	320	210
20 or 80	6400	1600	710	400	260
30 or 70	8400	2100	930	530	340
40 or 60	9600	2400	1070	600	380
50	10 000	2500	1110	630	400

Approximate size of sample required to estimate the percentage specified in Column 1 with the specified level of precision, on 19 times out of 20.
For example, if an *estimate* is 10%, then 900 observations are needed to ensure that there is a 95% chance that the *true value* lies in the range 10% ± 2%, namely between 8% and 12%.

Consider an instance when a pilot sample estimated the machine stopped time at 10 per cent and it was important to know that the true stopped time was not less than 8 per cent or not more than 12 per cent. Using the precision required ± 2 per cent, and the estimated true percentage, 10 per cent, the table shows that in total a sample of 900 observations is needed. This number of observations would ensure that nineteen times out of twenty the correct decisions would be made.

Clearly the economics of the investigation will dictate whether or not it is better to take a large sample, with the consequent expense and delay before the results are known, in order to have a very small risk of being misled by the data collected from the sample.

(ii) *Estimating a measurement.* In many industries the standard practice of checking a machine setting is to examine the first item produced. Checking only one item is inadequate when the process is subject to appreciable variation and this fact is often recognised intuitively by the setter when he examines several items. It is possible to determine objectively how many items should be examined and Table 3.4 gives the appropriate sample size for a

Table 3.4. Factors affecting the choice of sample size when checking process setting

Risk of making unnecessary adjustment	1 in 3		1 in 20	
Risk of failing to adjust when necessary	1 in 40		1 in 1000	
Required accuracy of setting (standard deviations)	Size of sample	Limit on median of sample	Size of sample	Limit on median of sample
		(standard deviations)		(standard deviations)
0.8	22	0.37	Too large for practical use	
1.0	14	0.34		
1.2	10	0.40	27	0.48
1.4	7	0.47	20	0.56
1.6	6	0.51	15	0.65
1.8	4	0.63	12	0.72
2.0	3	0.72	10	0.79
3.0	2	0.89	4	1.25
4.0	1	1.25	2	1.77
5.0	X	X	2	1.77
6.0	X	X	1	2.51
7.0	X	X	X	X

Approximate size of sample, with limit on the accuracy of process setting measured by the median of the sample. Designed to control the risk of making an unnecessary adjustment, and also the risk of failing to adjust when necessary at 'first off' inspection of a production process.

number of specific instances. In this table the accuracy required has been related directly to the variability of the process by choosing as a unit of measurement the standard deviation of the characteristic being measured (the process standard deviation).

The sample size and the limit on the median of the sample have been chosen to control the risk of making two alternative mistaken decisions. On the one hand, a lucky sample would suggest that it was unnecessary to adjust an incorrectly set process; on the other, an unlucky sample would suggest that it was necessary to adjust a correctly set process.

This table illustrates clearly how the number of items needed in the sample decreases when, firstly, the risk of making the wrong decision and secondly, the required limits of accuracy can be increased.

The following example illustrates the use of Table 3.4. A process with a standard deviation of 0.001 inches has tolerances of 0.5 ± 0.005 inches, and consequently it is decided that the process setting must be accurate to ± 0.002 inches. The choice of the risk of making each of the two mistaken decisions would be related to the cost of making scrap and the cost of the lost time spent on re-setting the machine. In this instance the risk of making an unnecessary adjustment was chosen as one in three, and the risk of failing to adjust when it was really necessary at one in forty. From these columns a sample size of three corresponds to the required accuracy of setting of 2.0 standard deviations. The table also shows that the median of the three observations must lie within 0.72 standard deviations (.00072 inches) of the required setting if the process is to be allowed to run. Limits of 0.5 ± 0.00072 would be established, and if the median of the three observations lay between these limits, the setting would be accepted.

The previous sections have dealt with the principles of using samples in management. They have outlined some of the difficulties to be faced and indicated how they can be overcome. In the following sections of this chapter the use of samples in work study, quality control and management investigations is examined.

3.3. Applications of sampling principles in industry

3.3.1. Work sampling

(a) *Purpose of work sampling.* Work sampling is a tool of work measurement and its specific purpose is to obtain an outline picture of a working situation such as a factory, a building site or even a hospital. The observations which are made are usually designed to measure the efficiency of management's use of its workforce and equipment. For instance, on a civil engineering site, work sampling would be used to measure:

1. the percentage of time lost, on each section of the site and on each unit of plant;
2. the work output, for instance the man hours earned by each gang;
3. the relative importance of areas of activity in order to identify areas worthy of detailed work measurement and method study.

(b) *Principles of work sampling.* Work sampling is carried out by an observer who records at specific instances of time the nature of the work being done by a worker or by a piece of equipment. The observation procedure should provide a series of unbiased snap shots of the working activity. From the observations on the civil engineering site, records would be accumulated of the number of instants that each piece of plant was observed whilst working and the number of instants whilst stopped. It is reasonable to assume that if these instants were an unbiased sample of all the possible instants of the survey period, then the percentage plant utilization can be estimated by the following ratio:

$$\text{Percentage plant utilization} = \frac{\text{No. of instants plant working}}{\text{No. of instants plant observed}} \times 100$$

(c) *Choice of sample.* In order to eliminate the possibility of bias in selecting when to observe, the choice of this instant should be as impersonal as possible. Random numbers are frequently used to select either the specific instant of each observation or the instant at which to commence a series of observations of the work situation. Such a series of observations could readily be made both of the work force and equipment on a tour round a construction site, a drawing office or a hospital. One procedure often adopted is to use random numbers to select the intervals between commencing successive tours. This can be done simply by means of a conversion table such as that shown in Table 3.5.

In drawing up this table it has been assumed that the minimum feasible interval between the start of successive tours is fifteen minutes, and that the average interval between tours should be twenty minutes, so as to yield on average twenty-four tours during the eight hour working day.

(d) *Bias in measurement.* The very presence of an observer is likely to introduce bias when the worker has control of his work cycle. This is a well known effect in work measurement by time study and an effort is made, wherever this is possible, to eliminate such bias by careful choice of the operator to be studied. Since in work sampling the observer is only present for an instant he is likely to introduce less bias than during a standard time study. Nevertheless, such an effect does exist and it is common practice to discard as unreliable the results of the first one or two days of a work sampling investigation.

Bias can also arise when the observers are either incorrectly or inadequately briefed. A pilot survey is often useful in identifying many of the problems which will be faced by the observers. It enables definite rules to be made covering both the method of collecting observations and the interpretation of the different work phases. Without such rules a subjective element is introduced into the classification of activities and the instant of making the observation. Bias in measurement is minimized when this subjective element is eliminated. One final point, the period over

Table 3.5. Table used to convert random numbers into intervals between times of starting successive tours

Tour interval (Mins)	Random numbers
15	00-08
16	09-17
17	18-26
18	27-35
19	36-44
20	45-53
21	54-62
22	63-71
23	72-80
24	81-89
25	90-98

Number 99 is not used

which the sample is taken should be sufficiently long so that it contains a sample representative of the normal working of the operation being studied. For instance, if plant overhaul is normally concentrated during the summer shut down period, a separate study of the activity of maintenance workers covering this period would probably be needed to supplement a work sampling study taken during the normal factory working period.

3.3.2. Sampling in quality control

(a) *When sampling is appropriate.* There are instances where it would be completely inappropriate to assess the quality of a product by the examination of samples. Every weld in the vessels used in nuclear powered generating stations has to be examined. The cost of a failure is so prohibitive that a possibility of failing to detect a faulty weld cannot be tolerated. Several X-ray or Gamma ray photographs must be taken and the photographs scrutinized by several people: only in this way can the near perfection of this inspection procedure be ensured.

On the other hand when destructive tests are applied it is impossible to avoid assessing quality on the results of a sample. A soldier's life may depend on a rifle bullet, the quality of which has to be inferred from the results of tests on other bullets.

Between these two extremes there are numerous instances where speed, cost and practicability make it desirable to assess the quality of a product on the basis of samples. Samples are used in quality control in two fields. Firstly, where batches of work are offered for acceptance, either at goods inwards or at despatch, and secondly where a product is being manufactured and quality being created.

(b) *Acceptance sampling.* One of the principal objectives in acceptance inspection is to detect and reject faulty work. Where it is unimportant if a few faulty items get through either into one's own production shops or into those of customers, sampling can be used to detect and reject faulty batches. It is clearly also important that the relative quality levels achieved by different suppliers should be monitored and this information taken into account when purchase orders are placed. Furthermore, the very existence of acceptance inspection should stimulate suppliers to send in work of an acceptable quality. Some sampling procedures such as the Defence Specification DEF 131A, published by the Ministry of Defence, go even further and modify their severity according to the quality level being achieved by each supplier. (These procedures are also available as British Standard BS9001.) Moreover, when properly used, acceptance sampling schemes allow inspection effort to be concentrated where it is needed. A typical sample plan would be to take a sample of 200 items, selected as five separate samples of forty items. If there are less than two items in the sample not up to the specified standard of quality, accept the batch without further inspection. If there are two or more items in the sample not up to the quality standard, inspect the remainder of the batch. If the batch consisted of 20 000 items, the sample would be merely 1 per cent of the batch, provided the quality level was satisfactory. In contrast, bad batches, provided they are rejected by the sample plan, would be subjected to 100 per cent inspection.

There is of course always a risk of being misled by the results obtained by the sample. Fig. 3.2 shows the percentage of batches accepted by the above sample plan. It demonstrates how on the one hand 10 per cent of batches with a level of faulty items as low as 0.25 per cent will fail to pass the sample plan, and yet on the other hand 10 per cent of batches with a level of faulty items

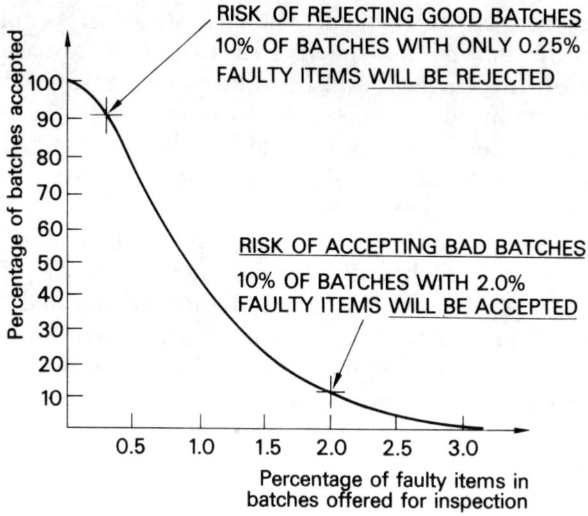

Figure 3.2 Risks involved in using acceptance sampling schemes

as high as 2 per cent will be accepted without further inspection. The real art of using acceptance sampling plans lies in the choice of management objectives. Ideally, policy decisions are needed on the following questions:

1. What level of faults can we tolerate very occasionally?
2. What level of faults will be acceptable every day?
3. Do we really want the sample plan to isolate the bad batches from the good batches?
4. Do we wish to use the inspection effort to screen the incoming work so that on average the percentage of faulty items is reduced to an acceptable level, or
5. Do we merely wish to monitor the quality performance of our suppliers and use the inspection effort as a means of stimulating their quality performance?

Once these decisions have been made, an appropriate sample plan can be selected from published tables, such as DEF 131A.

(c) *Controlling the achievement of quality.* When production processes are working satisfactorily and regularly making products which meet the tolerance, it is clearly unnecessary to inspect every unit produced. One approach would be to check samples of the product from a batch after it has been made. An alternative and preferable approach is to take samples during manufacture and to use these, first to check that the process has been set correctly and subsequently to check whether the average level and the process variability remain unchanged. The advantages of sampling during manufacture lie in the speed with which information can be obtained on the current level of quality. As a result more effort is concentrated on achieving satisfactory quality at the instant that quality is created. Savings inevitably arise as losses incurred by scrapping, rectification, blending and relegation to lower categories of quality are reduced.

It is often appropriate to collect the information needed to control product quality by taking measurements of a sample consisting of several identical components, such as machined parts, bars of chocolate or packets of biscuits. In these instances perhaps the simplest summary of this quality information is a control chart for the medians and the ranges of the measurements on each sample.

The measurements collected by sampling the product are plotted in a simple chart so that the order in which the measurements were collected can be readily seen. Fig. 3.3 shows a control chart of this kind which was used to control the dough weight of biscuits before they were cooked.

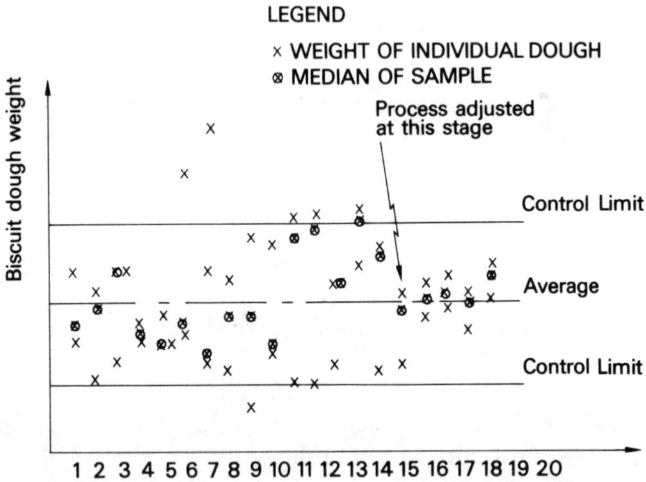

Figure 3.3 Control chart for medians showing detection and adjustment of biscuit overweight

A sample of three pieces was selected at regular intervals and the weight measured and recorded on the chart. A circle was drawn round the middle reading of each sample, namely the median. A target average and upper and lower control limits on the medians had been previously established and the process was allowed to run without adjustment provided the medians remained within the control limits.

The chart for medians is used solely to monitor the average setting of the process. A similar check on the variability of the process may be made by monitoring the range of the weights in each sample. Provided that the average setting and the process variability are known to be acceptable, the process quality needs no further check. In the case of the biscuit doughs it would be both impracticable and uneconomic to check the weight of every dough.

When there are a large number of quality characteristics on each component or when measurement of one or more of them is difficult or lengthy, components are often checked by gauging or by visual inspection. A simple method of monitoring the quality level in such instances is to select and gauge a sample of (say) twenty-five items from the process as close as possible to the instant of manufacture. The number of items failing to meet the specification are then counted, and this number is plotted in sequence on a simple control chart so that the order of manufacture can be readily seen. These charts are the most commonly used method of providing information on which to control the quality achieved during manufacture. Fig. 3.4 is an

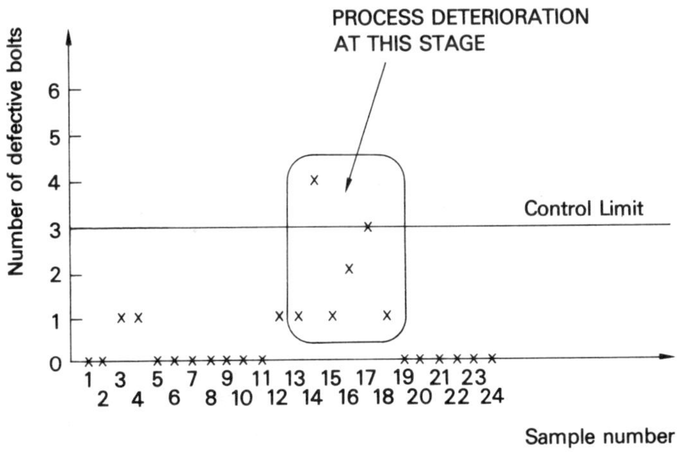

Figure 3.4 Control chart for number of defective items in samples of 10 bolts

example of control charts of this kind. It shows how the process deteriorated for a short period, was detected and eventually brought under control.

(d) *Investigations to improve the quality level.* Control charts are intended to control the quality level of processes which are running satisfactorily. Often when they are introduced they focus attention on faulty equipment, methods or material and result in an immediate improvement in quality. However, when a production process is not working at an acceptable level, sampling can be used to reduce the effort of investigation.

In such investigations it is desirable to measure the quality characteristics causing the unacceptable quality, rather than counting the number of defective items. When the quality check is subjective, an immediate switch to measurement may not be readily made. In such instances the product may be graded into five grades and scores of 0, 1, 2, 3 and 4 allocated to the different grades.

The samples should be chosen to examine reasons for variation in the measurements and to collect information to assess the magnitude of each source of variation. For instance, in biscuit manufacture it is highly desirable to reduce the variation in biscuit weight to the lowest practical amount. A schematic diagram of the production process involved is shown in Fig. 3.5. Samples would

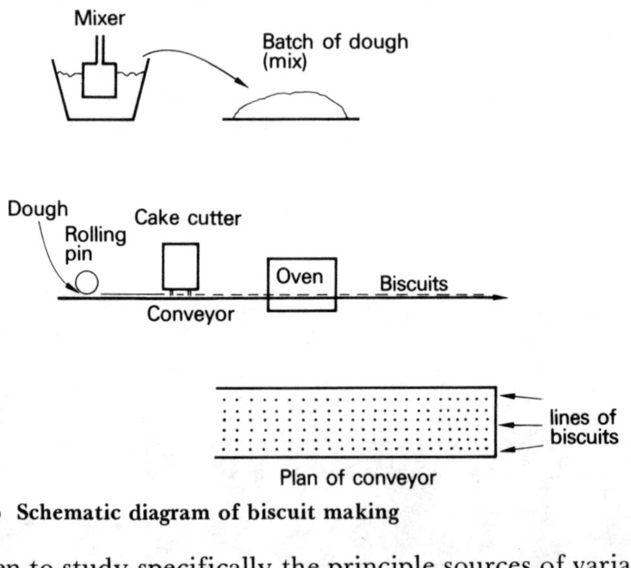

Figure 3.5 Schematic diagram of biscuit making

be chosen to study specifically the principle sources of variation in weight, such as the variation from batch to batch in the dough mixing and the variation from line to line in the cutting and cooking of the biscuits. In one particular investigation five biscuits were taken on each of three well spaced occasions from each of five lines and for each of four mixes. By careful analysis of the measurements it was possible to determine whether it was better to concentrate on reducing line to line variation or mix to mix variation, and to estimate the potential benefits if one or both could be reduced.

3.3.3. Management investigations

(a) *Field of Application.* Whenever information has to be collected to form the basis of management decisions, the use of samples to collect this information should be considered. The potential area of applications is vast and includes:

- Checking of invoices, particularly on sales between different units within a group of companies;
- estimating the value of year end stocks;
- marketing appraisals, for instance into the watching habits of television audiences;
- establishing costing formulae as a basis for standard costing;
- special investigations such as a study of the scale and nature of the engineering alterations within a company making mechanical equipment.

In many instances the cost or the time needed for a complete investigation makes the use of samples inevitable. Often, moreover, it is felt intuitively that a sample will provide the information required with a sufficient degree of accuracy. The following section describes a method of choosing a sample which allows the reliability of the sample to be measured in a very simple manner.

(b) *Example of application.* The problem posed by the company in question was 'What are the potential savings, if, instead of our present methods of re-ordering, we were to apply mathematical rules to determine when to re-order and how much to re-order?'

The company had sixty branches of varying sizes and carried from 3000 to 10 000 different items of stock at a branch. Its policy was to provide a high level of service from stock to its many customers. It was organized in four geographical regions, and each region had approximately fifteen branches.

The first step was to spread the investigation throughout all the regions, each of which would provide a responsible member of staff to collect the relevant information. Five branches were selected at random from each of the regions, so spreading the sample to eliminate as far as possible bias arising from choosing a 'typical' branch.

At each of these branches ten separate samples were chosen, each sample containing between fifteen and twenty-five stock items. The first sample was selected by the following procedure:

1. choosing a random starting point in the first tray of stock cards and,
2. selecting cards at regular intervals throughout the remaining trays.

The same procedure was adopted for each of the remaining nine samples.

By this approach ten 'identical' samples were chosen, spread over the twenty selected branches. The variation from sample to sample could be used to measure the reliability of the deductions made from the investigation. One of these deductions concerned the size of stock savings if the frequency of re-ordering stocks was doubled, and the estimates provided by each of the ten samples are shown in Table 3.6.

Table 3.6. Ten independent estimates of potential savings

Sample number	Estimated saving	Averages
1	£155 000	
2	£170 000	First Five
3	£185 000	£166 000
4	£134 000	
5	£188 000	
6	£242 000	
7	£208 000	Second Five
8	£138 000	£187 000
9	£165 000	
10	£182 000	
Average over all ten samples		£176 000

From these results the best estimate was given by the average, namely, £176 000. The reliability of this estimate can be assessed by calculating the average of the first five samples (£166 000) and the average of the second five samples (£187 000), and comparing the two estimates. A slightly more sophisticated method of assessing the reliability of the estimate is described in the following chapter on page 61.

3.4. Summary

Samples can be used to provide management with information more quickly and more cheaply than a full investigation. On the other hand, there are inevitable risks when samples are used. The risks of choosing a biased sample can be minimized by taking a number of small samples each independent of one another, rather than one large sample and by making the choice of the individual items in each sample as impersonal as possible.

When carrying out investigations, the purpose for which the information will be used should be decided before the sample is designed to collect it. By careful design the reliability of the information of the samples can be readily assessed although it is desirable, whenever possible, to look for a check of the results which is independent of the samples.

The use of samples is well established in the fields of work study and quality control and has considerable benefits to offer in all areas where management investigations are being made.

Finally, the ruse of subdividing a sample into identically chosen sub-samples cannot be too strongly recommended. It helps to eliminate sampling biases and more especially provides a direct measure of the reliability of the total sample.

List of terms used

Sample	*Standard deviation*
Population	*Median*
Sampling	*Work sampling*
Bias in measurement	Pilot survey
Bias in sampling	*Quality control*
Random sampling	Batch
Random	*Sample plan*
Random numbers	*Average*
Structure of the population	*Range*
Precision	Control chart
Risk	Sources of variation
Variation	*Reliability of estimate*

Italicized terms are defined in the glossary (page 262) as well as in the text where appropriate.

4. Patterns in figures

4.1. The rewards and risks in analysing figures

Sales forecasting, standard costing, and work study are just three of the many fields in which a manager makes estimates and then decisions on these estimates. If he knows that there is a systematic pattern, such as a seasonal pattern in the sales figures, he can make a better estimate and so a better decision from the estimate. Rewards appear in such forms as more efficient use of machines and manpower, reductions in stock levels, better delivery promises and better marketing and pricing policies. In particular, a rational wage policy based on the estimates of job evaluation can contribute significantly to improved industrial relations.

There are obviously obstacles to be overcome before such prizes can be won. The principal task in analysing figures is to identify the major sources of variation in the figures, and then to measure the nature and the amount of the *systematic* variation arising from each source. There will always be *random* variation arising from the innate variability of industrial and commercial activity and in many instances this tends to mask the systematic pattern. In other instances what appears at first glance to be a systematic pattern in the figures does not subsequently repeat itself and must be written off to chance fluctuations.

A further risk lies in the choice of the yardstick of performance. Are we really comparing like with like? For example, is it reasonable for the sales director to compare the performance of the manager of the northern division with that of the manager of the eastern division simply by measuring the sales per head of population? Would it not be better to compare the rate of growth of sales per head? Perhaps the pattern of the relationship between sales and population is such that a simple ratio of one to the other can never provide a fair comparison. It could be that in the more populated areas there is greater competition and a more complex relationship needs to be established. If comparisons are made subjectively they will be coloured by the personalities of the managers concerned, and whilst personality is important it is performance which should count. A rational and consistent assessment of comparative performance may, in some instances, be easily established through simple measurements and in others require a more sophisticated evaluation. An analysis of the pattern in the sales figures will help the sales director to choose the correct performance criterion.

4.2. Random pattern of variability

4.2.1. How reliable is the average?

There will always be some random pattern in management measurements which prevents the next result being forecast accurately. Where the random pattern dominates and completely masks any systematic pattern the analysis of the figures is simple. Basically, the more figures there are, the more reliable the answer.

The usual summary measure of a set of figures on which decisions are based is the average. Just how much faith to place in the average, bearing in mind the inevitable variation in the figures it summarizes, can be visualized from Figs. 4.1 and 4.2.

The first of these figures illustrates that no matter how the individual figures may vary, the average will lie in the middle.

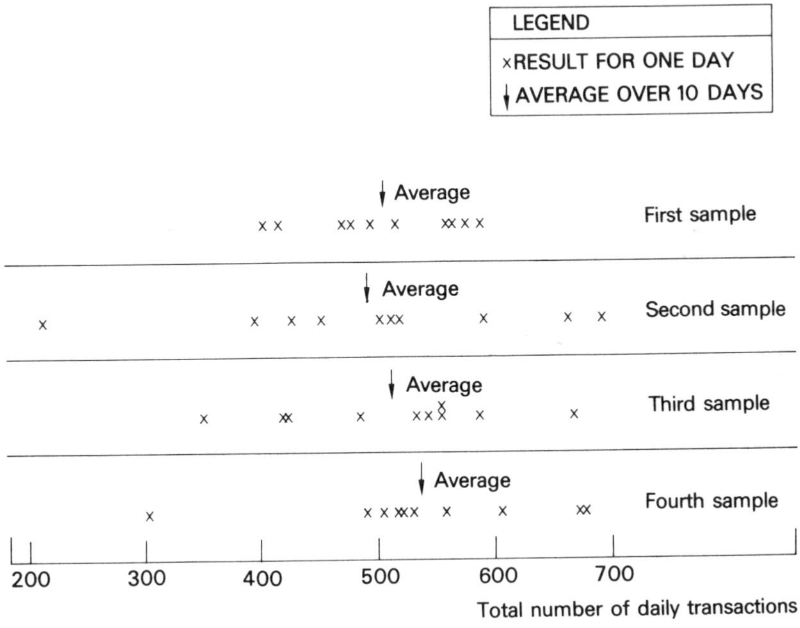

Figure 4.1 No matter how the individual observations scatter—the average lies in the middle

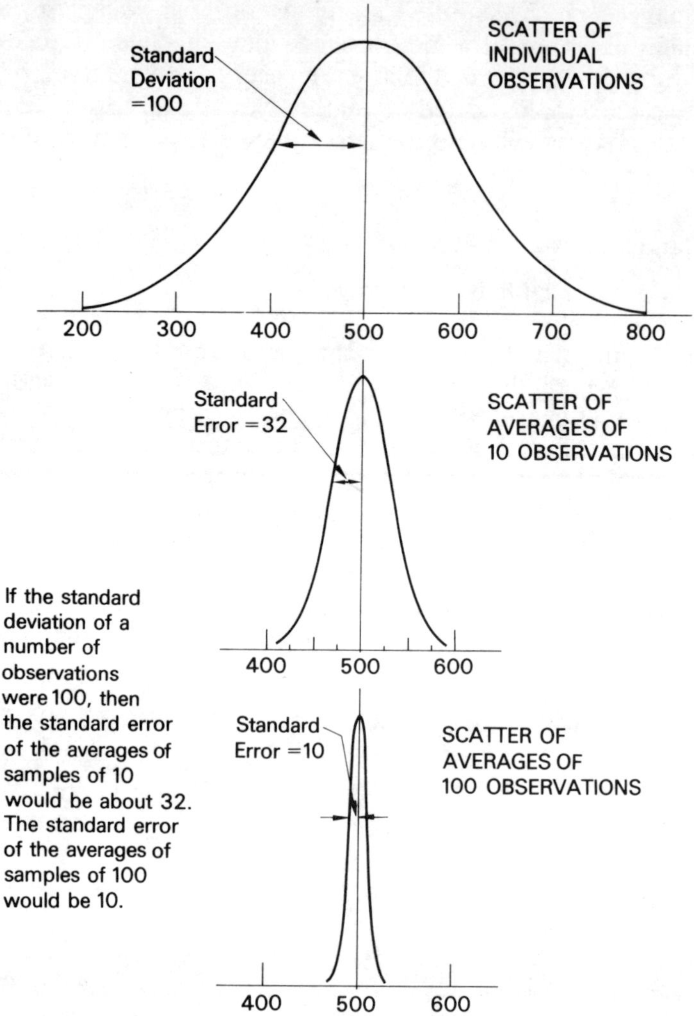

Figure 4.2 The larger the sample, the more reliable the average

Consequently, when repeated samples are taken (in this instance each sample consisting of ten observations), the average will vary far less from sample to sample than the individual figures vary from one to another. Fig. 4.2 shows what happens when a very large number of samples of ten are taken and the average of each sample is determined and also, in the bottom portion, what would happen if repeated samples of 100 were taken. In both cases, the averages form frequency diagrams which are spread symmetrically about the same average value as the frequency diagram of the individuals, but with a smaller scatter. The amount of variation in this particular case is such that the total number of individual daily transactions by the office can vary from day to day between 200 and 800 but the average of ten daily figures will fall between 400 and 600, and the average of 100 daily figures between 470 and 530.

One could be very confident that whatever the true average may be an individual observation would not differ from it by more than 300 transactions; that the average of ten observations would not differ from it by more than 100 transactions, and the average of 100 observations by more than thirty transactions. The averages of course follow a frequency diagram and so have a degree of variation which can be assessed by a measure equivalent to the standard deviation. This measure has been given the name 'the standard error' of the average. If the variability amongst the individual observations follows a random pattern then the standard error of the average can be estimated from the standard deviation of the individual figures.

Fig. 4.2 shows that the standard error of the average of ten observations $= \dfrac{\text{standard deviation,}}{\sqrt{10}}$

and the standard error of the average of 100 observations

$$= \frac{\text{standard deviation,}}{\sqrt{100}}$$

In general terms,
the standard error of the average of n observations

$$= \frac{\text{standard deviation of individual figures}}{\sqrt{n}}$$

It is particularly worth noticing from the above relationship that just doubling the sample size will not double the reliability of the average: to halve the standard error the sample size has to be quadrupled.

4.2.2. Confidence limits on the average

The frequency diagram of averages will always be more bell-shaped than the frequency diagram of individual figures. Consequently, it will be even more justifiable to use the proportions of the normal distribution to determine limits on the degree of scatter of the averages. This has been illustrated in Fig. 4.3 from which it can be readily seen that 95 per cent of all the possible sample averages differ from the true average by less than twice the standard error. Consequently, if only a single average is determined there is a 95 per cent chance that it will differ from the true average by less than twice the standard error.

The scale below the frequency diagram in Fig. 4.3 shows the standard error of the average of 100 observations of the daily total

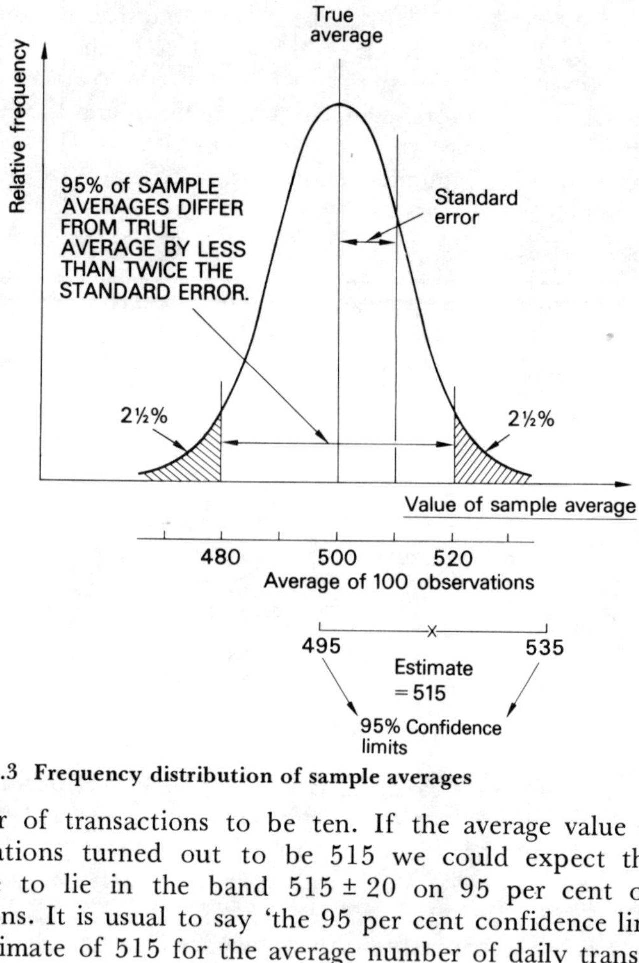

Figure 4.3 Frequency distribution of sample averages

number of transactions to be ten. If the average value of 100 observations turned out to be 515 we could expect the true average to lie in the band 515 ± 20 on 95 per cent of such occasions. It is usual to say 'the 95 per cent confidence limits on the estimate of 515 for the average number of daily transactions are 515 ± 20, namely 495 and 535'.

In practice the true average and the true standard error are never known and have to be estimated from the observations forming the sample. The variation amongst the observations is used to estimate their standard deviation and the relationship

$$\text{standard error} = \frac{\text{standard deviation}}{\sqrt{\text{number of observations}}}$$

is used to estimate the standard error. The 95 per cent confidence limits are then based on the sample average and this estimate of the standard error, and are:

sample average ± twice (estimate of standard error).

4.2.3. Several averages

Some of the advantages of splitting a sample into several identical sub-samples have been described in the previous chapter. A further advantage lies in the ease with which the standard error of the average over all the sub-samples can be estimated.

Fig. 4.1 showed the result of taking forty daily observations of the total number of transactions carried out in an office, by means of four sub-samples of ten observations. The appropriate averages are summarized in Table 4.1.

Table 4.1. Averages of sub-samples

Sub-sample No.	Average
1	508
2	492
3	512
4	536
Overall	512

Range of sub-samples = 44

In instances such as this, where there are between three and ten identically chosen sub-samples, the standard error of the average over all the sub-samples may be estimated by:

$$\text{standard error} = \frac{\text{range of sub-samples}}{\text{number of sub-samples}}$$

The standard error of the average of the forty observations

$$= \frac{44}{4} \text{ namely } 11;$$

the 95 per cent confidence limits for the estimate based on the average of the forty observations are:

$$512 \pm 22$$

4.3. Systematic pattern of variability

4.3.1. Is there a pattern?

Measurements used in management are bedevilled with fluctuations from several sources. It is common sense to accept the many small fluctuations due to the trivial sources as inevitable and to concentrate on isolating the important few. If the important few sources of variability are systematic then appropriate action can be taken to reduce their effect, otherwise it is far better to measure the total amount of variability and to take it into account in determining management policy.

Management's choice of what may or may not be a major source of systematic variation depends on the structure of the situation. Machine utilization could vary systematically from one machine group to another; output in man hours earned from one department to another; profit contribution from one division to another; orders received from one quarter to another, or from one month to another. This choice can be limited either by the availability of figures, or the ability to collect figures in a suitable form. Furthermore, even before the analysis is carried out careful thought should be paid to what can be done to accommodate systematic variation, and what is the economic angle—where is the payoff? Can the batch to batch variation in raw material be appreciably reduced by blending? Can the packet to packet weight variation be appreciably reduced by changing the method of packaging? Can the reliability of a sales forecast be appreciably improved by taking separate notice of seasonal changes?

In those instances where only two alternative performance levels are being compared the pattern can often be highlighted by careful arrangement of the figures. Consider, for example, the results contained in Table 4.2.

Table 4.2. Simple comparison of performance
Profit contribution (£000's) of different divisions

Division	Last year	This year
I	135	151
II	152	161
III	119	165
IV	212	225
Average	154.5	175.5
95% Confidence limits	± 46.5	± 37.0

The average profit contribution for this year is clearly £21 000 up on last year. However this increase is small compared against the 95 per cent confidence limits of £46 500 and £37 000 on the average contributions. At first glance it would appear that this improvement could be readily due to chance, due to the random fluctuations in performance. This is illustrated in Fig. 4.4a where the confidence limits on the respective averages are seen to overlap considerably.

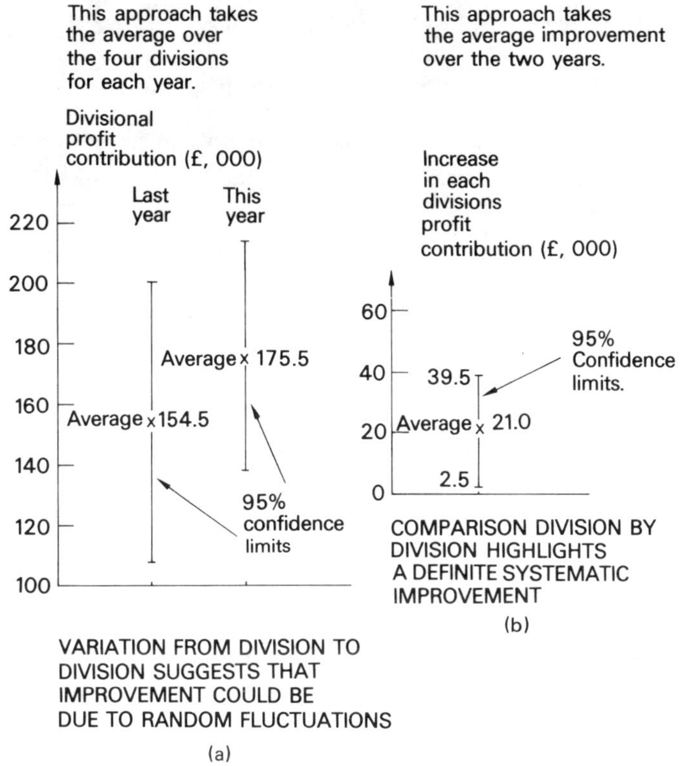

Figure 4.4 Careful arrangement of figures can highlight their systematic patterns

If there is no reason why one division should turn in the same performance as another division, then the division to division variation should be treated as systematic variation. Making a comparison of the increase in profit over last year, division by division, as shown in Table 4.3 on page 66, could well be the correct form of analysis.

The average increase of £21 000 is larger than these 95 per cent confidence limits and this shows that there has been a definite systematic improvement in profit contribution (Fig. 4.4b).

The first analysis would say that the new sales promotion was possibly working but that the improvement could be due to chance. The second analysis would say that sales have definitely improved and could justify further expenditure on sales promotion.

This simple example typifies the advantage of a careful arrangement of figures to highlight their pattern. In this case there were only two alternatives being compared, this year's performance and last year's, and the difference between them, division by division, was the correct comparison to make.

Table 4.3. Comparison of increase in profit, division by division

Profit contribution (£000's) of different divisions

Division	Increase
I	16
II	9
III	46
IV	13
Average increase	21.0
95% Confidence limits	± 18.5

4.3.2. Graphical representation

Where several alternatives are compared, the method of analysis is more sophisticated unless the pattern in the figures is very marked and then simple graphical methods may be adequate. The key to making the analysis straightforward is to collect the information in a systematic manner. In the comparison on profit contribution, there may have been only three divisions in the year before last, or the divisional structure may have been shuffled. If this were so, the only common measure over the three years would be the total company profit contribution. Any deduction about the sales promotion drive would be much more tentative without a measure of the innate variability of the total company operation.

Consider the biscuit making process shown in Fig. 3.5. Because of the variability in biscuit weight, it is essential to pack overweight to meet the law on weights and measures. The greater the variability, the greater the overweight, and so an analysis of the nature of this variability could lead to savings. Fig. 3.5 is on page 54. To examine the sources of variation in biscuit weight *six* biscuits were taken, at each of *three* ten minute intervals, from each of *five* positions across the conveyor belt, on each of *four* mixes of dough making *sixty* (3 x 5 x 4) samples of *six* biscuits. The first stage of the analysis was non-graphical, it was to compare the variability within each sample of six biscuits against the total variability in biscuit weight. The range of the six biscuits was calculated for each sample and the size of this very short term variability was found to be about one third of the total variability. Because it is so small, the very short term variability has been ignored in the subsequent graphical analysis and the average weight of the sample of six biscuits used to measure the process's performance at a point of time.

The following figures illustrate three extreme situations in which a simple graphical representation will produce useful information.

(a) *Short term variation.* Fig. 4.5 shows an instance in which

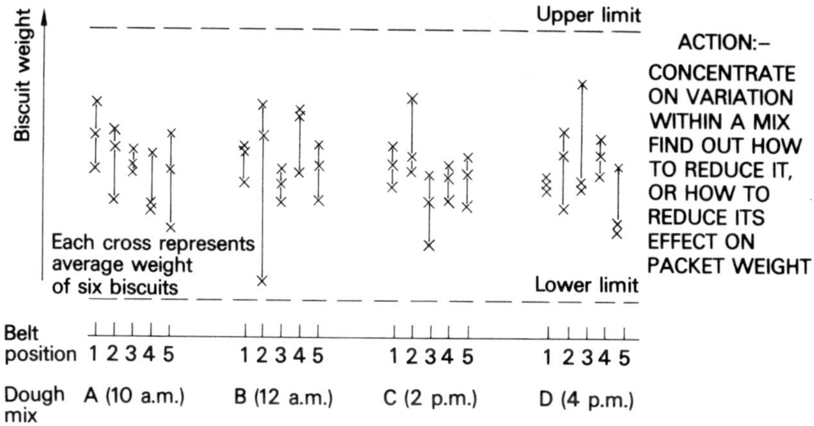

Figure 4.5 Principal source of variation: short term variation within a mix

it is quite clear that the principal source of variation arises from the differences between the samples taken within a mix. There appears to be little or no variation from mix to mix or from one belt position to another and in this case effort to reduce process variation should be concentrated on short term sources. Why are there such differences from one sample to the next? How can this be reduced? How can the effect of this short term variation be eliminated or reduced at the packaging stage or immediately before it?

(b) *Systematic differences between mixes.* Alternatively the diagram might show that the principal source of variation arose from systematic differences between the mixes. This could point to the need for a closer control of the mixing process. The particular pattern of Fig. 4.6 suggests that the difference between mixes is changing systematically throughout the day and that it could be due to systematic changes in the temperature in the factory. However, four mixes are not enough to make firm deductions, except for the need to concentrate on reducing differences between them.

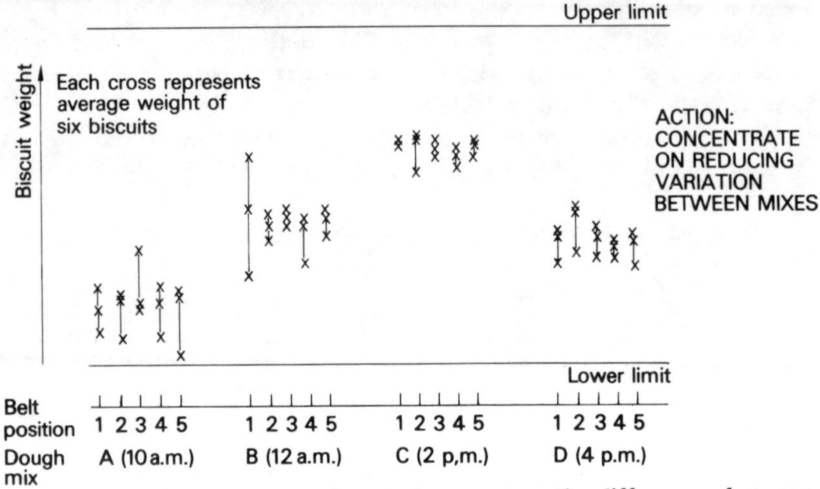

Figure 4.6 Principal source of variation: systematic differences between mixes

(c) *Systematic differences between belt positions.* In the previous figures the results were displayed in a natural time sequence. This enabled biscuits being made at the same time to be compared with biscuits being made at a different time and so highlighted mix to mix differences. In Fig. 4.7 all the results from one belt position have been grouped together to highlight the systematic differences between belt positions. In this case,

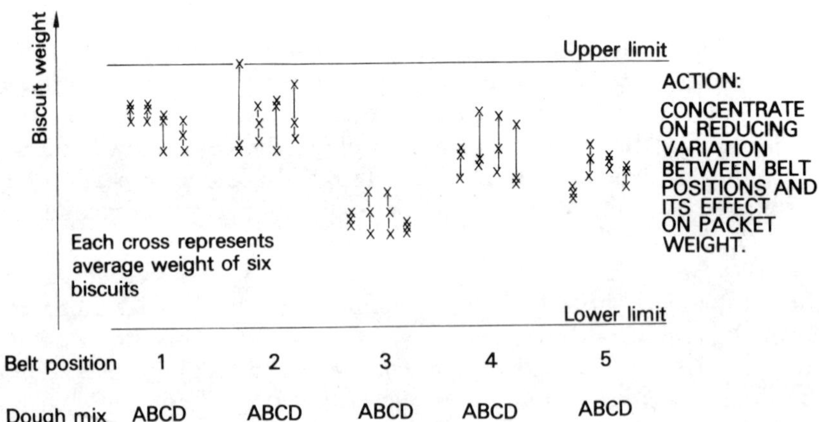

Figure 4.7 Principal sources of variation: systematic differences between belt positions

position to position differences appear to be the principal source of variation and efforts should be concentrated on eliminating them. If the method of packaging arranges the biscuits so that the heavy positions compensate the light positions, these systematic differences are unimportant. If not, an appropriate method of packaging should be developed.

4.4. Pattern of associated figures

4.4.1. Purpose

Determining whether or not two measurements are related and the nature and degree of this relationship can often be of practical importance. Probably the most important application of such relationships is to forecast or predict what would happen under different conditions. For example, the weight of a casting might be used to estimate the time needed to fettle it, or a trend in past sales extended forward to predict future sales. Furthermore, a knowledge that two measurements are related may help in understanding the fundamental mechanism being studied as occurred in an investigation into factors affecting market price at public auction. The analysis led to a greater understanding of the market mechanism and a more profitable marketing strategy.

4.4.2. Scatter diagrams

The simplest procedure for determining the pattern of associated measurements is to plot one measurement against the other to form points on a diagram called a *scatter diagram.*

Consider the set of figures shown in Table 4.4, the planned and actual delivery times of twenty production batches. The respective figures for each batch determine the points in the scatter diagram shown in Fig. 4.8. (Table 4.4 and Fig. 4.8 are on page 70.)

This diagram shows that the actual delivery time tended to increase as the planned delivery time increased. Although this is useful information, it is more important to determine the exact nature of the relationship in order to be able to estimate actual delivery times. In many instances a reasonable approximation would be to fit a straight line through the plotted points and to use this to predict the value of the characteristic to be estimated. The best straight line represents an average relationship with points scattered on either side of it. The amount of this scatter determines the precision with which an estimate can be made. The problem of how to draw the best straight line through the points

Table 4.4. Delivery times of production batches

Batch	Delivery time (days) Planned	Actual
1	5	4
2	5	6
3	5	7
4	6	4
5	6	5
6	7	7
7	7	17
8	8	6
9	8	11
10	8	13
11	9	6
12	9	12
13	9	15
14	10	10
15	11	11
16	12	13
17	12	15
18	12	18
19	14	15
20	15	21

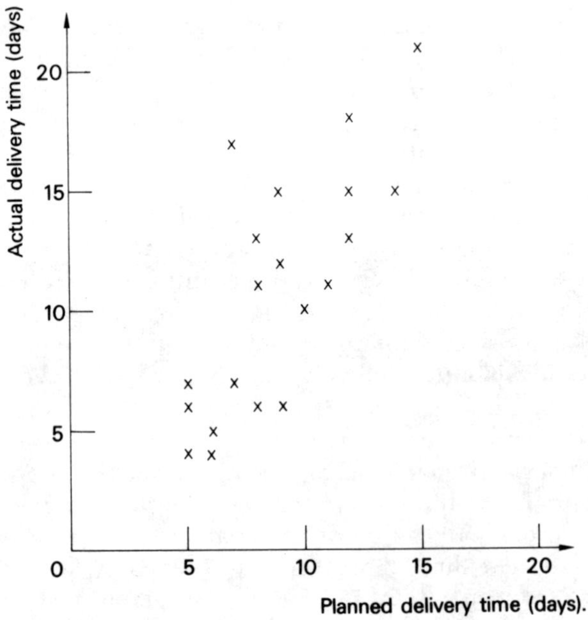

Figure 4.8 Plot of actual against planned delivery times

forming a scatter diagram, and then how to measure the amount of the scatter about it, is tackled in the next section.

4.4.3. Simple steps for drawing the best straight line

A simple method of drawing the best straight line through the scatter diagram is defined by the following steps:

(a) Divide the plotted points into four equal groups by lines drawn in the vertical direction, the direction in which the prediction is being made. When the number of points is not exactly divisible by four, the outer groups should contain an equal number and more points than the inner groups. The procedure is illustrated in Fig. 4.9, for the data shown in Table 4.4, and in this case there are five points in each group.

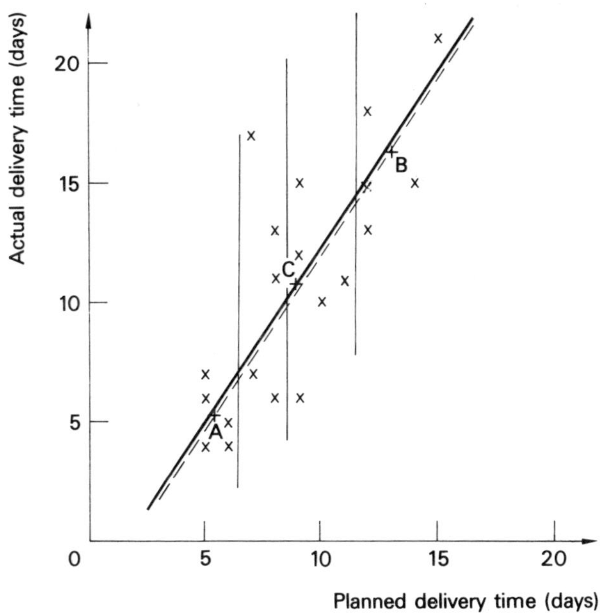

Figure 4.9 Best straight line through plot

(b) Calculate for the points in the extreme left hand group, the average of the characteristics plotted on the horizontal axis (the planned delivery time) and the average of the characteristic plotted on the vertical axis (the actual delivery time). Use these values to determine a point, denoted by A in Fig. 4.9. In this instance the respective averages, shown in Table 4.5, are 5.4 and 5.2.

Table 4.5. **Average delivery times**

Batch	Average delivery time (days) Planned	Actual
First five	5.4	5.2
Last five	13.0	16.4
All twenty	8.9	10.8

(c) Repeat the prcvious step for the points in the extreme right hand group to determine averages of 13.0 and 16.4 and call the resulting point B in Fig. 4.9.

(d) Repeat the previous step but in this case determine the averages of all the groups together, namely, 8.9 and 10.8, and call the resulting point C.

(e) The best straight line through the plotted points passes through C with a slope determined by the line AB. This line is shown in Fig. 4.9 as a full line.

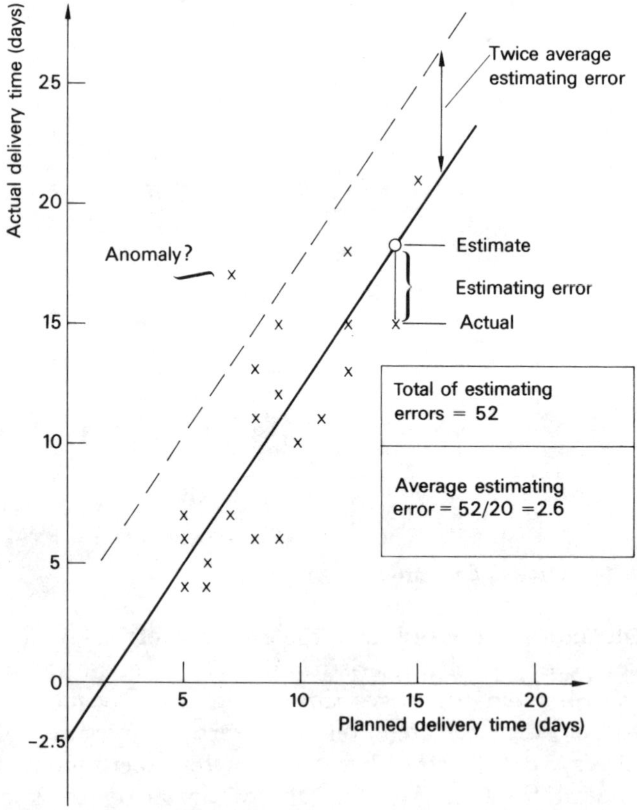

Figure 4.10 Scatter about best straight line

The value estimated by the best straight line is the average actual delivery time corresponding to a specified planned delivery time, the value which would occur if all the random variation about the best straight line were eliminated. In fact this random variation cannot be eliminated, and it may be measured by the average of the distances of the points from the line. These distances which represent the estimating error must be measured in the direction of the vertical axis, the axis of the characteristic which is being predicted. They can in practice be read off the diagram, Fig. 4.10, with sufficient accuracy. In this example they add up to 52.0 giving an average distance of 2.6—an average estimating error of 2.6 days.

It is reasonable to assume that the distances of the points from the line follow a normal frequency distribution. Consequently, 60 per cent of all future estimates based on the best straight line should be in error by less than the average estimating error, and 90 per cent in error by less than twice this value. (See Fig. 2.8).

4.4.4. Practical use of associated pattern

(a) *Revise planned delivery times.* The full line in Fig. 4.10 could be used to correct the existing planned delivery times so that they are correct on average. However this would mean that 50 per cent of the batches were in fact late against planned delivery times. The dotted line drawn twice the average estimating error above the best straight line could be used instead to ensure that 95 per cent of the batches are made within the planned delivery time. It is worth noting that batch No. 7 with actual delivery time of seventeen days appears to be an anomaly and worthy of a detailed investigation.

(b) *Understand why batches are late.* The best straight line shows that batches planned to take five days to deliver do on average take five days. Batches which are planned to take fifteen days will on average take twenty days to deliver. Since the batches with longer delivery times were those which required more than one manufacturing stage, the inference to be drawn from the best straight line is that insufficient time has been allowed for the delay between successive stages. Alternatively, something should be done to reduce the amount of this delay.

(c) *It is worthwhile estimating delivery times.* In this example the plotted points show clearly that the actual delivery time of a batch depended on its planned delivery time. This need not necessarily be so, and the actual delivery time could have been estimated from its average value, namely 10.8 days. If this average value had been used instead of the best straight line, (Table 4.6) the average estimating error would have been 4.2 days, almost twice as large as the average error arising from estimates based on the best straight line.

Table 4.6. Size of estimating error if linear relationship is ignored

Batches	Actual delivery time	Deviation from average
1	4	6.8
2	6	4.8
3	7	3.8
4	4	6.8
5	5	5.8
6	7	3.8
7	17	6.2
8	6	4.8
9	11	0.2
10	13	2.2
11	6	4.8
12	12	1.2
13	15	4.2
14	10	0.8
15	11	0.2
16	13	2.2
17	15	4.2
18	18	7.2
19	15	4.2
20	21	10.2
	Total	84.4

Mean Deviation = 4.2

4.4.5. Equation of best straight line

A straightforward relationship between two factors can be represented graphically as has been done in Fig. 4.10. When the relationship is of a more complex form, in particular if the planned delivery time had depended on two or more factors, graphical representation cannot be used. Instead, the relationship has to be expressed as an equation in mathematical shorthand.

The slope of the best straight line is measured by the amount by which the actual delivery time increases for every unit of planned delivery time. Fig. 4.10 shows that as the planned delivery time increases by ten days from five to fifteen days, the actual delivery time increases by fifteen from five to twenty days. Consequently, the increase for every unit of planned delivery time is 15/10, namely 1.5.

Fig. 4.10 also shows that when the planned delivery time is zero the actual delivery time read from the best straight line is −2.5 days. Consequently, the mathematical equation of the best straight line is:

Actual delivery time = 1.5 x (planned delivery time) – 2.5 days.

4.5. Multiple associations

4.5.1. The nature of multiple associations

Very often the characteristic we want to predict depends on more than one factor. For example, the profit arising from the different branches of a dry cleaning company depends not only on the branch's turnover but also on the rent paid for the branch's premises; the selling price of a house in a particular locality depends on the size of the house, the proximity of railway stations, of schools and shops, and of open spaces; the work load in a bank depends on the level of each of thirteen significant clerical activities; and the points evaluation of jobs and consequently their relative worth in terms of basic wage rates depends on responsibility for other people's work, for equipment, for other people's safety, on the time and effort needed to acquire the basic skills, on working conditions, and so on.

The technique for determining the appropriate relationship has a sophisticated name *multiple regression analysis,* but it is just a procedure for determining the relationship in the form of a mathematical equation. In the case of the profitability of the branches of the dry cleaning company, the equation could take the form:

Annual profit (£) = 0.3 x (annual turnover in £s)
– 0.2 x (annual rent in £s)
+ £1000

This is a simple instance with only two factors, annual turnover and annual rent, being used to estimate annual profit. In this case the amount of the calculations necessary to fit the best relationship to the basic data collected from the sixty branches of the company is not excessive. However, if many more factors were taken into account, the calculations become extensive and they would be best carried out on a computer. This in practice presents little trouble since most of the people who sell time on computers are familiar with the calculations needed in multiple regression analysis.

4.5.2. How to determine complex relationships

There will always be some random variability which cannot be removed however complex a relationship is fitted to the basic data. This must be tolerated, but nevertheless measured and used to determine confidence limits on the estimates based on the calculated relationship. In practice the simpler the relationship which enables satisfactory estimates to be made the better and the techniques of multiple regression analysis are aimed at identifying the simplest acceptable relationship.

The first step is to choose those factors which are likely to affect the value of the characteristic being estimated. For instance, what affects the unit price of a particular kind of agricultural produce sold by auction in the open market? After much discussion the factors, ten in all, were chosen as:

1. The amount sold in the previous week; in the current week; in the forthcoming week;
2. The amount available for sale in the previous week; in the current week; in the forthcoming week;
3. The amount of competitive produce available in the previous week; in the current week; in the forthcoming week; and
4. The proportion of the season which had elapsed.

Adequate data over the past few years was available and a computer program was used to fit the best equation containing these ten factors to the data. The computer program calculated the constants (called coefficients) to be used in the equation together with confidence limits on their values. For example, the multiplying coefficient for the amount sold in the forthcoming week was 0.1 with 95 per cent confidence limits of ± 0.3. Since this coefficient could easily be zero, it was assumed to be zero and ignored, so simplifying the estimating equation. Seven of the factors introduced into the equation were eliminated in this manner leaving a simpler equation of the form:

Unit price = 10.0 – (0.01 x amount sold in previous week)
– (0.008 x amount of competitive produce available next week)
– (0.02 x proportion of the season which had elapsed)

Several of the factors were closely related to one another. Once the key factor had been taken into account, the others which were closely related to it had nothing to add to the quality of the estimation and so they were dropped out of the equation.

This particular result was one of the few where the pundits did not say 'I told you so–we knew that already'. In fact it was not until a sound logical explanation was deduced, based on the way competitive produce was sold that the analysis was finally accepted. The investigation was repeated for several alternative markets and the results were used to improve the present marketing strategy.

As with the simple straight line relationship there was a degree of random uncertainty associated with each estimate of the week's unit price. This was measured by the computer program and provided a vehicle for identifying freak situations both in the past and on current operations.

4.5.3. Example–Inter-branch staffing comparison

The data shown in Table 4.7 is typical of that collected to assess staff requirements at different branches of a bank. The total number of man hours worked in a particular week, together with the total number of transactions handled in that week and the total number of overnight wallets cleared in the week was determined at each of sixteen different branches.

Table 4.7. Data for inter-branch staffing comparison

	Total number in the week of		
Branch No.	Man hours worked	Transactions	Overnight wallets
1	1130	12500	30
2	1240	10000	230
3	1270	10000	410
4	1270	9500	230
5	1060	9000	70
6	1070	8000	265
7	810	8000	120
8	1300	7000	650
9	850	6000	90
10	1070	6000	250
11	960	6000	215
12	810	5000	105
13	970	4500	520
14	860	3000	215
15	800	3000	295
16	940	2500	310

Using a simple computer program, the best equation for estimating the man hour requirements was calculated as:

$$\text{Man hours} = 515 + 0.05\,(\text{Number of transactions}) + 0.65\,(\text{Number of wallets})$$

The standard deviation of the estimating error was calculated as 86.3 man hours.

Table 4.8 shows the difference between the actual man hours worked and the estimated requirements based on this equation. There are no great anomalies between the actual and the estimated

Table 4.8. Differences between actual man hours worked and estimated requirements

Branch No.	Man hours worked		Difference
	Actual	Estimate	(actual-estimate)
1	1130	1167	−37
2	1240	1170	70
3	1270	1288	−18
4	1270	1145	125
5	1060	1006	44
6	1070	1092	−22
7	810	998	−188
8	1300	1292	8
9	850	877	−27
10	1070	981	89
11	960	958	2
12	810	836	−26
13	970	1081	−111
14	860	807	53
15	800	859	−59
16	940	843	97

values. Nevertheless, any requests for extra manpower from branches No. 4 or No. 16 should be scrutinized with special care, and similar requests from branches No. 7 or No. 13 are potentially justifiable.

4.5.4. Potential misinterpretation and limitations

When data collected as a routine is subjected to multiple regression analysis there is always a possibility that one of the factors not being measured is not being held constant. This change could be associated with one of the measured factors in which case that factor would be incorrectly regarded as an important factor. On the other hand, the changes could be interpreted as being due to random causes and result in a large estimating error.

For instance, suppose that the number of transactions were divided into two parts, the number of transactions for private accounts and the number for business accounts. The number of business transactions handled by a branch could be closely associated with the number of night safe wallets handled by that branch. In this case the number of business transactions could well be a better indicator of the branch work load than the number of wallets. The estimating equation would then be based on the number of private transactions and the number of business transactions.

On the other hand, the number of business transactions might not be closely associated with the number of wallets handled, and still be an important factor. The existing estimating equation would regard it as having a random effect from branch to branch and would have in consequence a large estimating error. If the estimating equation were expanded to include the number of private transactions; the number of business transactions; and the number of night safe wallets handled, then the estimating error might be considerably reduced.

Furthermore, the range over which some of the factors are allowed to vary can be quite restricted and the effect of an important factor can show up as insignificant. The analysis is correct within the range of the results: nevertheless, management often wishes to make deductions outside the current range of values. Such deductions are fraught with danger.

4.6. Planning investigations

4.6.1. Objective

The three principal reasons for carrying out investigations into the sources of systematic variability are:

1. to reduce the total variability of the process;
2. to manipulate the factors affecting the process in order to effect a significant improvement; and
3. to determine underlying relationships as a means of simplifying the task of estimating, or of controlling.

The first reason has been illustrated by the investigation of the principal sources of variation in the packet weight of biscuits described earlier in this chapter. The objective was to measure how much of the total variability arose from systematic differences between different batches (mixes) and between different positions across the conveyor belt. This knowledge would then enable technical and managerial staff to concentrate on reducing or eliminating the effect of the principal sources of variability in order to reduce the variability in packet weight.

Investigations carried out to improve the profitability of a paint manufacturing plant, to reduce the downtime on a new integrated tube mill, and to improve the success rate of new carpet designs are not aimed at reducing variability. Identifying the principal sources of variability is only a step on the way to determine the operating conditions which produce the greatest improvement in profitability, in downtime, or in design success rate.

The third objective, namely to simplify estimation, may be illustrated by an instance in which the length and diameter of a number of products were used to estimate their product cost. There were sixty-three potential combinations of length and diameter of a product, all being made on the same or similar machines. Fig. 4.11 shows how twelve of these combinations were chosen for

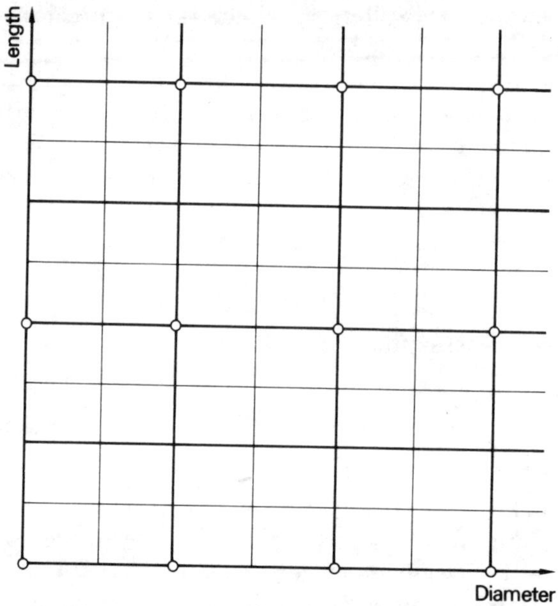

Only the twelve circled combinations of length and diameter were costed. These costs were used to establish an equation from which the remaining 51 combinations of length and diameter were costed.

Figure 4.11 Investigation to simplify estimation

costing. The resulting costs were used to establish an equation of the form:

$$\text{Product cost (pounds/1000)} = 0.27 + 0.061\,(\text{length in inches}) + 0.073\,(\text{diameter in inches})$$

From this equation the product costs of the remaining fifty-one combinations of length and diameter were estimated.

4.6.2. Basic principles

In the field of scientific investigation one of the most important skills of the investigator is his ability to arrange experiments so that unwanted variation is eliminated completely or reduced to a very low level. As a result, a fundamental principle can be demonstrated or a constant measured, and in laboratory conditions this can be done. There is still a need for the investigator in industry to eliminate as much variability as it is practical to achieve. Nevertheless, since he is not working in laboratory conditions, there will still remain a large amount of unwanted variability masking the underlying patterns in the figures. The objective of the investigator is to identify this pattern as quickly and as cheaply as possible in the face of the unwanted variability.

(a) *Eliminate ambiguity.* Investigations should be planned and executed in such a way that the results can be analysed without ambiguity. Suppose that the packaging of a consumer product was revamped and at the same time a customer discount was offered on the product as shown in Table 4.9. These changes could well result in increased sales but one would never know whether the increase was due to the discount or the new package, or indeed how much each of the two factors contributed.

Table 4.9. What's the reason for the increased sales?

	With no discount	With customer discount	
With old package	'Old product' —low sales		
With new package		'New product' —high sales	New packaging improves sales?
		Discount improves sales?	

In order to remove this ambiguity a series of balanced trials are necessary, combining all the four alternatives, as shown in Table 4.10 on page 82. The average of Trials 1 and 2 determines the performance of the old package, the average of the results of Trials 3 and 4 that of the new package. Since both packages were used alternatively with and without the customer discount, comparison of the average for the new package with that for the old package determines the effect of changing the package—independent of the effect of the customer discount.

In a similar manner the average of the results of Trials 2 and 4 determines the sales performance with a customer discount and the average of the results of Trials 1 and 3 the performance without the discount. The difference between these averages measures the effect of the customer discount—independent of the effect of changing the packaging.

Table 4.10. Balanced trials eliminate ambiguity

	With no discount	With customer discount
With old package	Trial 1	Trial 2
With new package	Trial 3	Trial 4

Average 'old' / Average 'new' — Unambiguous comparison

Average 'with no discount' / Average 'with discount' — Unambiguous comparison

(b) *Achieve efficiency.* The balanced design shown in Table 4.10 is a very efficient way of collecting information. All the results are first used to measure the effect on sales of changing the package and then they are all used again to measure the effect of giving the customer discount.

Moreover, if the four trials had each been repeated, all eight results could be used first to measure the effect of altering the package; then to measure the effect of giving the customer discount; and finally to see if these two factors were completely independent of one another, or if there was any interaction between them. An example of such an interaction is shown by the results listed in Table 4.11 and illustrated in Fig. 4.12.

These results show clearly that giving the discount was the principal reason for increased sales, but that this effect was increased very considerably by the introduction of a new package. Furthermore, without the discount, the new package had no beneficial effect on the sales level—it appears to have resulted in a slight decline in sales.

In such an instance the average increase due to introducing the new package and the average increase due to offering the customer discount could be quite misleading. The averages (Table 4.11)

Table 4.11. Results of eight field trials

Sales achieved (units)

	Without discount	With discount	Average
Old package	99	110	
	99	112	
	Average 99	Average 111	105
New package	95	127	
	97	127	
	Average 96	Average 127	111.5
Average	97.5	119	

suggest that changing the package had increased the sales by 6.5 units and offering the discount had increased the sales by 22.5 units. What is more important, if the investigation had considered first the change of package without offering a discount it would appear that sales would fall by three units. If then it had examined

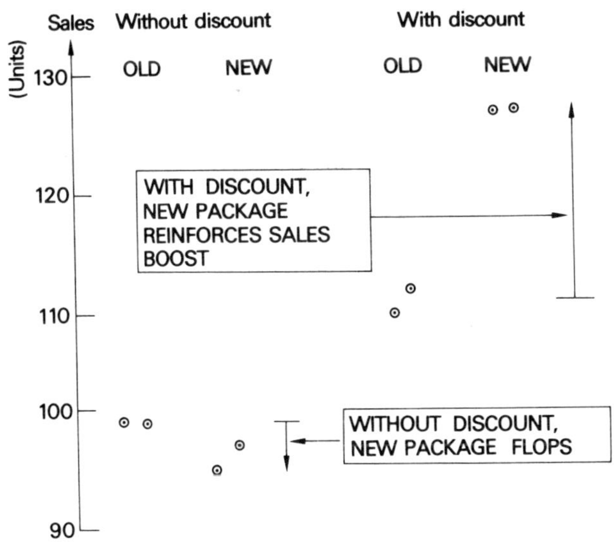

Figure 4.12 Interaction of factors affecting sales, shown by pattern of eight field trials

the effect of the discount without changing the package, sales would be expected to rise by only twelve units, from 99 to 111. By using the balanced design, the interaction of new package and customer discount was discovered showing a rise of twenty-eight units and indicating that, in spite of the poor response from a simple change of package, it was worthwhile making the change if a customer discount was offered.

Table 4.12. Steps in allocating trials randomly

Step 1 Identify each trial by a number

Number	Trial
1	Old: No discount
2	Old: No discount
3	New: No discount
4	New: No discount
5	Old: Discount
6	Old: Discount
7	New: Discount
8	New: Discount

Step 2 Select a sequence of random numbers

Sequence of random numbers				
07	54	32	69	75
84	03	27	45	32
26	17	64	19	29

Step 3 Order of random numbers fixes order of trials

Sequence allocations trials							
7;	5;	4;	3;	2;	6;	8;	1;

Step 4 List trial selected for each supermarket

Supermarket	Trial	Supermarket	Trial
A	7–New: Discount	E	2–Old: No discount
B	5–Old: Discount	F	6–Old: Discount
C	4–New: No discount	G	8–New: Discount
D	3–New: No discount	H	1–Old: No discount

(c) *Eliminate unsuspected biases by randomization.* It has already been mentioned that one of the problems of carrying out experimental trials in the laboratory or investigations in the factory is how to eliminate all sources of variation except those being investigated. When systematic variation is known to be present, for example if it is expected that the response to the trials would differ from district to district, then it is possible to arrange to balance out these biases by careful design. However, should systematic variation be present but its presence remain hidden, then an improvement arising from this source could be incorrectly attributed to one of the factors being deliberately changed in the experimental trials. In order to insure against the risk of such misleading results the sequence of carrying out the trials, or the allocation of materials or facilities should be chosen in a formal random manner, such as by means of random numbers.

If the eight trials based on changing the package design and the customer discount had been carried out at eight different supermarkets, the supermarkets would have each been asked to stage one of the eight trials chosen at random The numbers 1, 2, 3, . . . 8 could each be used to identify a specific trial, as has been shown in Table 4.12. The sequence in which these numbers occur in a table of random numbers could then be used to determine the sequence of allocating the trials to any previously determined sequence of supermarkets. The precise method of making the allocation has been illustrated in Table 4.12.

Table 4.13. All trials with discount in northern supermarkets

Sales achieved (units)

		Without discount		With discount	Average
Old package		89		120	
		89		122	
	Average	89	Average	121	105
New Package		85		137	
		87		137	
	Average	86	Average	137	111.5
Average		87.5		129	

(d) *Design the investigation to eliminate major sources of variation.* In this series of market trials, it is quite likely that there would be a well known systematic source of variation amongst the supermarkets; for instance, four of the supermarkets could have been in the north and four in the south and the results could be biased by the difference in regional buying habits. The results quoted in Table 4.13 and illustrated in Fig. 4.13 show what would have been the result had all the trials with a discount been carried out in the northern supermarkets and all the trails without a discount been carried out in the southern supermarkets.

Taken at their face value, without recognizing the bias present, the effect would be to over-estimate the sales with discounts by twenty units over the country as a whole.

The allocation of trials to supermarkets by means of random numbers would turn the systematic variation into random

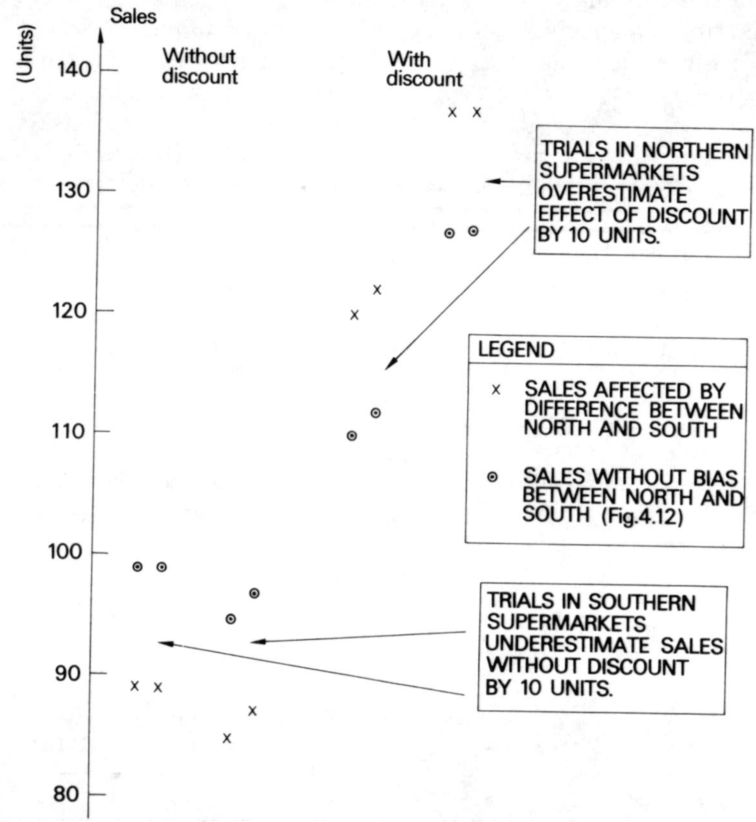

Figure 4.13 Results biased by systematic differences

variation and probably eliminate the bias. However, this would be achieved at the expense of increasing the size of the total random uncertainty in the results. Table 4.14 and Fig. 4.14 show that random allocation will reduce the effect of these biases but at the expense of increased uncertainty in the deductions. In fact, the random allocation of the trials without discount arranged for both the trials on the old package to be carried out in the south and

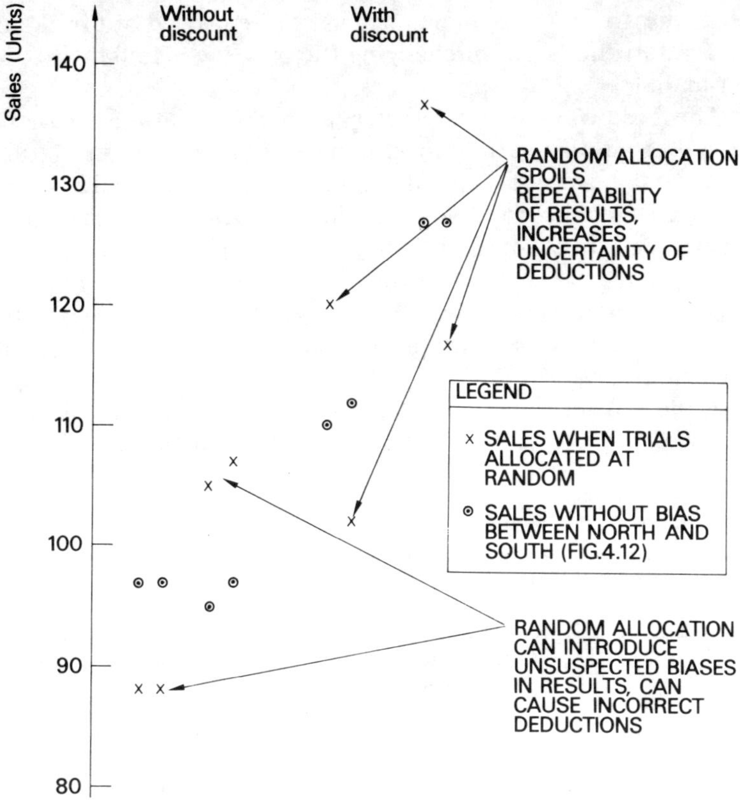

Figure 4.14 Random allocation to eliminate systematic differences

Table 4.14. Trials allocated to supermarkets by random numbers

Sales achieved (units)

		Without discount		With discount	Average
Old package		89		120	
		89		102	
	Average	89	Average	111	100
New package		105		137	
		107		117	
	Average	106	Average	127	116.5
Average		97.5		119	

both the trials on the new package to be carried out in the north. As a result the effect of changing the package would be incorrectly estimated.

The best way to handle such a source of potential bias is to design the investigation to eliminate it. In this investigation the four trials denoted by odd numbers in Table 4.12 would be arranged for the four supermarkets in the north and the four identical trials denoted by even numbers would be allocated to the four supermarkets in the south. Then, during the analysis of the results, comparisons could be made separately both within the four northern supermarkets and also within the four southern supermarkets.

Table 4.15 shows the results when the trials are arranged to balance out the difference between the northern and southern

Table 4.15. Trials arranged to balance out difference between northern and southern supermarkets

Sales achieved (units)

		Without discount	With discount	Average	Average (North and South)
	Old	109	120	114.5	
North	New	105	137	121	
	Average	107	128.5		
	Old	89	102	95.5	105
South	New	87	117	102	111.5
	Average	88	109.5		
Average		97.5	119		

supermarkets. Having collected the information in this way, it is important to ensure that it is analysed correctly. Fig. 4.15 shows how this analysis is made—separately for the southern and then for the northern supermarkets—so that the effect of the biases are eliminated.

(e) *Consider the analysis before any trials are made.* It is a basic rule of all sound investigations that the analysis of the data should be planned before any data is collected. If necessary, hypothetical results should be used to decide how the real data should be analysed and careful thought devoted to deciding what action is likely to be needed and how this can be put in train.

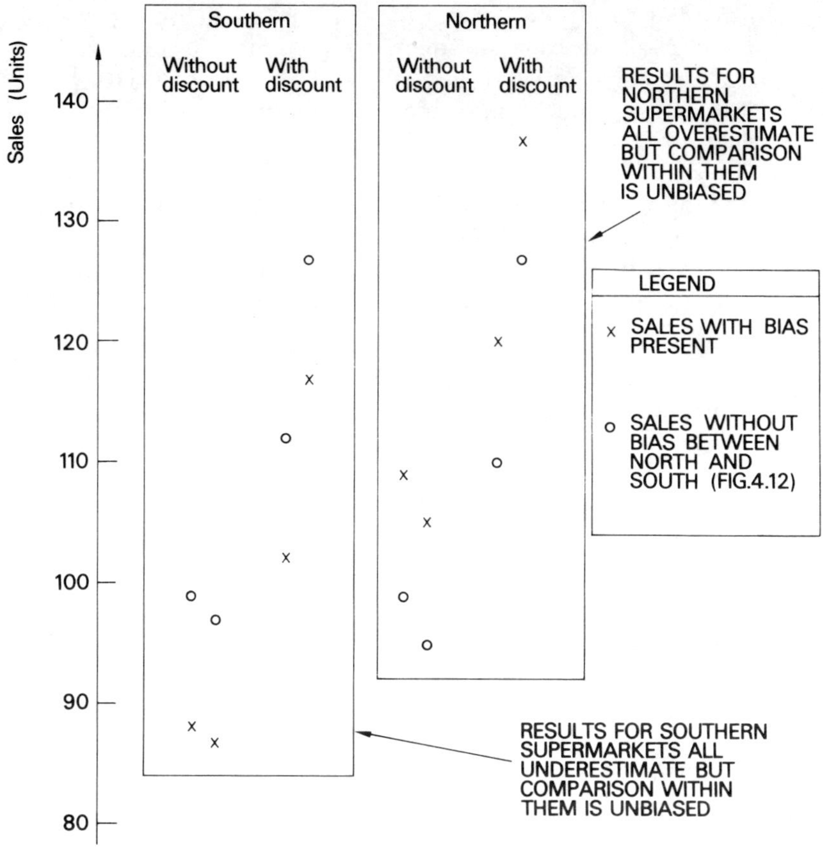

Figure 4.15 Careful design and analysis can eliminate effect of systematic differences

4.7. Applications

The principles outlined in this chapter are relevant to the whole field of management activity. It is a field where variability abounds and a greater understanding of the nature of this variability, coupled with positive action based on this understanding, will inevitably lead to increased profitability. This section examines the principal areas of management and illustrates the potential of analysing patterns in figures.

In summary, the principles to apply are:

1. Determine if there is any systematic variation in the figures. If there is, take it into account when making the relevant decisions.

2. Check if associated measurements are available or can be made available, measurements which may account for, or explain some of the variability. If there is a pattern of association, take it into account when making the relevant decisions.
3. Whether or not systematic variation exists, there will always be random variation causing the measurements to fluctuate. Determine the confidence limits of estimates arising from the measurements and if necessary increase the number of measurements to give the desired confidence band.

Finding patterns in figures will not help management with immediate day to day problems. It will, however, provide management with an analysis of the total picture, so that they can devise improved methods and procedures and reduce the number of day to day problems which arise.

4.7.1. Marketing

(a) *Forecasting.* Forecasting demand is riddled with uncertainty and yet it is an essential step before planning can start. Weekly or monthly orders will vary from one week or one month to the next. Is there any seasonal pattern in them? Is this pattern truly systematic, repeating itself year after year? If it is, forecasts based on seasonally adjusted figures will be more accurate. Estimates of demand over the next four weeks will improve if a correct assessment of seasonality is incorporated in short term forecasts. A correct assessment of seasonality incorporated in medium term forecasts will allow management to calculate how much stock would have to be built up in the slack months to anticipate the demand in the high season; would allow management to estimate the excess production capacity needed to meet the high season demand; and would allow management to estimate the way in which a backlog of orders will build up during the high ordering season.

Even if correct allowance can be made for a seasonal pattern of ordering, there will always remain a residual pattern of random variability. The size of this uncertainty is a measure of the short term flexibility required from the enterprise. The forecast for each planning period should be accompanied by upper and lower limits: the wider these limits, the greater the flexibility which will need to be achieved to maintain a consistent customer service. In short term planning the upper limit can be used to set a target stock figure, but the uncertainty associated with medium term forecasts will need to be offset by carrying excess capacity or by fostering subcontract capacity.

(b) *Factors affecting the market.* There are so many factors affecting the market that it is difficult, without painstaking analysis, to assess which are the important factors and to measure their relative importance. The principal tool of such an analysis is multiple regression since it can be applied to past records and does not call for experimental trials of alternative marketing strategies.

In one such investigation, the results over a period of four years for each of fifteen product groups were examined for each of four selling regions–making a total of 240 potential sets of information. Each set contained information relating to the sales of one product group, for a specific region, during a particular year. This information included:

Turnover (£),
Profit contribution (£),
Number of salesmen per million in population,
Percentage of product sold direct to retail outlets,
Number of lines in product group,
Population (millions) in selling region,
Advertizing expenditure on product group (£).

There were measurements for considerably more factors included in each set, but they were found to have little or no effect either on turnover or profit contribution. The equations resulting from this analysis were:

Turnover (£) = 15 000 + 1300 per salesman
–200 (percentage retail) + 400 per line
–600 (per million population)
+500 (per £1000 advertising), and

Profit (£) = 20 000 + 250 per salesman
–40 (percentage retail) + 90 per line
–100 (per million population)
–350 (per £1000 advertising).

The equations show that the effect of selling direct to retail outlets inhibits both turnover and profit. Presumably a day spent calling on wholesalers is more valuable than a day spent calling on retailers. They also show that if more money is spent on advertising it would increase turnover, but reduce the profit contribution. They suggest strongly that it would be better to cut the advertising appropriation and increase the number of salesmen in each region.

4.7.2. Manufacturing

(a) *Supplies of materials and components.* The delivery times and usage rates of materials and components are just as affected by uncertainty as other management measurements. How much of this uncertainty can be attributed to systematic variation? Almost certainly a seasonal pattern in order intake will produce a seasonal pattern in usage rate. In some instances a knowledge of current outstanding orders enables the usage rate to be predicted with a minimal amount of uncertainty. Even here there will be some uncertainty, to be measured and allowed for in stock holding or flexible production programming.

Is there a pattern in delivery times, making it possible to classify them either by supplier or by group of products? Do the promised delivery times of suppliers provide a viable means of estimating their actual delivery times? Again, whatever improvement can be achieved in estimating delivery times there will be a residual amount of uncertainty to be measured and allowed for to ensure that only an acceptably small percentage of deliveries are late. It is seldom adequate to have the average delivery time correct, and in consequence half the deliveries late.

(b) *Utilization of manpower.* Operation times for a group of workers carrying out the same operation will almost certainly vary from worker to worker and from occasion to occasion. Different conditions of machinery, different methods of working, different individual efforts, speeds and fatigues, all combine to produce this variation. Furthermore, the operation itself may vary in work content from one occasion to the next. How much of this variation can be attributed to systematic causes, which can either be remedied or allowed for in planning? How much of it is random, calling for some degree of over-staffing and an extra ration of management attention?

(c) *Utilization of equipment.* Machine breakdowns are just as unpredictable. When will a breakdown occur, and how long will it take to repair? Machine utilization is of course affected by other factors. Changeovers occur from time to time, so do shortages of work, materials and manpower. Where is the systematic pattern? Is there a difference from setter to setter, shop to shop within the factory, site to site within the construction company? How much of the variation is systematic and so can either be remedied or allowed for by planning—how much is random and needs to be covered by excess capacity?

(d) *Control of excess costs.* Excess costs arise from using the wrong grade of labour, of machines or material; from quality losses; from overtime and waiting time. Is there a pattern in the weekly/monthly estimates of excess costs? Is there a systematic difference from one department to another? Are they seasonal, associated perhaps with holiday periods? Does the analysis point to an area needing special attention, or perhaps to a review of the standard costing and excess cost reporting system? As previously mentioned, the techniques described in this chapter are designed to provide an assessment of the total picture and not a week by week, or month by month monitoring of performance. However, the size of the residual random variation does provide a measure of the week to week or month to month variation to be expected, and the basis for measuring the reliability of the average level of excess costs.

4.7.3. Personnel

All companies, large or small, are concerned about comparative wage rates. In its simplest form this will be a straight comparison of take home pay for people doing similar jobs. There is bound to be variation from one man to the next. Is there any systematic pattern in this variation, and if so does it call for management action to straighten out anomalies before they lead to industrial unrest?

Within the large companies and also within different smaller companies in a particular sector there have been deliberate moves to rationalize the pattern of comparative wage rates. Unions and management agree that there are a large number of factors which affect the basic rate for a job. What job evaluation sets out to do is to ensure that the effect of each of these factors is taken into account in a fair and impartial manner when the worth of every job is assessed. Past history of supply and demand, changes in the skills needed for the job and other factors irrelevant to the present day situation have all tended to distort the wages pattern.

In order to develop a rational wages structure, a basic framework is established using only jobs which both unions and management agree to be fairly paid. The particular skills and requirements of each of these jobs are then assessed. A typical list would be:

Mental demands and skills: basic education; training for the job; previous experience; length of initiation period; variety of work; analytical ability; alertness of observation.

Responsibilities: for labour; for material; for equipment; for clerical work; for contracts; for originality and initiative; ability to manage others.

Job conditions: monotony; disagreeableness; risk of accident.

Physical demands and skills: abnormally heavy; abnormal position; dexterity.

Each of these nineteen factors would be scored separately working across the jobs for each factor in turn. This enables a comparison to be made within each factor, but how much weight should be given to each factor when making a comparison of the relative worth of the jobs? It is here that multiple regression again plays its part and calculates the relative weighting to give to the scores. A simplified form of job evaluation could result in the following equation:

$$\begin{aligned}\text{Weekly wage (pounds)} = {} & 12.5 + 0.75\ \text{(mental skills score)} \\ & + 2.0\ \text{(responsibilities score)} \\ & + 0.25\ \text{(job conditions score)} \\ & + 0.5\ \text{(physical skills score)}\end{aligned}$$

This result indicates that the company currently rates an additional point for responsibility to be four times more valuable than an additional point for the application of physical skills.

Even after fitting equations containing several factors there will still be a residual random uncertainty. Once more it should be measured and the difference between the actual and the estimated wage rates examined to identify the exceptions. In such a sensitive area as this, the reason for every exception should be carefully established and whatever steps are practical should be taken to eliminate the anomalies.

Lists of terms used

Sales *forecasting*
Standard costing
Work study
Systematic variation
Seasonality, seasonal pattern
Random variation, fluctuations
Reliability of estimate
Sample
Average
Frequency diagram
Standard deviation
Standard error
Confidence limits
Sources of variation
Associated figures/measurements
Scatter diagram
Relationship
Precision
Slope
Normal frequency distribution
Multiple associations
Multiple regression analysis
Computer program
Interaction
Random numbers
Turnover

Chance
Sub-sample
Range

Profit contribution
Planning
Job evaluation

Italicized terms are defined in the glossary (page 262) as well as in the text where it is appropriate.

5. Monitoring

5.1. Monitor what and why?

It would be impossible to travel by car over any worthwhile distance if you could not check from time to time just where you were. Over well travelled routes, the check would be against your memory: over infrequent journeys the check would almost certainly take a different form and on a rally it would be against a formal route plan.

Monitoring is as essential to a business as it is to a car journey. Just how is the business progressing? Regular checks on sales volume, cost of goods sold, profit before tax, stock turn, outstanding debts, fixed assets will detect when significant changes have occurred in the company's operating position. More frequent checks of cost variances against standard; of orders received against targets; of the utilization of materials, manpower and machines provide week by week situation reports.

These checks are needed so that management can discharge one of its major responsibilities, namely to control the present situation. But to do this effectively management has to detect when a real change calling for immediate action has occurred and not to be misled by random fluctuations which could readily have occurred by chance. It is far too easy to follow the will o' the wisp indications of the random fluctuations rather than concentrate on the hard graft of achieving an overall improvement in performance and profitability.

The prizes of effective monitoring and control lie in increased efficiency; in the reduction of losses and increased output; in more meaningful control information, leading to a greater understanding of the business; and in increased confidence–resulting in speedier and more accurate decisions.

5.2. The meaning of control

'Control' in industry is often confused with the keeping of records. Clearly without records or measurements there can be no true control, but they are not enough. The meaning of control to a manager is illustrated in Fig. 5.1.

A typical example of this type of control is provided by a thermostat in a hot water tank. The controller determines the measure of efficiency, namely the water temperature. This measurement is then compared against a predetermined standard, and the difference is used to determine whether or not to adjust the heating process. If necessary, the appropriate adjustment is made automatically.

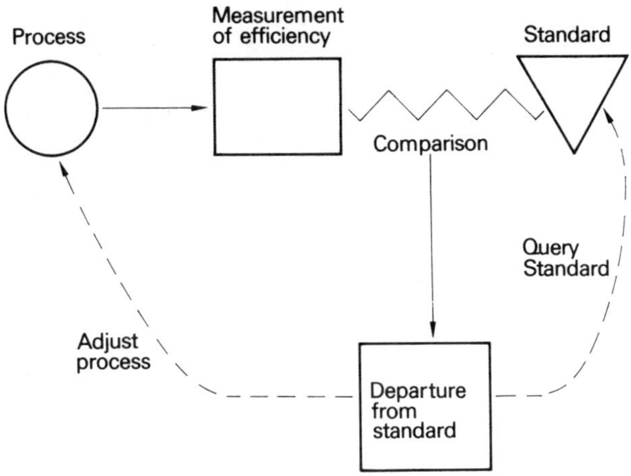

Figure 5.1 The meaning of control

Figure 5.1 highlights the needs of management control:

1. To set a standard and to be willing to modify it when it is no longer relevant;
2. To be able to measure the efficiency of the process (be it design, production, clerical or selling process) in the units used for setting the standard;
3. To be able to detect real departures from the standard and be willing to ignore the inevitable random fluctuations; and,
4. To be able to adjust the process. Without the ability to take corrective action, control, if it can be called control, is tenuous indeed.

5.3. The statistical approach

The statistical approach of taking the emphasis away from individual figures and putting it on the pattern of management performance over a period has to be built into the monitoring procedure. The major implication is that the standard in the control loop (Fig. 5.1) cannot be regarded as a specific value. It has to take the form of a frequency diagram, as shown in Fig. 5.2, from which the limits of variation in the measure of management performance can be determined. Provided that future measurements fall between these limits, the process being managed is regarded as conforming to the standard. Only when a future measurement falls outside the limits does the process depart from standard and need to be adjusted.

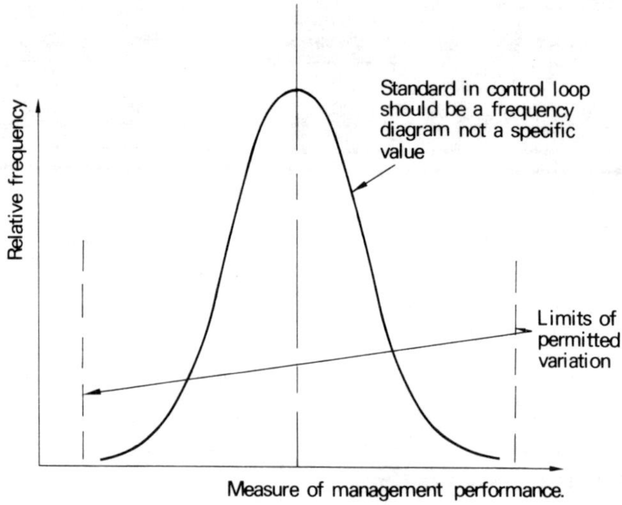

Figure 5.2 The statistical standard

An elementary form of monitoring can be achieved by plotting on a simple chart the measurement of efficiency taken at regular intervals of time (for instance the weekly output in tons). If the plotted points look as though they had come from a single frequency diagram, two lines which enclose most of them could be drawn and these lines projected into the future as shown in Fig. 5.3. These lines, derived empirically from past performance, would become the limits of the variation permitted in the future. Provided all the future measurements of performance fall between these limits the change from one measurement to the next should not be used to infer either an improvement or a deterioration in performance.

Experience with monitoring charts indicates very strongly that more benefit is gained by telling people when action is *not* required, rather than when action is required. However, when action is required the chart only indicates that it is required. Management action has to be taken to complete the control loop.

Monitoring of performance after the event cannot put things right. When they do go wrong it is essential that corrective action is taken quickly to prevent the poor performance continuing into the future. However, the aim of control through monitoring is to reduce to a minimum the need for corrective action. This is achieved by providing the responsible manager with up to date information on how he is performing, with guidance in what to do

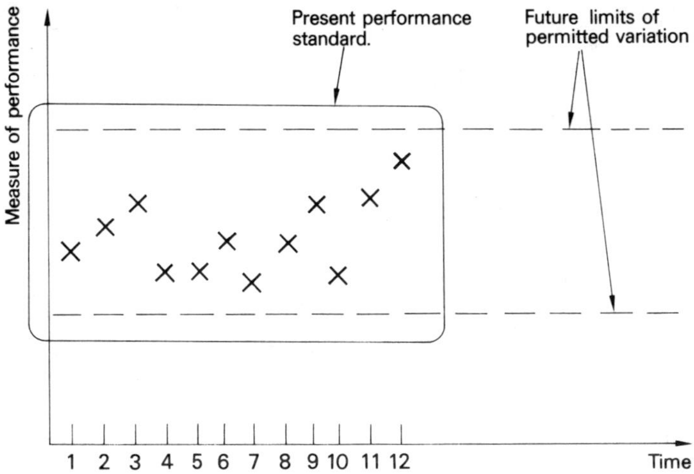

Figure 5.3 Elementary form of monitoring

when he is not meeting the limits of the performance standard, and finally with the right motivation to respond when the controls indicate that action is needed.

5.4. Monitoring through measurement

In situations where it is possible to take several measurements over a short period of time, for instance in the field of quality control, it is possible to use the median as a measure of the central value of the process and the range to measure its short term variability. The method adopted is to set a standard both for the central value and also for the variability of the process and then to take samples from the process to ascertain whether or not these standards are being maintained.

The standard would be assessed by measuring fifty to one

hundred items. The data contained in Table 5.1 which was obtained from nine samples, each containing seven items would be typical.

Table 5.1. Set of nine samples each of seven items used to set quality standard

Sample No.	Readings 1	2	3	4	5	6	7
1	5.0	3.2	4.0	6.4	3.6	2.8	4.4
2	3.0	3.6	4.8	5.0	4.0	4.2	4.8
3	4.8	4.6	3.0	5.6	5.0	4.4	4.6
4	6.8	4.6	3.6	4.6	3.0	3.6	3.4
5	3.8	4.8	3.6	3.0	4.2	3.6	4.2
6	1.0	3.6	3.2	3.4	3.6	3.0	3.4
7	3.4	3.8	4.4	4.4	3.4	5.0	3.0
8	3.6	4.2	5.2	5.6	3.0	3.4	4.0
9	4.4	4.0	4.2	4.0	4.0	6.2	4.6

These observations would be plotted on a simple chart against a time scale to show the order in which each sample was collected. Design or similar tolerances on the individual items would be marked on the chart, as shown in Fig. 5.4 and the plotted measurements compared against these tolerances.

When each sample has been plotted on the chart, the median of the sample is easily determined by counting and ringing the measurement which in this case is fourth from the bottom in each sample. The range of the sample can also be determined simply from the plotted points and noted at the foot of the chart. The medians and ranges of the nine samples are tabulated for convenience in Table 5.2.

This table also shows that the median of the medians is 4.0, and the median of the ranges is 2.6.

Table 5.2. Medians and ranges of nine samples

Sample No.	Median	Range
1	4.0	3.6
2	4.2	2.0
3	4.6	2.6
4	3.6	3.8
5	3.8	1.8
6	3.4	2.6
7	3.8	2.0
8	4.0	2.6
9	4.2	2.2
Median:	4.0	2.6

The medians of the samples show variation from sample to sample, but there is a limit to the amount by which each median can be expected reasonably to differ from the median of the medians 4.0. Calculating the limits of reasonable variation has been simplified by statisticians who have determined the factors tabulated on page 102 in Table 5.3. The action limits, exceeded by

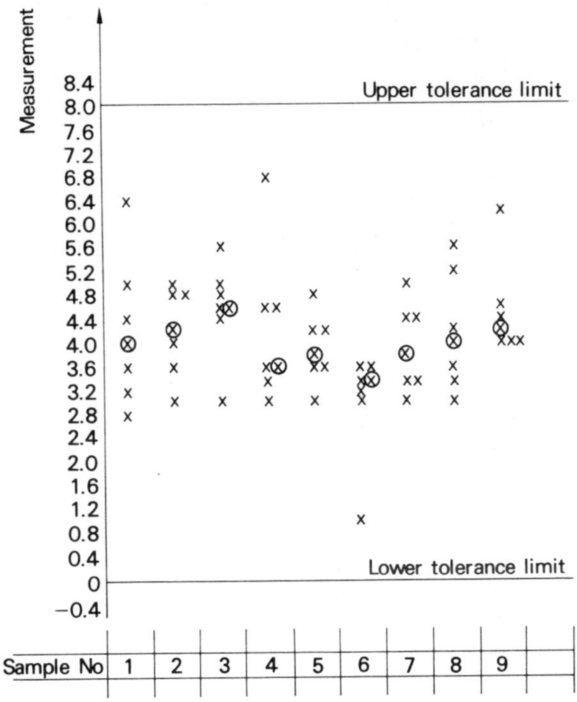

Figure 5.4 Plot of individual measurements against tolerances

chance fluctuations only once in 1000 samples, turn out to be 2.6 and 5.4. These limits have been shown in Fig. 5.5. The nine medians fall well within these limits indicating that all the samples are consistent with the standard for the central value.

In a similar manner, an action limit which should be exceeded by chance only once in 1000 samples can be determined for the range of the samples. Only an upper action limit is needed to detect an undesirable increase in process variability. Using the tabulated factors shown in Table 5.4, the action limit for the range is calculated as 5.7.

The nine ranges are all well below this value, indicating that the

Table 5.3. Table of factors for control limits on chart for medians

Sample Size	Action factor a (1 in 1 000)
2	2.87
3	1.41
4	0.98
5	0.77
6	0.64
7	0.55
8	0.49
9	0.44
10	0.40
11	0.37
12	0.35

To obtain action limits on the chart for medians multiply the median range by the factor a appropriate to the sample size. Then add and subtract from the median of the medians.

Example: Median of ranges (each of 7 measurements) = 2.6
Median of medians (each of 7 measurements) = 4.0
Action gap = 0.55 × 2.6 = 1.4
Upper action limit = 4.0 + 1.4 = 5.4
Lower action limit = 4.0 – 1.4 = 2.6

Table 5.4. Table of factors for control limits on ranges

Sample size	Action factor b (1 in 1 000)
2	4.9
3	3.2
4	2.7
5	2.4
6	2.3
7	2.2
8	2.1
9	2.0
10	1.97
11	1.94
12	1.90

To obtain the action limit for the range of each sample, multiply the median range by the factor b appropriate to the sample size.

Example: Median of ranges (each of 7 observations) = 2.6
Action limit on range = 2.2 × 2.6
= 5.7

samples are also consistent with the standard for short term variability. Now, provided that the quality standard established represents the best commercial practice, the limits may be used to control the process in future. Provided that the medians continue to scatter evenly about the median of the medians (4.0) and fall between the limits, and the sample ranges continue below 5.7, the

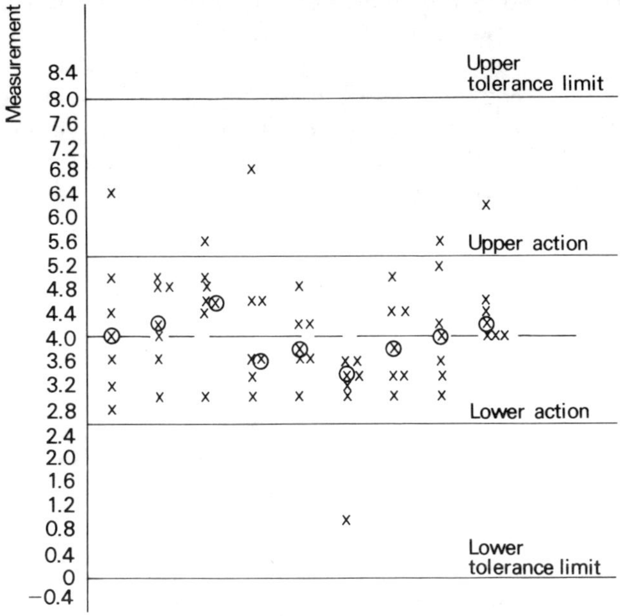

Sample No.	1	2	3	4	5	6	7	8	9	
Range	3.6	2.0	2.6	3.8	1.8	2.6	2.0	2.6	2.2	

(Action Limit for range = 5.7)

Figure 5.5 Plot showing medians against action limits for medians

process would be allowed to run without adjustment. A median outside the action limits would call for an adjustment to the average setting of the process. A range above the action limit would call for an adjustment to reduce the process variability.

5.5. Control through counting

Management performance can be monitored by counting the number of exceptions occurring over a regular review period, and in many cases this results in the simplest form of control. How many new accounts were opened during the past week; how many new customers placed orders during the past month; how many complaints about quality; how many debtors with accounts outstanding more than three months; how many customers waiting for items supposed to be available from stock; how many items of unacceptable quality in a sample of fifty items?

The collection of information by counting has been described in chapter 2 and it was seen that the frequency distribution of data arising from counting can be quite unsymmetrical. In fact the shape of the frequency distribution depends on the average of the count, the lower the average count the more unsymmetrical the frequency distribution. The manner of applying these principles to establish monitoring procedures is best shown by a simple example.

Table 5.5. Weekly record of 'idle' job cards

Week number	1	2	3	4	5	6	7	8	9	10
Number of cards	4	6	2	5	9	7	3	3	4	2
Week number	11	12	13	14	15	16	17	18	19	20
Number of cards	7	5	1	1	5	5	5	5	4	9

As with monitoring by measurement, the inherent variability of the data calls for a statistical standard in the control loop, and this standard is estimated from immediate past history. The data shown in Table 5.5 would be used to assess the shape and position of the frequency distribution of the weekly number of job cards claiming payment for idle time. The frequency diagram of the data, Fig. 5.6, shows an average of 4.6 cards each week but a scatter which could result in as many as eleven or twelve claims for payment in a week. By using the Poisson distribution as the statistical standard, an action limit which is exceeded only once in 1000 weeks can be determined once the average count is known. Table 5.6. shows the appropriate action limit values. In this instance, the average count of 4.6 lies between 4.05 and 4.61 showing that the appropriate action limit is thirteen.

The control chart is prepared by plotting the number of 'idle' cards in time sequence instead of in the form of a frequency diagram, and inserting lines to show the average count and the action limit. Provided all the points scatter evenly about the

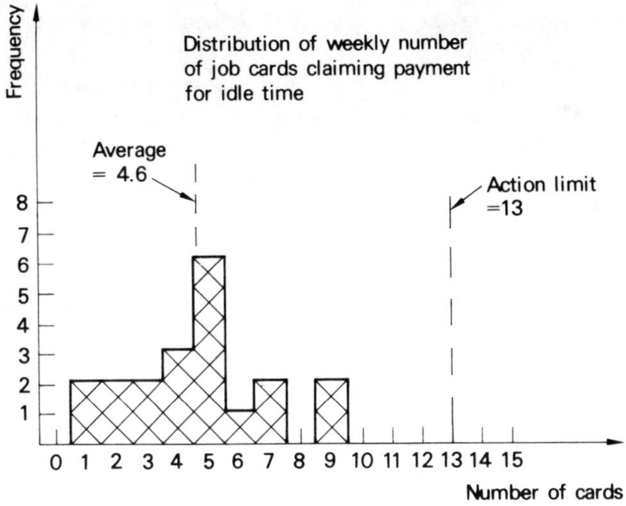

Figure 5.6 Statistical standard for counting

average and none exceeds the action limit, as in Fig. 5.7, the individual counts are consistent with the statistical standard. If, furthermore, the average number of weekly claims for idle time is at a tolerable level, then subsequent monitoring would only call for special action if the action limit of thirteen was reached. If the average number is considered to be too high then a sustained

Table 5.6. Action limit values for monitoring charts for counting

Average number of count	Action limit	Average number of count	Action limit
Up to and including 0.001	1	2.97 to 3.49	11
0.002 to 0.045	2	3.50 to 4.04	12
0.046 to 0.20	3	4.05 to 4.61	13
0.21 to 0.43	4	4.62 to 5.20	14
0.44 to 0.74	5	5.21 to 5.79	15
0.75 to 1.11	6	5.80 to 6.40	16
1.12 to 1.52	7	6.41 to 7.03	17
1.53 to 1.97	8	7.04 to 7.66	18
1.98 to 2.45	9	7.67 to 8.31	19
2.46 to 2.96	10	8.32 to 8.96	20

When the average number of the count (m) is larger than the values tabulated take the action limit as: $m + 3\sqrt{m}$

effort would need to be mounted to lower that level, provided of course that the financial benefits outweigh the cost of achieving them. In the quality control field, many instances have been recorded where simply displaying the control charts provided adequate motivation and information to enable the workman or woman to make a significant improvement.

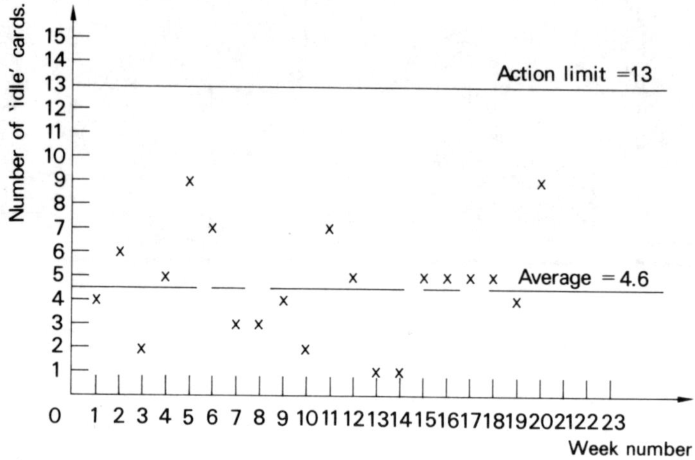

Figure 5.7 Control chart for counting

5.6. Cumulative sum charting

The development of cumulative sum techniques arose out of specific needs in industrial quality control. In some applications it is necessary to detect small changes in the average level of a process, for example, when controlling the breaking strength of nylon yarn. The standard control chart procedures which rely on an individual point falling outside the control limits do not provide a sufficiently sensitive method of detecting these small changes. A more powerful technique, the cumulative sum chart, was developed to accumulate evidence of change over a long series of points. Although its initial applications were in industrial quality control, it is an ideal technique for monitoring all management indices.

5.6.1. Cumulative plotting

The weakness of the standard control chart and the power of the cumulative sum chart to detect small changes in average level can be seen from an analysis of the production figures shown in

Table 5.7. Production yields—each figure represents the average of four weeks output

Weekly production yields in tons

Sample No.	Average	Sample No.	Average
1	149	7	153
2	151	8	147
3	150	9	148
4	148	10	149
5	146	11	145
6	157	12	148
13	145	19	149
14	147	20	143
15	146	21	144
16	144	22	145
17	142	23	141
18	153	24	144

N.B. The bottom half of the table was obtained by subtracting 4 tons from each of the figures in the top half.

Table 5.7. The first set of figures represents the average weekly yield over twelve four weekly periods, omitting the weeks containing Easter, Christmas and the August fortnight holidays. The second set was obtained by subtracting four tons from each of the twelve figures in the first set.

When these figures are plotted on a standard control chart (Fig. 5.8) the inherent variation from period to period is sufficient to mask the deliberate change in the average level. None of the points

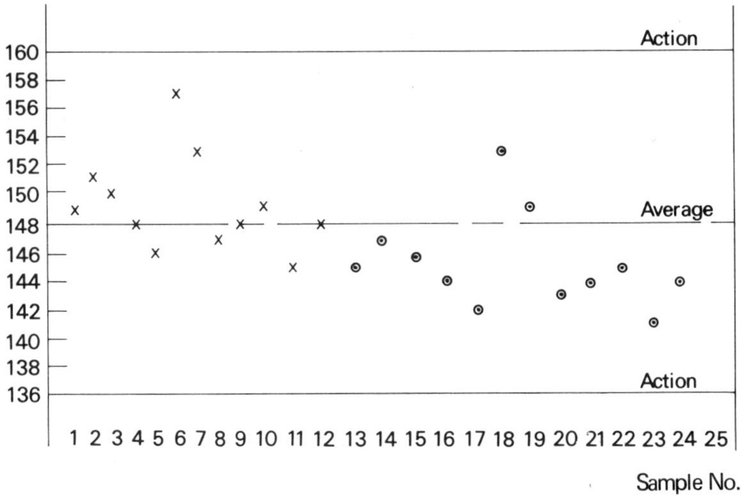

Figure 5.8 Control chart for averages shows no change in average level

falls at all near the action limits. However, the practised eye might observe that the last twelve points tend to fall below the average level and taken as a group they might indicate a change. The cumulative sum approach is designed to show this total picture by combining together in a formal manner the information given by the individual points.

Table 5.8. Build up of cumulative sum above standard

Sample No.	Average	Excess over 148	Cumulative sum
1	149	1	1
2	151	3	4
3	150	2	6
4	148	nil	6
5	146	−2	4
6	157	9	13
7	153	5	18
8	147	−1	17
9	148	nil	17
10	149	1	18
11	145	−3	15
12	148	nil	15
13	145	−3	12
14	147	−1	11
15	146	−2	9
16	144	−4	5
17	142	−6	−1
18	153	5	4
19	149	1	5
20	143	−5	nil
21	144	−4	−4
22	145	−3	−7
23	141	−7	−14
24	144	−4	−18

Table 5.8 shows how the individual results are first compared against a reference value, in this instance the past average performance of 148, and the amount by which they exceed or fall short of this value is recorded. The final column of Table 5.8 shows the cumulative sum of these excesses, and it is this cumulative sum which is used to monitor changes in the average output level.

When the cumulative sum of these excesses is plotted on a simple chart (Fig. 5.9) it shows dramatically the nature of the change in the average output level. The slope of the points on the cumulative sum chart represents the average, and the change in

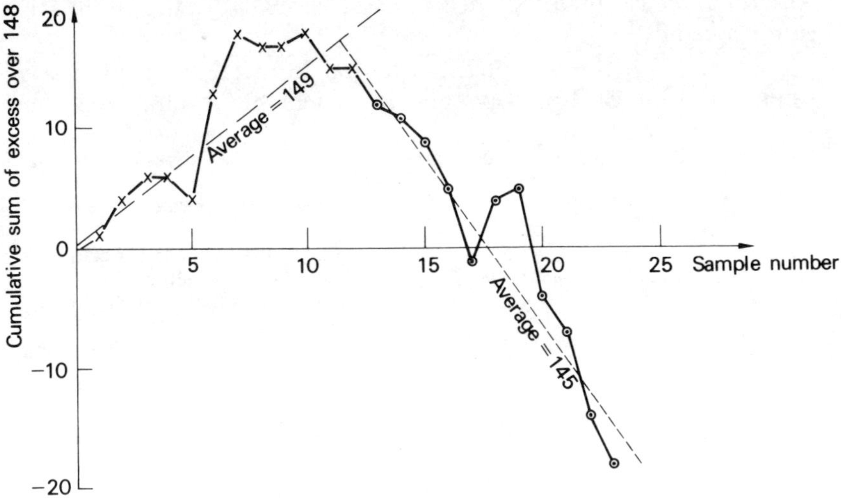

Figure 5.9 Cumulative sum chart shows dramatically that average level has changed

slope indicates very clearly how the average output level has fallen from 149 tons to 145 tons a week.

5.6.2. Decision limits for cumulative sums

Naturally there will be fluctuations in the slope of the cumulative sum chart due to the inherent variability of the individual values. It is possible to establish action limits related to the slope but this is clearly not as simple as determining the limits for standard control charts. Moreover, even after making adjustments to give horizontal or near horizontal slopes this type of chart needs a considerable width of paper. As a result, slightly more sophisticated ideas have been used to develop practical control procedures called 'decision interval schemes'.

Decision interval schemes first require management decisions on what is an 'acceptable level' and what is a 'rejectable level' of performance. When the average level of performance is at the acceptable level, the cumulative sum chart should continue to run for a long time before a fluctuation incorrectly indicates that a change has occurred. On the other hand, when the average performance level changes to a value which is just unacceptable, the rejectable level, this change should be detected quickly by the cumulative sum chart. These basic principles are illustrated in Fig. 5.10. It should be borne in mind that individual weekly results can differ considerably from the average and it is these fluctuations which can cause incorrect decisions to be made by the cumulative sum procedure.

In Fig. 5.10, the acceptable level has been taken at an average weekly output of 150 tons, and the rejectable level at 142 tons.

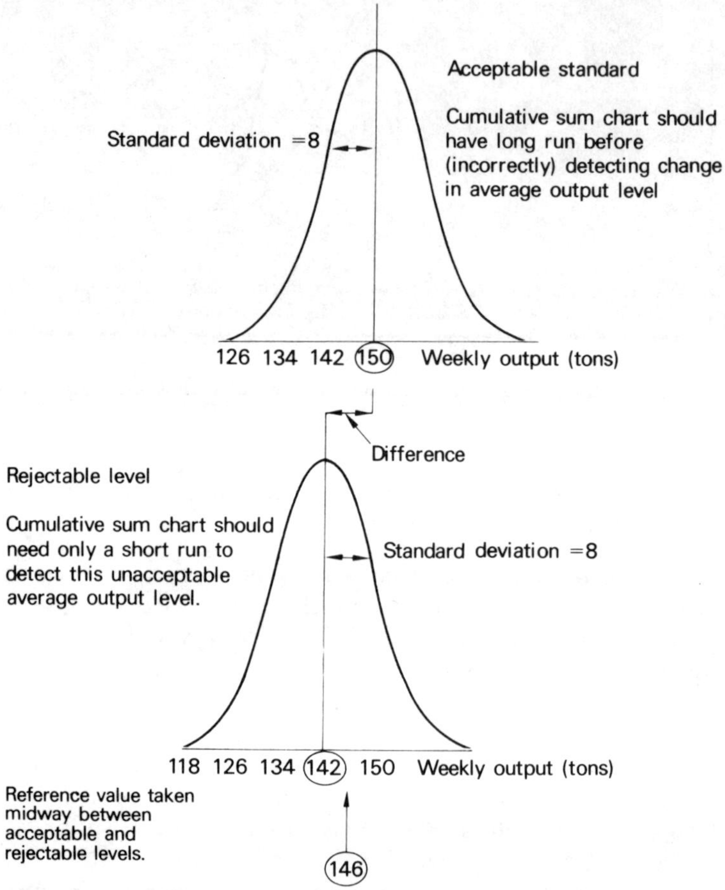

Figure 5.10 Basis of establishing decision interval type cumulative sum monitoring procedure

Provided the weekly output figures scatter evenly about 150 tons, the cumulative sum chart should have (say) 500 or 1000 observations before a fluctuation incorrectly indicates a change in the average output level. Should the average level drop to 142 tons, there would be occasional weeks when the output was above 150 tons. However, the cumulative sum chart should need on average only (say) three or four observations to detect this drop in the average output level. The average number of points on the cumulative sum chart before the cumulative sum exceeds the specified action limit (the decision limit) has been called the 'average run length'.

The monitoring procedure (Table 5.9) takes as its reference

Table 5.9. Decision interval scheme at work

Sample No.	Average of 4 weekly outputs	Excess over reference value of: 146	Cumulative sum (decision limit: −9.04)
1	149	+	Cumulative sum not started since values above reference value
2	151	+	
3	150	+	
4	148	+	
5	146	+	
6	157	+	
7	153	+	
8	147	+	
9	148	+	
10	149	+	
11	145	−1	−1
12	148	+2	+*
13	145	−1	−1
14	147	+1	+*
15	146	+	
16	144	−2	−2
17	142	−4	−6
18	153	+7	+*
19	149	+	
20	143	−3	−3
21	144	−2	−5
22	145	−1	−6
23	141	−5	−11†
24	144	−2	−2

* Cumulative sum stopped since it had become positive

† Cumulative sum stopped (change in average output level detected) since it exceeded the decision limit of −9.04

value the figure which lies halfway between the acceptable and the rejectable levels, namely 146 tons. Output figures over the reference value would lead to a cumulative sum which would quickly go off the top of the chart. Since these values are acceptable no cumulative sum is determined. However, should an output figure fall below the reference value, a cumulative sum is started. It will have negative values, indicating that the output is below the reference value and will be continued provided it stays negative. Should the cumulative sum cross the decision limit, it is concluded that a change has occurred in the average output level.

In Table 5.9, the first ten results all lie above the reference value of 146 and so a cumulative sum was not started. Over the next eight results a cumulative sum was started and stopped when it became positive, on three separate occasions. Four out of the last five results were sufficiently low that their cumulative sum (–11) crossed the decision limit (–9.04). This particular decision interval scheme is one of many which could be developed. Details of how to construct such a scheme, including determining the value of the decision limit, are given in Table 5.10. In outline, it is necessary to determine:

1. The acceptable level of performance;
2. The desired average run length at this level;
3. The rejectable level of performance;
4. The desired average run length at this level; and,
5. The standard deviation of the individual observations.

From these five values it is straightforward to calculate:

1. The reference value, to be subtracted from each value;
2. The number of observations to be grouped together to form a sample; and,
3. The value of the decision limit for the cumulative sum.

Table 5.10. Factors for decision interval schemes

Average run length at Acceptable level	Average run length at Rejectable level	$\frac{\text{Difference}\sqrt{N}}{\text{Standard devn.}}$	$\frac{\text{Limit}\sqrt{N}}{\text{Standard devn.}}$
1000	3	2.24	2.40
1000	7	1.30	4.06
500	3	2.08	2.26
500	7	1.20	3.80
250	3	1.88	2.11
250	7	1.08	3.51

Example of use

1. Choose the desired average run length at the acceptable level, say 500.
2. Choose the desired average run length at the rejectable level, say 3.
3. By reference to column 3 of the above table, this choice determines

$$\frac{\text{difference}\sqrt{N}}{\text{standard deviation}} \text{ to be } 2.08$$

The difference between an acceptable level of 150 and a rejectable level of 142 is 8.

The standard deviation, from past observation, is also 8.

4. From this relationship, $\sqrt{N}$ is calculated as 2.08 and so the number of observations to be grouped together to form a sample should be 4.

5. The choice of average run lengths also determines, from column 4 of the table,

$$\frac{\text{limit}\sqrt{N}}{\text{standard deviation}} \text{ to be 2.26, so limit} = 2.26 \times \frac{\text{standard deviation}}{\sqrt{N}}$$

6. Since $\sqrt{N}$ is 2 and standard deviation is 8, the value of the limit of the cumulative sum is 4 x 2.26, namely 9.04.

This illustration of the use of the decision interval scheme for monitoring by means of cumulative sums, has considered only the instance in which a fall in the characteristic being monitored has to be detected. The application to detect an increase in its average level is almost identical, except in this case the cumulative sum is started when the measurement exceeds the reference value. It will have positive values and be continued provided it stays positive until it crosses a positive decision limit. Furthermore, by combining two schemes, one to detect a fall and the other to detect an increase, cumulative sum charts can be applied in those instances where performance has to be maintained at a steady level.

Further extensions of the decision interval scheme have been made to cover cumulative sum monitoring of variability and the instance where control is through counting, rather than measurement.

5.6.3. How to handle individual observations

Since cumulative sum charts are so powerful, they are of particular value for the control of management indices. In such instances there is only a single observation, a weekly output, a monthly order total or a monthly cost variance, and so the sample size must be *one.* Table 5.11, on page 114, has been extracted from published nomograms to cover this special case.

The method of using these tables may be illustrated by an application to the monthly cost variances in a foundry. Here:

1. The acceptable level for the average cost variance was £0;
2. It was decided that an average run length of 500 at the acceptable level would be satisfactory;
3. The standard deviation of the monthly cost variances was £50; and,
4. The rejectable level was chosen at an average excess cost variance of £100, and so the difference between the acceptable and rejectable levels was £100.

The appropriate scheme would have a reference value midway

Table 5.11. **Factors for decision interval schemes based on individual measurements**

Difference / standard deviation	1000 Limit / St. devn.	1000 L (R)	500 Limit / St. devn.	500 L (R)	250 Limit / St. devn.	250 L (R)	125 Limit / St. devn.	125 L (R)
2.0	2.7	4	2.4	3	*	*	*	*
1.9	2.8	4	2.5	3	2.1	3	*	*
1.8	3.0	4	2.6	4	2.2	3	*	*
1.7	3.2	4	2.8	4	2.4	4	*	*
1.6	3.4	5	2.9	4	2.5	4	2.1	3
1.5	3.6	6	3.1	5	2.6	4	2.2	4
1.4	3.8	6	3.3	5	2.8	5	2.4	4
1.3	4.1	7	3.5	6	3.0	5	2.5	4
1.2	4.4	8	3.8	7	3.3	6	2.6	5
1.1	4.7	9	4.1	8	3.5	7	2.9	6
1.0	5.1	10	4.4	9	3.8	8	3.2	6

Average run length at acceptable level (1000, 500, 250, 125).

L (R) denotes average run length at rejectable level
* Do not use these values.

Example of use

1. Difference between acceptable level (£0) and rejectable level (£100) is £100.
2. Standard deviation from past observation is £50.
3. Enter the tables on the line $\frac{\text{difference}}{\text{standard deviation}} = 2.0$.
4. Choose one of the four average run lengths at the acceptable level, say 500 and read off the tabulated values, namely

$$\frac{\text{limit}}{\text{standard deviation}} = 2.4, \text{ and L (R)} = 3.$$

5. From this relationship, the limit for the cumulative sum is calculated, 2.4 x standard deviation, namely £120.
6. Note that the cumulative sum chart will need on average three observations to detect a change to the rejectable level.

between the acceptable and rejectable levels, £50; from the tables, a decision limit of £120, and would take on average three observations to detect a change to the rejectable level. The application of this scheme to a particular set of results is shown in Table 5.12.

Two isolated high variances in Periods 1 and 3 caused cumulative sums to be started, but these were quickly stopped as compensating low variances occurred. Subsequently, sustained high variances in Periods 7 to 14 inclusive resulted in the cumulative sum exceeding the decision limit, indicating that the true average period variance could not be as low as zero. The average variance over Periods 7 to 14 was in fact £69.

The first column of Table 5.11 has a limited range, from 1.0 to 2.0, and so the acceptable and rejectable levels have to be chosen so that the difference between them lies between 1.0 and 2.0 standard deviations. This should, in practice, be easy to do since the average run length at the acceptable level can be chosen to give a

Table 5.12. Decision interval scheme for control of foundry cost variance

Period	Foundry cost variance	Excess over £50	Cumulative sum (limit = £120)
1	93	43	43
2	0	−50	—*
3	131	81	81
4	25	−25	56
5	−2	−52	4
6	30	−20	—*
7	71	21	21
8	122	72	93
9	1	−49	44
10	47	−3	41
11	57	7	48
12	58	8	56
13	78	28	84
14	118	68	152†
15	34	—	
			Cumulative sum not started
16	−4	—	since values
17	39	—	below
18	−2	—	reference
19	−73	—	value
20	20	—	

* Cumulative sum stopped since it has become negative.
† Cumulative sum stopped since it exceeded the decision limit of £120.

reasonable average run length at the rejectable level. However, individual observations which are subject to considerable variation cannot reasonably be expected to detect small changes. Table 5.11 shows what can be done.

5.7. One assessment only

The previous section has dealt with the situation in which repeated checks are made to monitor performance and the decision on whether or not to take action is based on an accumulation of the information gathered by these checks. There are instances in which there is only one opportunity to check, where only one assessment is possible, before making a decision. Perhaps the best example of monitoring, where the decision has to be made as a result of only one assessment, is the use of acceptance sampling procedures for goods inwards inspection. The basic principles for applying acceptance sampling procedures, as well as their advantages, are described in chapter 3 (page 49). In outline, a sample of (say) 200 items is taken from a batch of (say) 5000. If there is only *one* defective item in the sample, the batch is accepted without further check, if two or more are defective the batch is not accepted. It may be returned to the supplier, or subjected to 100 per cent inspection before use. This type of procedure is operating in many factories on a routine basis, and each batch is treated as an individual.

Table 5.13. Procedure for control through DEF-131-A

If normal inspection is in force, then

1. Reduced inspection may be introduced if:
   - (a) all the previous 10 batches have been accepted
   - (b) the total number of defective items in the samples from the previous 10 batches does not exceed an appropriate limit *and*
   - (c) production remains at a steady rate.
2. Tightened inspection would be introduced if:
   2 out of the last 5 batches were rejected

If tightened inspection is in force then normal inspection may be introduced if:
the supplier's average quality level is better than the acceptable quality level.

If reduced inspection is in force then normal inspection must be introduced if:
- (a) a batch is rejected *or*
- (b) production becomes irregular or delayed

If tightened inspection is in force then 100% inspection must be introduced and action taken to improve the quality level if:
the last 10 batches have been on tightened inspection

There is no doubt that this scientific approach to the inspection function is a sound economic investment but making individual decisions does not build up a history or an experience, against which to judge and perhaps discount freak results. Consequently, the development of procedures designed to judge a supplier's performance, rather than an individual batch, such as those of the Defence Specification DEF-131-A are to be welcomed.

DEF-131-A contains an important set of sampling plans

designed to cover the purchasing of defence materials. The main objective of the procedure accompanying these plans is to put pressure onto the producer to achieve an average quality level which is at least as good as an arbitrarily specified 'acceptable quality level'. This is achieved by a formal procedure, based on the supplier's past performance, for adjusting the amount of inspection and the criterion for accepting a batch. The nature of this procedure is shown in Table 5.13 and a specimen of the sampling plans which would be used with this procedure is shown in Table 5.14.

Table 5.14. Specimen of sampling plans in DEF-131-A control scheme

Normal inspection:	Sample size 200, accept if 2 or less defective.
Criterion for reduced inspection:	Less than 4 defectives in last 2000 items inspected.
Reduced inspection:	Sample size 80, accept if 2 or less defective.
Tightened inspection:	Sample size 200, accept if 1 or less defective.
Acceptable quality level:	0.40%.

One of the problems of implementing such procedures is to achieve the degree of discipline which ensures that records are kept in the correct manner and that they are correctly interpreted and acted upon.

5.8. Applications

Management is concerned with two roles, or two different phases of activity. The first of these roles is to control the present situation, to hold the status quo. The second role is to introduce improvements when the present level of performance is unacceptable. Improvement plans should be concentrated on a limited number of areas, those with the greatest profit potential, whilst maintaining at the same time a holding operation on the remainder. The principles and procedures described in this chapter provide an efficient means of carrying out the holding operation. Putting the short term fluctuations in performance in proper perspective and identifying only the exceptional situations calling for remedial action frees management energy and time to concentrate on the improvement projects.

5.8.1. Principles

The principles of monitoring control described in this chapter are in summary:

1. Turn performance into figures.
2. Set a standard in terms of these figures, a standard in the form of a frequency diagram incorporating the inherent variability of performance.
3. Detect significant changes in performance level, changes calling for management action.
4. Know how to restore performance to the standard level. Have a formal check list to help identify what needs to be done.
5. Motivate. Make it in management's interest to measure, compare against a standard and to take action only when necessary.

Standard monitoring control charts are designed to identify change in those situations where the results of individual samples can be expected to show the change. On the other hand, cumulative sum charts allow a number of samples to be combined in order to show small but important changes in the pattern of performance which would not be detected by the standard control chart.

5.8.2. Company performance

Once a year the financial director has the task of preparing a snapshot of the financial state of the company. As with any formal family photograph, a special clean up takes place to show the world the best possible picture. However, there are certain essential factors in the composition of this picture which need to be monitored by management if a satisfactory year's performance is to be recorded. W. B. Rice* several years ago proposed the charting of nine pairs of indices of company performance based on monthly data shown in Table 5.15.

Whether or not you agree that these financial indices are appropriate to your company, the message is clear. Monitoring of the appropriate indices will detect when significant changes have occurred in the company's operating position. The inevitable random fluctuations would be measured and action limits displayed on the charts so that undue meaning is not attached to a

* 'Statistical Control Applies to Financial Statements' *The Accounting Review*, vol. 21, no. 3 July 1946 pp. 267-272.

Table 5.15. Nine pairs of indices of company performance

Measure of performance	
Monetary value	Ratio
Net sales	Net sales, cumulated for each year
Net profit before taxes	Expressed as a percentage of net sales
Cost of goods sold	Expressed as a percentage of net sales
Administrative, general and selling expenses	Expressed as a percentage of net sales
Working capital	Turnover of working capital
Total inventories	Turnover of inventories
Outstanding debts	Collection period
Net worth	Turnover of net worth
Fixed assets	Expressed as a percentage of net worth

large fluctuation occurring within the normal band of variability.

In this field cumulative sum charts are more appropriate and much more powerful than the standard monitoring control charts in detecting change. They are straightforward in operation, and in particular the band between upper and lower reference values, within which no cumulative sum is started, provides an excellent means of filtering out unnecessary action.

5.8.3. Production planning and control

The units and the frequency of measurement used in monitoring production will depend on the nature of the production facilities. However, monitoring should involve a regular comparison of output against target and a regular comparison of costs against target. In manufacturing industries, the same or similar products are being manufactured week by week or month by month either within a department, within a factory or within a division. Where products are diverse, a major problem is to set up a common yardstick for measuring output. Once this problem has been solved cumulative sum charts, based on individual results, are the most appropriate tool although standard control charts have been used in practice.

In the field of project management, especially in civil engineering, senior management are usually responsible for several projects. Monitoring, in this instance, should be aimed at controlling the output and cost against target on individual projects and identifying those projects which need special attention. One tool which has proved valuable in this field has been called the *value envelope*. The control limits of the value envelope are determined by the use of network analysis (critical path method). The cumulative value of the work done either in monetary value or man hours if all jobs start at their earliest possible time is used to determine the left hand limit. The cumulative value if all jobs start at their latest possible time determines the right hand and most critical limit. The type of chart and the nature of the control is shown in Fig. 5.11. Should the line of crosses

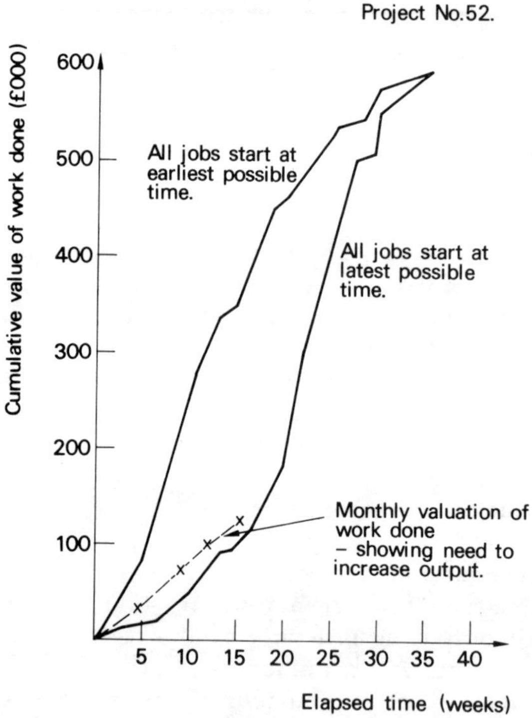

Figure 5.11 Value envelope showing performance limits if project is to be finished on time

representing actual achievement (at monthly or fortnightly intervals) fall outside the value envelope by crossing the earliest possible limit line they would indicate the project was ahead of schedule. Should they cross the latest possible limit line, they would indicate that the project could not be finished on time without drastic replanning and restaffing.

A value envelope for each project will enable senior management to determine at a glance the projects under their control on which they should concentrate.

5.8.4. Sales performance

Sales performance can be monitored either through the value of orders received or by the value of sales achieved. In many companies the results would be the same but when failure to deliver a satisfactory product in time causes customers to cancel and purchase elsewhere, monitoring of orders can provide a more satisfactory measure of sales performance. In practice, all companies collect information on weekly or monthly sales in value but by no means all have a similar analysis for orders. Monitoring control can be just as easily applied to product performance as to representatives' performance, and charts can be prepared for individual products just as readily as for individual salesmen. A straightforward and desirable extension, the monitoring of products grouped according to their profit contribution, can provide a control of gross profit.

Tables 5.16 and 5.17 show how a two-sided decision interval scheme for monitoring the cumulative sum of weekly sales would be established and applied.

The acceptable and rejectable sales levels would be established

Table 5.16. Establishing decision interval scheme for weekly sales level

1. Acceptable sales level = 35 rolls a week.
2. Average run length at acceptable level = 125.
3. Rejectable sales level = 25 rolls a week.
4. Reference value = 30 rolls a week.
5. Difference = 10 rolls a week.
6. Standard deviation from past weekly sales figures = 9.1 rolls a week.
7. $\dfrac{\text{Difference}}{\text{standard deviation}} = 1.1$
8. From Table 5.11, $\dfrac{\text{limit}}{\text{standard deviation}} = 2.9$,

   and so the limit of the cumulative sum = 26.4
9. Note that the cumulative sum chart will need on average *six* observations to detect a change to 25 rolls a week.
10. An upper 'rejectable' sales level of 45 rolls a week could be used to detect an increase in sales on this product.
11. The appropriate reference value is 40 rolls, and the limit of the cumulative sum is also 26.4.

from past performance and from the amount of change which can be tolerated. The choice of average run length at the acceptable level would be arbitrary, bearing in mind the average run length which would arise at the rejectable level. Since the upper and lower rejectable sales levels were equally spaced about the acceptable level, two identical schemes were established. The first

Table 5.17. Decision interval scheme used to monitor weekly sales
Stock item: 6345

Week no.	Seasonally adjusted sales	Below 30 Diff.	Cu. sum. limit – 26.4		Above 40 Diff.	Cu. sum. limit 26.4
8/1	32			✓		
2	36			✓		
3	26	–4	–4			
4	27	–3	–7			
5	26	–4	–11			
6	33	3	–8			
7	32	2	–6			
8	43	13	+		3	3
9	31				–9	–
10	36			✓		
11	44				4	4
12	52				12	16
13	48				8	24
14	21				–19	5
15	39				–1	4
16	37				–3	1
17	62				22	23
18	27				–13	10
19	40				nil	10
20	27	–3	–3		–13	–
21	17	–13	–16			
22	16	–14	–30*			
23						
24						

* *Action:* sales on this item have fallen. What are *you* going to do about it?

had a reference value of thirty, halfway between the acceptable level of thirty-five rolls and the rejectable sales level of twenty-five rolls. The average run length at the acceptable level of 125 was chosen arbitrarily within Table 5.16 to keep the average run length at the rejectable level as low as possible, namely six. The resulting decision limit for this scheme was calculated as –26.4. This scheme would be used to detect instances in which the sales level fell below the acceptable level. It is clearly also important to detect an increase in sales and to ensure that production facilities are capable of meeting the extra demand. To do this, the second scheme was chosen to detect when the average sales level had risen from its acceptable level of thirty-five to a 'rejectable' level of forty-five. The reference value of this second scheme was forty and a cumulative sum only started when the weekly sales exceeded this figure. In those instances in which the sales are seasonal, the cumulative sum charts would monitor seasonally adjusted sales figures.

Table 5.17 illustrates the use of the combined schemes. Provided that the sales are between thirty and forty, the central column is ticked and a cumulative sum not started. Weeks three to eight show a period when sales appear to be low but the cumulative sum shows that the average is certainly not as low as thirty. Over a subsequent period, weeks eleven to twenty, high weekly sales started a cumulative sum, but because the average level was not above forty it died away. The sales in the three weeks twenty to twenty-two were all below thirty and the cumulative sum built up to –30, which is below the lower decision limit of –26.4, calling for action to restore the normal sales level.

5.8.5. Quality control

The use of monitoring charts for the control of quality is now well established and all personnel working in the field of monitoring quality should be skilled in their practical use.

Acceptance sampling schemes, either designed to identify the bad batch or to provide an insurance against holdups in production have been operating for over thirty years. They have been used both in goods inwards departments and also to audit quality before despatch to customers.

Standard control charts, and more recently cumulative control charts have been used to enable production staff to know quickly and cheaply how they are meeting quality standards. These charts have been based both on measurements of vital characteristics of the product and also on a simple count of how many in a sample were of unsatisfactory quality. One of the key features of their use has been to produce information on the level of quality being achieved by measuring it at the point at which it is created. Only in this way is it possible for speedy action to be taken to prevent further defective work being produced.

List of terms used

Cost variance	Cumulative sum chart
Random fluctuations	Standard control chart procedures
Control	Reference value (cumulative sum)

Control loop
Frequency diagram
Monitoring charts
Quality control
Median
Range
Central value
Variability
Sample
Drawing *tolerances*
Action factor
Action limits
Control limits
Counting
Poisson distribution
Cumulative sum

Decision interval schemes
Acceptable level
Rejectable level
Average run length
Standard deviation
Acceptance sampling procedures
DEF-131-A: Normal inspection
Tightened inspection
Reduced inspection
Sampling plan
Short term fluctuations
Significant change
Project
Value envelope
Seasonally adjusted
Computer program

Italicized terms are defined in the glossary (page 262) as well as in the text where it is appropriate.

6. Forecasting

Forecasting is simply the application of the maxim 'look before you leap', with an additional maxim 'the further you are going to leap, the further you should look forward'.

A forecast of sales for a long period ahead is needed if policies on research, product development, expansion of capacity and management development are to be chosen to meet the needs of the future company. This is the field of long-range forecasting, often full of pitfalls and gross uncertainties and subject to the vagaries of governmental policies.

A medium-range forecast covering a period of up to fifteen months in the future is usually employed for establishing sales, production and financial budgets. Short term forecasts, usually covering a period less than three months, may be used for production planning and stock control.

Classical management theory makes forecasting, closely linked with planning, the first of the functions of management. So it is inevitable that some kind of forecasting will be done in all situations, however subjectively. The forecast may be hidden in decisions on how the product is to be sold or on the method of production, but nevertheless it was made.

The better the forecast, the better the plan, the more co-ordinated the effort and the bigger the profit.

6.1. Systematic way of preparing forecasts

Forecasts provide information for management's plans, information which should be based on facts, not just on opinions. The pattern of past orders or sales reflects the performance of the company. It may miss the anecdotes and idiosyncracies of individual customers but it mirrors the company's total sales experience. What is needed is a systematic method of extracting this experience and assessing its relevance to the future.

The pattern of the future cannot of course be entirely determined by the past. Management's ability to take hold of a moribund company and bring it back to life cannot be discounted.

Moreover, the forecast of what is likely to happen in the future may not measure up to management's intention of what they want to happen. If not, there is need for a change in marketing tactics or strategy, to transform the picture shown by the forecast into an acceptable budget or plan. But, however you look at it, the forecast is the starting point of the plan.

6.1.1. What kind of forecast

Two factors have to be determined when choosing the form of the forecast. They are the degree of detail and the forecasting horizon: how much detail should a forecast contain, and how far forward should it look.

The degree of detail depends solely on the purpose of the forecast. In a carpet manufacturing company, a forecast for stock control or for loom loading (short term production planning) would need to be made for every design of carpet in every quality and every width. A forecast for the annual budget could be in product groups—typical product groups would contain all carpets of the same quality (and profitability) and width (using the same looms).

For longer term planning, a forecast in terms of the total demand for each quality, and the total demand for each width of carpet would provide the information needed to assess future profitability and future long term investment in plant.

The position of the forecasting horizon is determined by the time needed to implement policy changes which result from the sales forecast. For example, if a reasonable change in production capacity requires two or three months to implement, then there would be little point in forecasting to a horizon less than three months ahead. How long does it take to arrange systematic overtime; short time working; a second or third shift; to buy and instal new equipment; or to build a new factory?

Forecasts are usually classified as short term, medium term or long term (Table 6.1) but what is short term to a steelworks, with a rolling cycle of three months' duration, is medium or possibly long term to a fashion goods company. Nevertheless, both companies will need short term, medium term and long term plans based on different degrees of detail and different horizons each appropriate to their peculiar situations.

The degree of detail needed in the forecast helps to decide the source of demand information which can be used. If total industry information is all that is needed then statistical returns published by government departments or trade associations may be adequate. Such information is only of value for long term forecasts where a broad outline of the future economic climate will suffice. If some degree of detail, relating to the company's different products, is needed then the only source of information will lie in the company's past sales performance. Occasionally some special information is available—when the company has a long forward order book, when trial marketing of a new product has been done, or as occurred in a mail order firm where the firm's 'key agents' were able to order high fashion goods from a black and white catalogue over a month ahead of the despatch of the multi-coloured, multi-paged full catalogue.

Table 6.1. Classification of forecasts

Horizon	Typical purpose	Degree of detail
Short term	Immediate production plan; stock replenishment	Full for detailed planning
Medium term	Company budget Seasonal build up of stocks Recruitment and training of labour	Adequate for control
Long term	Capital investment plans	Broad outline

In long term forecasting where a broad outline is sufficient, sophisticated models based on input/output analysis have been prepared by a number of the larger companies. These models allow the planner to conjecture 'What would happen if we were to reprice our product; if we spend more money on sales promotion; if we were to cut advertising expenditure and employ more salesmen; if . . . ?' Their purpose is to allow the long term planner to envisage the consequences of alternative situations so that a number of alternative plans can be prepared. Long term forecasting in this sense is concerned with trying to envisage all the likely major changes affecting the future and to estimate their consequences in terms of sales, manpower, finance, and equipment. Fig. 6.1 on page 128, shows a basic forecasting model used on an industrial product. This model would allow alternative rates of growth, industry by industry; alternative price/demand relationships, industry by industry; and alternatively timed sales effort/sales relationships to be conjectured. It would then take the present total market; predict the future total market, year by year; and forecast company sales, industry by industry and year by year.

It is usually considered that much simpler methods should be used for short and medium term forecasting. These forecasts have to be made in more detail and sophisticated models would result in confusion rather than clarity. The steps necessary to make short and medium term forecasts are outlined in the following section.

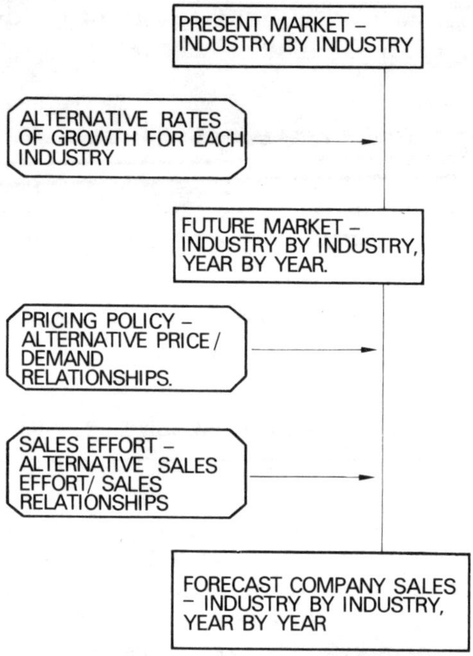

Figure 6.1 Basic model for long term forecasting for an industrial product

6.1.2. Step by step approach

All short and medium term forecasting techniques are based on analysing the past pattern of sales and projecting this into the future. To be successful they all need to take the following steps.

(a) *Analyse past figures.* Collect together sales or order figures covering the past four or five years, for each of the main product areas. Check that these figures are a true representation of the past pattern of demand, and then determine the nature of the seasonal pattern ensuring that it is truly systematic, repeated year after year, as shown in Fig. 6.2.

(b) *Examine seasonally adjusted figures.* Once the seasonal pattern has been established, make appropriate adjustments to eliminate it. Then chart the seasonally adjusted figures and examine the pattern in them. In many instances the pattern can be represented by a simple linear trend, together with a measurable amount of variation about the trend. See Fig. 6.3 on page 130.

(c) *Project into the future.* Project the pattern (Fig. 6.3) into the future to provide forecasts of the seasonally adjusted sales or orders and then readjust them to build in the appropriate amount of seasonality.

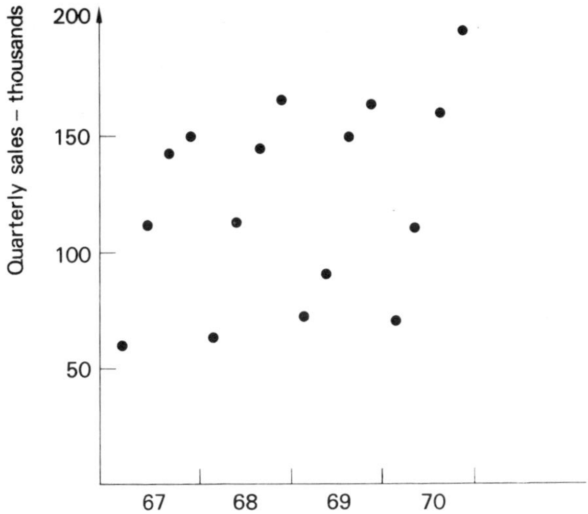

Figure 6.2 Seasonal pattern of sales

(d) *Measure and monitor the error in forecasting.* The variation about the trend shown in Fig. 6.3 provides a measure of the uncertainty in forecasting. It is as important a piece of information as the forecast itself since it can be used to measure the amount of flexibility needed in production and financial resources. Once the forecasting procedure becomes routine, each actual result should be compared against the forecast to detect abnormal errors. Abnormal results need to be checked carefully, not only to eliminate arithmetical mistakes but also to provide commercial intelligence of changes in the pattern of demand.

(e) *Assess the effect of major changes.* The steps taken so far assume that the market in which the company is operating is mirrored by the company's sales or orders. If it is a dynamic market then the company figures will mirror this changing pattern. However, from time to time there will be large and dramatic changes due to:

a major change in company policy, as might occur after a merger;
a major change in competitive policy, for example when a major competitor brings out a new model; or
a major change in government fiscal policy, particularly hire purchase restrictions.

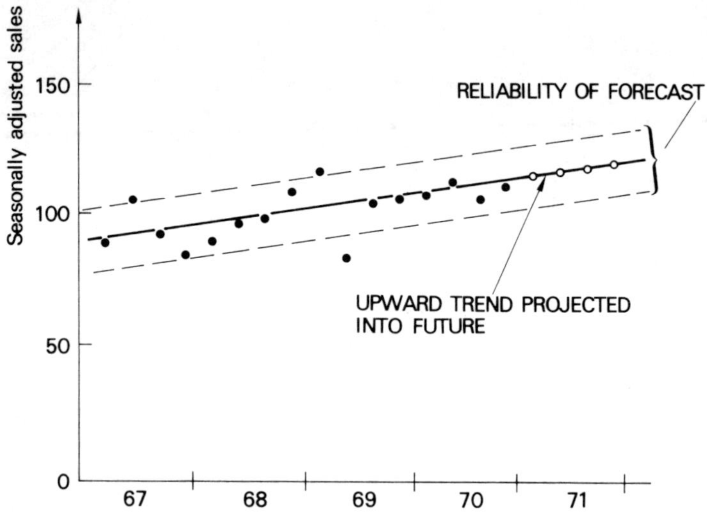

Figure 6.3 Pattern in seasonally adjusted sales: seasonal adjustment makes forecasting more reliable

(f) *Prepare for action.* A forecast is valuable management information and it should be issued at the earliest possible instant. Decide what to do *now* to change an unsatisfactory plan.

6.2. Steps in making a forecast

The step by step approach just described should apply to all forecasting techniques however simple or however complicated. The mechanics of carrying out these steps is described by means of a fairly simple but practical method of forecasting which has been particularly useful in the preparation of forecasts for a twelve month budget.

In this illustration of the method, the calculations have been kept to a minimum by working in quarterly sales. It has been tacitly assumed that the differences between the *three* months within each quarter is sufficiently small to be ignored. This will not be true of course in every application.

6.2.1. Measure the seasonal variation

Consider the quarterly sales shown in Table 6.2.

Table 6.2. Quarterly sales (thousands)

Quarter	1	2	3	4	Total
1967	66	114	155	146	481
1968	68	115	158	171	512
1969	79	100	166	170	515
1970	75	123	169	181	548
Total	288	452	648	668	
Average	72	113	162	167	

A quick examination shows a marked seasonal pattern of sales. Quarter 1 is systematically less than Quarter 2, which is less than Quarter 3 and this is almost the same as Quarter 4. This clear systematic pattern will not always exist and the quarterly sales data should be plotted on a chart showing the results over the years separately for each quarter (Fig. 6.4).

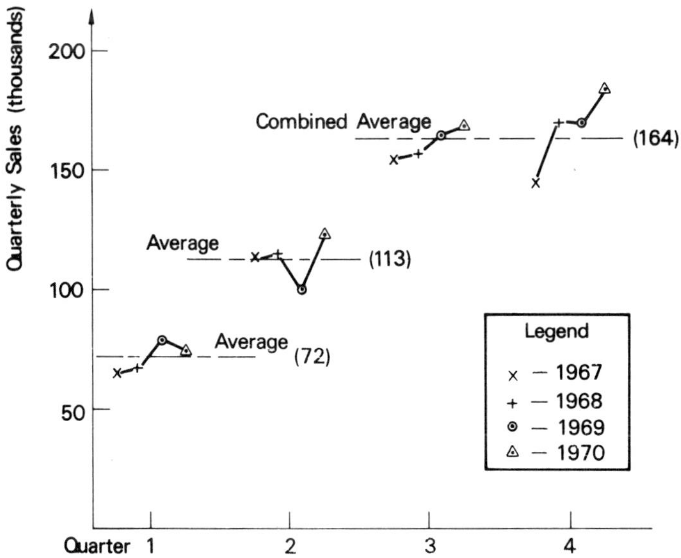

Figure 6.4 Quarterly sales figures arranged to highlight quarter to quarter variation

Assess whether the apparent differences in the average quarterly sales could be easily explained by the variation from year to year in the quarterly sales figures. In this instance the chart simply confirms the conclusion of a marked seasonal pattern of sales.

6.2.2. Find the pattern in seasonally adjusted figures

One simple means of adjusting the sales figures to eliminate the seasonal pattern is to express each quarter as a percentage of the appropriate average for each quarter. In this instance, because there is no difference between the last two quarters, the average over both quarters is used for both of these quarters. For instance, the quarterly adjusted sales for 1967 are:

Quarter 1 $\quad 66 \times \dfrac{100}{72} = 91$

Quarter 2 $\quad 114 \times \dfrac{100}{113} = 101$

Quarter 3 $\quad 155 \times \dfrac{100}{164} = 94$

Quarter 4 $\quad 146 \times \dfrac{100}{164} = 88$

The resulting quarterly adjusted sales are shown in Table 6.3.

Table 6.3. Quarterly indices (quarterly sales, seasonally adjusted by expressing them as percentage of average of appropriate quarter)

Quarter	1	2	3	4
1967	92	101	94	88
1968	94	102	96	104
1969	110	89	101	104
1970	104	109	103	110

These adjusted figures have been plotted against time in Fig. 6.5 and the best straight line has been drawn through the plotted points, using the method described in chapter 4. The same method was used to measure the average forecasting error and the limits within which 90 per cent of the plotted points should lie.

6.2.3. Project this pattern to estimate future sales

The straight line drawn on Fig. 6.5 has been projected forward and the values of seasonally adjusted sales for the next five quarters read straight off the graph, on the vertical axis. These

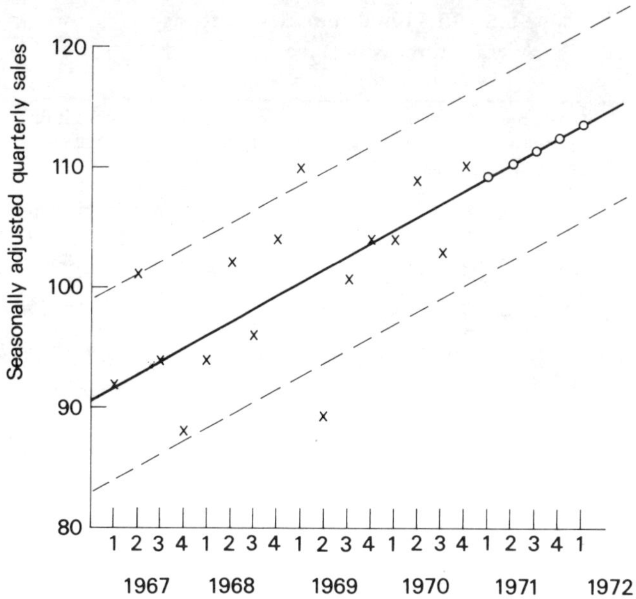

Figure 6.5 Seasonally adjusted quarterly sales and estimated trend

values which represent the percentage of the average quarterly sales are then expressed in actual sales units by building in the seasonality which had been eliminated previously. The details are shown in Table 6.4.

Table 6.4. Estimated forecasts based on graph of seasonally adjusted sales

Date	Forecast of seasonally adjusted sales (Percentage of quarterly average)	Average quarterly sales	Forecast actual sales
1971-1	109.5	72	79 000
1971-2	110.5	113	125 000
1971-3	111.5	164	183 000
1971-4	112.5	164	184 000
1972-1	113.5	72	82 000

6.2.4. Measure and monitor the error in forecasting

The average forecasting error was similarly projected forward to give estimated limits within which 90 per cent of future forecasts should fall. These limits are in terms of seasonally adjusted sales and are converted into actual units in the same manner by which the forecast was converted into actual units. These limits are shown in Table 6.5.

Table 6.5. 90% Limits on sales forecasts
Average forecasting error = 4.0
(Measured on Fig. 6.5)

Date	90% Limit of seasonally adjusted sales (Percentage of quarterly average)	Average quarterly sales	90% Limit (actual sales)
1971-1	± 8.0	72	± 5800
1971-2	± 8.0	113	± 9000
1971-3	± 8.0	164	± 13000
1971-4	± 8.0	164	± 13000
1972-1	± 8.0	72	± 5800

Subsequent forecasts: take action if forecasting error exceeds 12.0 on seasonally adjusted sales

On subsequent forecasts, any error (in seasonally adjusted units) in excess of three times the average forecasting error would warrant careful investigation.

6.2.5. Assess the effect of major changes

The effect of major changes in the company's, in competitors' and in government policy are difficult to assess. The commercial sales manager must have the right to make modifications to the projected figures and these will be based on his experience and judgment. However, a forecasting diary should be kept recording the initial projected figure, the modified figure together with the reason for the adjustment, and in due course the actual sales which occurred. If adequate discipline is employed, adjustments will be limited to those instances where they are sensible.

In the case of short term forecasting, experience suggests that the effect of these major changes may be ignored and the projected forecast used without adjustment. This approach is in fact being used by a number of companies to forecast weekly sales for each of several weeks ahead as a basis for production planning. The calculations are made by computer and apart from a check for abnormal errors, the forecasts are completely automatic.

6.2.6. Prepare a plan

This forecast was made during the first quarter of 1971, as soon as the results for the previous quarter were known and it would form the basis of the budget for 1971-72. This type of forecast would almost certainly be made for each of the company's product groups and the production feasibility and profitability of the forecasts would be assessed. If the forecast demand exceeded production capacity, action to increase this capacity either through

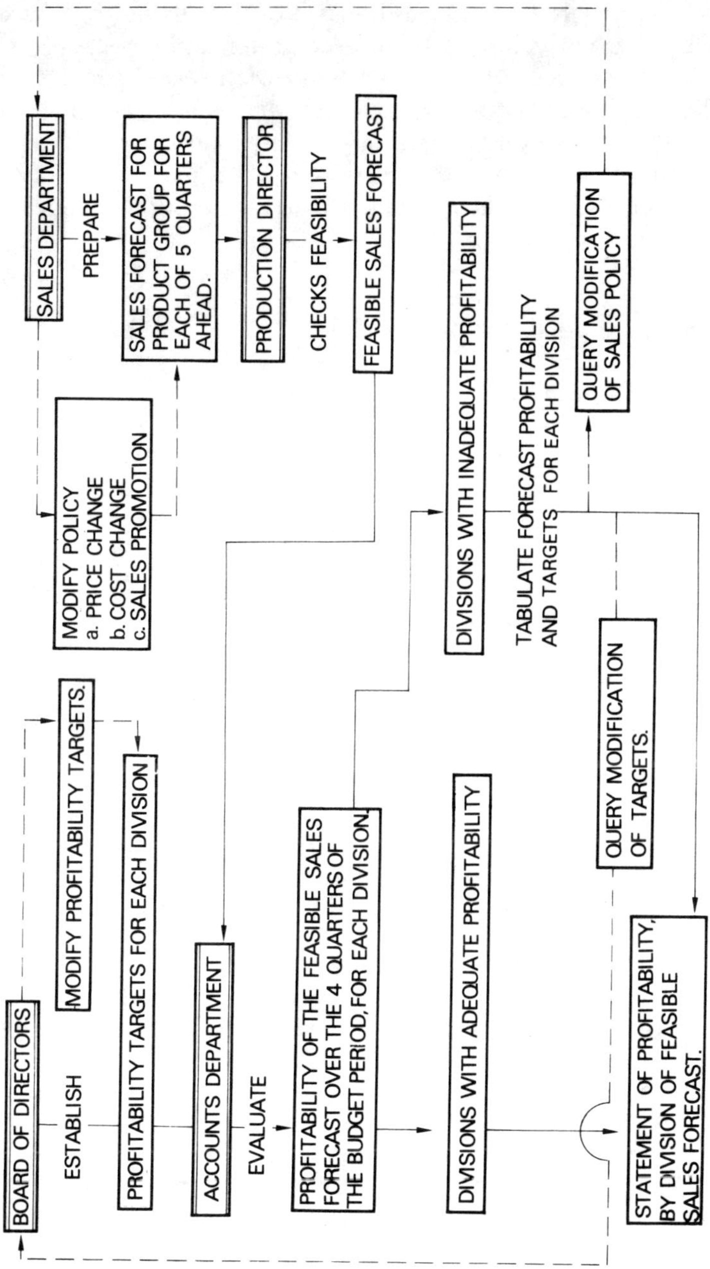

Figure 6.6 Profitability analysis of sales forecast

overtime working, subcontracting or an extra shift has to be taken *now*. If none of these is feasible the budget would be based on production capacity rather than forecast demand.

In a similar manner the profitability of the sales forecast (duly modified to take account of agreed production limitations), has to be assessed and action taken immediately to turn an unsatisfactory forecast into a satisfactory plan. Fig. 6.6, on page 135, illustrates the method used by one company to assess the profitability of the budget sales forecast.

6.3. Keeping the forecast up to date

6.3.1. Advantages of exponential smoothing

The techniques described in the previous section are ideally suited for making a single forecast. When forecasts are being revised at frequent intervals, as they should be, the task of revising the best straight line and the average forecasting error can become formidable. This is particularly true when short term forecasts are being made for a very large number of items as a basis for stock control. The technique known as exponential smoothing is probably the simplest method of keeping such forecasts up to date. The routine requires only a limited amount of arithmetic and can be readily delegated to a clerk or a computer.

Exponential smoothing is an averaging procedure, but it is so arranged that extra weight is given to the more recent results—as the manager would do in an intuitive analysis. The forecasting error can be averaged in an identical manner, so providing an up to date estimate of the reliability of forecasting and allowing freak results to be detected and discarded if this is appropriate.

6.3.2. How it is done in a simple case

The simplest situation is where there is no marked change in the level of demand. If seasonality exists, it can be accommodated by working with seasonally adjusted sales making a projection into the future and building back seasonality into the forecast. In many instances there is little or no growth or fall off up to the horizon covered by the short term forecast for stock and production planning, and it is adequate to assume that no trend exists.

Suppose, in such a situation, the average monthly sales over the last twelve months was 1460. The forecast for this month is 1460; for the next month is 1460; for the month after that is 1460, and so on. If this month's sales turn out to be 1560, should you

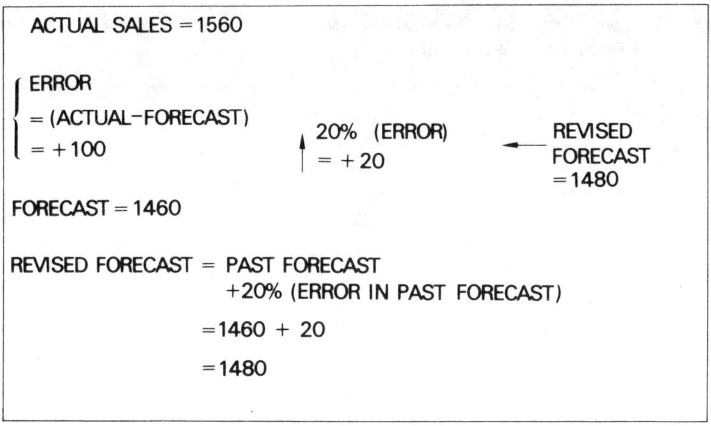

Figure 6.7 Exponential smoothing used to update simple forecast

continue with the old average of 1460, should you take the actual sales of 1560 as the basis for a new forecast, or should you take something in between? Exponential smoothing says: 'Take something in between', and experience suggests that the past forecast should be adjusted by about 20 per cent of the forecasting error, as shown in Fig. 6.7.

An example illustrating the routine of the calculations and a plot of the forecasts made one period ahead compared against the actual results are shown in Table 6.6 and Fig. 6.8 on pages 138 and 139.

The factor 20 per cent has been called the *smoothing constant* and the choice of this constant needs to be examined. If a smoothing constant of zero was chosen, all the immediate past history would be discarded and the old average maintained unchanged. If at the other extreme, a smoothing constant of 100 per cent was chosen, all the forecasting errors would be taken into account. In fact the forecast would be based only on the last result and the old history discarded. Consequently, the smaller the smoothing constant, the more the attention given to past history; and the larger the smoothing constant, the more the attention given to recent results. One computer program switches from a 10 per cent smoothing constant when the sales level appears to be steady (apart from random fluctuations) to a 30 per cent smoothing constant when the level appears to have changed.

The comparative importance given to current and past results is shown in Table 6.7. With a smoothing constant of 10 per cent it is

Table 6.6. Routine of calculation for simple exponential smoothing—updating of forecast based on average

Week	Actual sales (tons)	Forecast (tons)	Error (tons)	20% of error (tons)
1	32	Average		
2	36	= 29.4		
3	26			
4	27			
5	26			
6	33	29.4	3.6	0.7
7	32	30.1	1.9	0.4
8	43	30.5	12.5	2.5
9	31	33.0	− 2.0	− 0.4
10	36	32.6	3.4	0.7
11	44	33.3	10.7	2.1
12	52	35.4	16.6	3.3
13	48	38.7	9.3	1.9
14	21	40.6	− 19.6	− 3.9
15	39	36.7	2.3	0.5
		37.2		
Col. 1	Col. 2	Col. 3 = previous value + Col. 5	Col. 4 = Col. 2 − Col. 3	Col. 5 = 20% (Col. 4)

Table 6.7. How exponential smoothing gives less and less weight to past results

Date Yr.-Qtr.	Traditional average—gives equal weight to each result	Exponential smoothing—gives more weight to most recent results, less weight to past results Smoothing constant		
		10%	20%	30%
1971-4	12.5%	10%	20%	30%
1971-3	12.5%	9%	16%	21%
1971-2	12.5%	8.1%	12.8%	14.7%
1971-1	12.5%	7.3%	10.2%	10.3%
1970-4	12.5%	6.6%	8.2%	7.2%
1970-3	12.5%	5.9%	6.6%	5.0%
1970-2	12.5%	5.3%	5.2%	3.5%
1970-1	12.5%	4.8%	4.2%	2.5%
			and so on into the past	

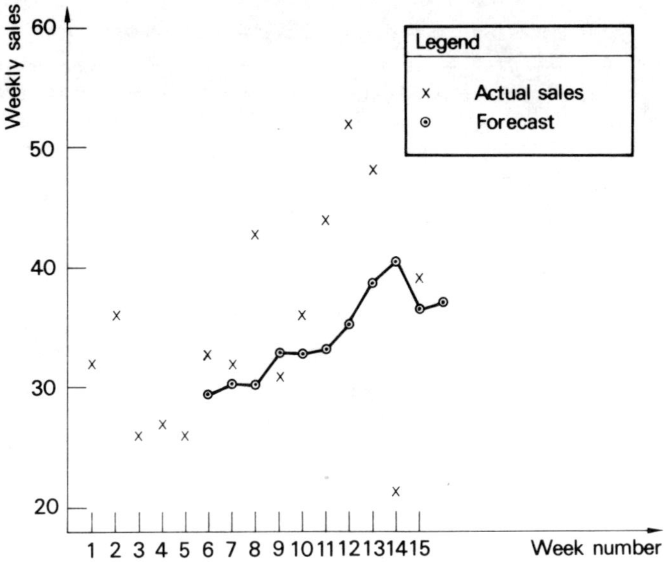

Figure 6.8 Comparison of actual sales with forecast one week ahead

seven periods back before the weight falls below 5 per cent, half the initial value; with 20 per cent, it is four periods; and with 30 per cent only two periods before the weight falls to below half its initial value.

6.3.3. Maintaining a measure of the average forecasting error

The average forecasting error can be kept up to date by exponential smoothing, just as the forecasts are kept up to date. However, in this instance, it is wise to take a much smaller smoothing constant since forecasting errors are very variable and their short term fluctuations should be ignored. A smoothing constant of about 2 per cent is recommended. The way of updating the average forecasting error is shown in Table 6.8 overleaf. From Table 6.6 the forecast for week 16 is 37.2 tons, and from Table 6.8 the average forecasting error is 4.5 tons. The 90 per cent limits on the forecast are: 37.2 ± 9.0 tons, namely 46.2 and 28.2 tons. If demand is to be met from stock, the stock in hand will need to be built up to the maximum likely demand, namely 46.2 tons—a fact on which the production plan for week 16 would be based.

Once formal forecasting procedures have been introduced, all instances where the error is greater than three times the average error should be investigated as potential anomalies. Such instances occur in Table 6.8 on week 12 and week 14.

Table 6.8. Routine updating of average forecasting error

Week	Error in forecast (tons)	Average forecasting error (tons)	Error—average error (tons)	2% x (Error—average error) (tons)
1	2.6			
2	6.6	Average = 3.7		
3	– 3.4	(N.B. Ignores		
4	– 2.4	– signs)		
5	– 3.4			
6	3.6	3.7	– 0.1	– 0.002
7	1.9	3.7	– 1.8	– 0.04
8	12.5	3.66	8.8	0.18
9	– 2.0	3.84	– 1.8	– 0.04
10	3.4	3.80	– 0.4	– 0.01
11	10.7	3.79	6.8	0.14
12	16.6*	3.93	12.7	0.25
13	9.3	4.18	5.1	0.10
14	– 19.6*	4.28	15.3	0.31
15	2.3	4.59	– 2.3	– 0.05
		4.54		
Col. 1	Col. 2	Col. 3 = previous value + Col. 5	Col. 4 = numerical value of Col. 2 – Col. 3	Col 5 = 2% of (Col. 4)

* Abnormally high forecasting errors. Should be investigated thoroughly before being used to revise average forecasting error.

6.3.4. What happens when trend is present

One of the main reasons for eliminating systematic seasonal variation from sales data is to be able to detect changes in the average level of sales, changes which may be regarded as forming part of a trend. The procedure of plotting the seasonally adjusted sales figures and representing the trend by a straight line and a scatter about it (as shown in Fig. 6.5 on page 133) may be used to determine the starting points for exponential smoothing.

In Fig. 6.5 the seasonally adjusted quarterly sales figure increases at about 1.1 units each quarter, and this would be expressed: Trend = 1.1. Exponential smoothing would then be used to maintain an up to date estimate of the trend.

When trend is present, the forecast is built up from two components: the revised forecast, assuming that no trend is present, and the revised trend. In summary:

new forecast = revised forecast + revised trend,

and, with typical smoothing constants:

Revised Forecast = Forecast + 20 per cent (Forecasting error), and

Revised Trend = Trend + 1 per cent (Forecasting error).

It is desirable to link the values of the smoothing constants for the revised forecast and for the revised trend, in order to maintain the best straight line for forecasting and still give most attention to the most recent results. A selection of appropriate smoothing constants is given in Table 6.9. To start exponential smoothing,

Table 6.9. Appropriate pairs of smoothing constants for revised forecast and revised trend

Smoothing constant for	
Revised forecast	Revised trend
0.51	0.09
0.36	0.04
0.19	0.01
0.10	0.003

initial values of a forecast; the trend; and the average forecasting error are needed and these would be read from a diagram such as Fig. 6.5.

Rather than starting exponential smoothing at the latest date, it is better to select a point someway back in time and use the

Table 6.10. Method of updating forecast and average forecasting error—in presence of trend

Position at 3rd quarter 1969

Actual	101	Trend	= 1.10
Forecast	102.8	Average forecasting error	= 4.0
Error	– 1.8	Change in error	= (1.8 – 4.0)
			= – 2.2

Revised forecast = 102.8 + 20% (– 1.8) = 102.4
Revised trend = 1.10 + 1% (– 1.8) = 1.08

Forecast for 4th quarter 1969 = 103.5

Revised average forecasting error
= 4.0 + 2% (– 2.2)
= 3.96

90% Limits on forecast for 4th quarter 1969 = ± 7.9

exponential smoothing procedures to bring the estimated forecast, trend and average forecasting error up to date. A suitable starting point on Fig. 6.5 would be the third quarter of 1969 which would give six updatings to allow the exponential smoothing procedure to run itself in. The forecast for this quarter, read from the best straight line, would be taken as 102.8. Initial values of the trend and the average forecasting error would be chosen as the values previously determined, namely 1.1 and 4.0. All of these values are in terms of the seasonally adjusted quarterly sales, and in due course the result for the third quarter of 1969 would be determined as 101. The precise method of updating the forecast and the average forecasting error, taking account of the trend and changes in trend, is shown in Table 6.10 on page 141.

Calculation routines similar to those shown in Tables 6.6 and 6.8 would be developed and by repetition of the steps shown in Table 6.10 the forecast and the average forecasting error would be brought up to date. The forecast for the first quarter of 1971 becomes 109.3, with a trend of 1.08, and an average forecasting error of 3.8. From these values the forecast for each of the five quarters ahead, together with 90 per cent limits on these forecasts, would be prepared. The results are shown in Table 6.11.

The pair of smoothing constants 0.19 (rounded to 0.20 to simplify the calculations) and 0.01 have been selected. Past experience suggests that they will produce forecasts with the smallest forecasting error in the circumstances.

Table 6.11. Forecasts based on exponential smoothing

Date	Average quarterly sales	Forecast sales		90% Limit on forecast	
		Seasonally adjusted	Actual units	Seasonally adjusted	Actual units
1971-1	72	109.3	78 000	±7.6	± 5500
1971-2	113	110.4	125 000	±7.6	± 8500
1971-3	164	111.5	183 000	±7.6	±12 500
1971-4	164	112.5	184 000	±7.6	±12 500
1972-1	72	113.6	82 000	±7.6	± 5500

6.4. The pros and cons of mathematical methods for forecasting

This assessment of the value of mathematical methods for forecasting is probably biased and perhaps the best advice to each manager is to 'suck it and see' for himself.

There is clearly a need to keep in touch with the plans of major customers, and in those instances where there are only three or four customers this intelligence, in numerical form, is probably as good as forecasting by mathematical methods. But subjective assessment of the future can be grossly unrealistic. For instance, TV executives were very worried when cigarette advertising on television was banned, and yet every second of advertising space which became available was sold without conscious effort.

Perhaps a key feature in assessing the value of mathematical forecasting is how long the past pattern of business is relevant to the company's future operations. This need not be a guess—examine what would have happened if mathematical sales forecasts had been used in the past. Even in those instances where the error in forecasting is large, the mathematical methods measure how inaccurate the forecast could be. This information is a bonus, far more valuable than the subjective assessment of accuracy bandied between sales and production managements.

These methods are not always readily applicable and special steps have to be taken. For instance, the company manufacturing chemical plant has to turn its sales into man hours or machine hours to combine small and large orders. In another company, the 'new' product with no sales history has to be identified with the predecessors to which it is most similar, and the previous growth pattern (incorporating a measure of variability) projected into the future.

Experience shows that mathematical forecasting, especially the exponential smoothing method has a lot to offer. This is particularly true when a large number of forecasts are needed and the calculations can be carried out by computer. In the ideal management information system, the end result would be a forecast and not a mass of data from which the manager has to extract a pattern and then decide what to do.

Finally, forecasting is like driving a car in the fog. You peer through the windscreen into the mists of time and try to make out the shapes ahead. For some companies there is only a thin mist and forecasts can be made with a fair degree of confidence. For others the future is almost completely obscured. No sales forecasting techniques can eliminate all the uncertainty—even the best fog lights have limited value in a very dense fog. But there is one difference, the forecasting techniques can measure the uncertainty of the forecasts of future demand, and this like the forecasts themselves, is valuable information for planning to meet the future. Remember the forecast is made to decide what to do *now* to deal with this uncertain view of the future. Don't hide the forecasts in a drawer, and don't have a committee meeting to decide whether or not to put your foot on the brakes.

List of terms used

Forecasting horizon	*Average*
Model	*Forecasting error*
Input/output	90% limits on forecast
Systematic pattern	*Exponential smoothing*
Seasonally adjusted sales	*Seasonality*
Linear trend	*Smoothing constant*
Abnormal errors	*Computer program*
Best straight line	Trend
Reliability of forecast	Management information system

Italicized terms are defined in the glossary (page 262) as well as in the text where it is appropriate.

7. Planning

Just as forecasting may be regarded as one of the processes of management, so may planning. It is just as important to use numerical methods to improve planning and so ensure that the other processes of management can be more easily and efficiently carried out. However it is essential to remember that without the other processes, planning is sterile and the plan becomes a worthless piece of paper.

7.1. Nature of planning

Planning is a wide ranging activity. It may concentrate on the adequate provision of resources of manpower, machinery, finance and materials, and their efficient use. It may concentrate on the correct sequence of activities to provide effective co-ordination between several groups working on a project. Wherever it is carried out, whether in research, design and drawing, purchasing, manufacture, maintenance, selling or servicing, it is imperative to measure the need for and use of resources if planning is to be done successfully. Moreover, the better the planning, the fewer the hold-ups, the more efficiently the critical resources can be used and the bigger the profit.

Planning can involve the balancing of conflicting expenditures and making the best use of limited resources. To do this effectively demands an understanding of the principles if not a knowledge of the techniques discussed in chapter 8. Without control, planning is meaningless. There is a continuing need to feed back information on progress to form a new plan or to revise the existing plan. Sometimes there are no practical formal methods of tackling these more sophisticated planning problems. They can only be solved by building a mathematical model of the situation and asking 'what would happen if . . . ?'—namely by using the simulation techniques described in chapter 9.

The basic requirements of any successful plan are:

1. The correct identification of all the activities being planned, in a form which allows the work content of each activity to be assessed;

2. The allocation of total resources in the light of the total requirement;
3. The assessment of the work content on each activity in turn;
4. The allocation of resources to each activity, within the limits of the total resources made available;
5. Estimation of the duration of each activity, based on its work content and the resources allocated;
6. The correct identification of the restrictions which make it necessary to carry out one activity before another; and,
7. In the case of project planning, the specification of deadlines for the completion of the project or a part of it.

7.2. Uncertainty and planning

Plans are always prepared in the face of uncertainty, and this fact must be borne in mind when they are being prepared. This is true whether one is planning the staffing of bank branches, the build up of stock in anticipation of seasonal sales, choosing the number of loading bays in a warehouse, or any similar activity.

In simple situations it is sufficient to measure the degree of uncertainty in the situation and to hold buffer capacity in the form of manpower and equipment, stocks, or perhaps even customers who are prepared to accept long delivery times. The case history (pages 69 to 75) dealing with late delivery of batches work illustrates how planning based on average delivery times will result in about 50 per cent of the batches being late. To ensure that only a small percentage are late there was a need to base the planned delivery times not on the average, but on values consistently beaten by the majority. Bank branches cannot be staffed to meet the average demand; warehouses cannot be planned to deal with average production rates and average customer demand, nor can the liquidity of a company be planned on average debtor levels and known cash drains alone. There is a need to cater for this variability, to plan to handle the uncertainty.

Where there is variability in the demand for such services, the strategy for improving the situation is:

1. Reduce the period of time over which build ups are allowed to occur without taking emergency action, the period of time covered by the 'buffer stocks' of these services. This will result in more frequent changes in the number of service points at the bank, in shorter delivery times to the

warehouse and in more frequent reviews of liquidity requirements. Since these changes may demand extra expenditure on manpower, machines or management effort there is clearly a need to ensure that the benefits achieved justify this expenditure.

2. Reduce the variability in the demand. Do not plan to cater for the abnormal demands for service. When these arise, expect people to wait to be served, warehouses to wait for delivery of exceptionally large orders, and make provision in advance to pay exceptionally large bills. On the other hand, stimulate demand during the slack period, as is done by the fuel industry who offer price reductions in the summer or in off peak periods, since this may well reduce the peak demand for these services.
3. By regular forecasting of the demand for services, estimate both the systematic changes in demand and the size of the random fluctuations. Build into the plan provisions to cater for the systematic changes—design the buffer to cope only with the uncertain, unpredictable fluctuations.

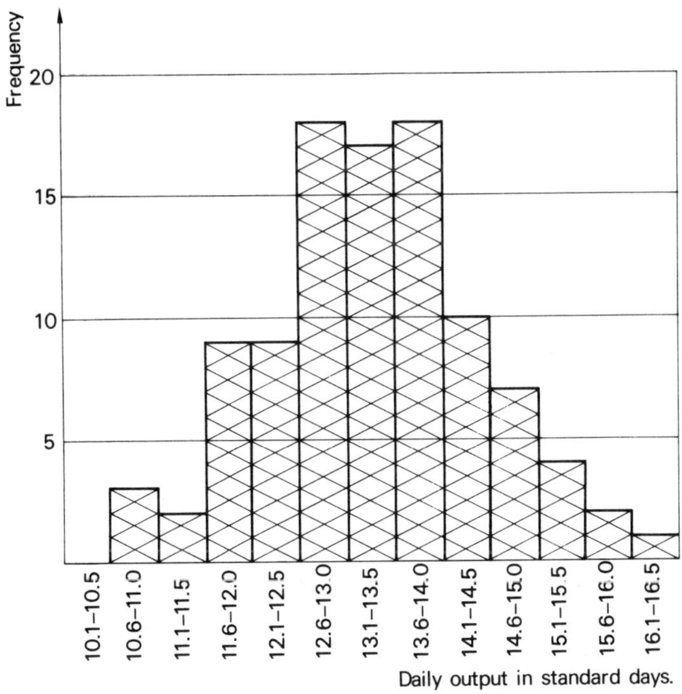

Figure 7.1 Variation in daily work load at branch of bank

In order to assess the importance of the role of variability in planning, consider the following illustration.

The work carried out on each of 100 days, in one branch of a bank was summarized in standard days. The results of this exercise have been expressed in the frequency diagram, Fig. 7.1 on page 147.

The manning of the bank was then examined on the assumption that the loss through failing to do all the day's work in that day was £100, ten times the cost per day of providing an extra man which was taken as £10 per day. The average daily activity was 13.3 standard days and so the average daily loss through idle time with fourteen, fifteen or sixteen men and the cost of this lost time can be easily determined. These calculations are shown in Table 7.1.

Table 7.1. Loss due to overstaffing

Staff	Idle time (Man days)	Cost at £10/day	Average loss over 100 days
14	0.7	£7	£700
15	1.7	£17	£1700
16	2.7	£27	£2700

The percentage of days on which work would be left unfinished can be read directly from the frequency diagram. This percentage and the cost of failing to complete the day's work is shown in Table 7.2.

Table 7.2. Loss due to failure to complete days work

Staff	Percentage of days with work unfinished	Cost at £100 per failure	Average loss over 100 days
14	24	£24	£2400
15	7	£7	£700
16	1	£1	£100

The total loss over 100 days' operation is shown in Table 7.3 and it is clear in this instance that it is more economical to run the branch with a staff of fifteen, rather than either fourteen or sixteen.

It is possible to make a more general analysis for this branch by calculating when the cost of an extra man just balances the savings it achieves. For instance, the extra cost of employing fifteen instead of fourteen men, (£10 a day), is more than offset by the reduction of the failure cost from £24 to £7 a day, (£17 a day). It is straightforward to calculate that this is true whenever the cost of failure is *six* or more times the cost of providing an extra man.

On the other hand, the extra cost of employing sixteen instead of fifteen men, £10 a day, is greater than the extra saving of £6 a day which it produces in the failure cost. This will be true whenever the cost of failure is less than *seventeen* or more times the cost of providing the extra man.

So, fifteen could still be the best number to employ even if the estimate of the ten to one ratio in cost was seriously adrift–provided that the cost of failing to complete the day's work the same day was between six and seventeen times the cost of employing an extra man.

Table 7.3. Total loss over 100 days' operation

Staff	Total loss over 100 days (£)
14	700 + 2400 = 3100
15	1700 + 700 = 2400
16	2700 + 100 = 2800

7.3. Adaptive methods

There are instances in which it is possible to take stock of a situation as things develop and take corrective action within the planning time scale. Techniques designed to speed up this corrective action have been called adaptive methods.

7.3.1. Planning projects

Detailed information on which the plan is to be based may be lacking. This is particularly true when planning new projects. It is consequently desirable to modify and adapt plans as the project proceeds, but essential nevertheless to get a plan down on paper on the strength of whatever information exists. The flight plan of a journey from London to Athens will be drawn up on the basis of a meteorological forecast of wind speed and direction. It is highly unlikely that the actual wind found during the flight will be identical to that forecast and the flight plan will need to be changed to ensure that the aircraft lands in Athens. In a similar way, to get a project back on its objective, the project plan has to be altered whenever an untoward event arises. The methods of network analysis which are highly appropriate to project planning are described later in this chapter.

7.3.2. Planning process improvements

The planning of process improvements also lends itself to adaptive methods. As each production trial is completed its results are available to help with the planning of the next. Adaptive methods are particularly appropriate to process plant making paint, chemicals, beer and so on. It may even be possible to run the production plant continually on experimental trials, introducing changes designed to speed up the evolutionary nature of process improvements.

Where raw materials change from season to season, for example the malt used in brewing can differ markedly from year to year, the process needs to be modified to accommodate this change. Adaptive trials which respond to the measured results of output and quality can be used to effect these modifications.

Consider as an illustration of the adaptive approach to process improvement the following hypothetical situation. A factory manufacturing what is basically a single product in batches has an average profit yield of £130 on a batch. However it is considered possible that the profit yield could be improved by altering the amounts of two vital additions, ingredient A and ingredient B. Since only twelve batches are made a week and the estimated profit varies considerably from batch to batch it is a recognised and sound practice to run a trial over a week's working. It has been agreed to plan a series of ten trials to investigate the effect of altering the amounts of ingredients A and B, using an adaptive method. Although the results of each week's trial can be determined before the next trial is run, these results are subject to considerable fluctuation: the current week to week variability in the average batch profitability has a standard deviation of about £10.

One method of planning the trials is to locate them at each corner of an equilateral triangle, as shown in Fig. 7.2. The values of the additions, ingredients A and B, for the first two trials are shown in Table 7.4. These trials combine with the past average

Table 7.4. First three trials

Trial	Amount of ingredient (% of current level)		Profit
	A	B	
1	150	100	108
2	120	60	99
3	120	140	

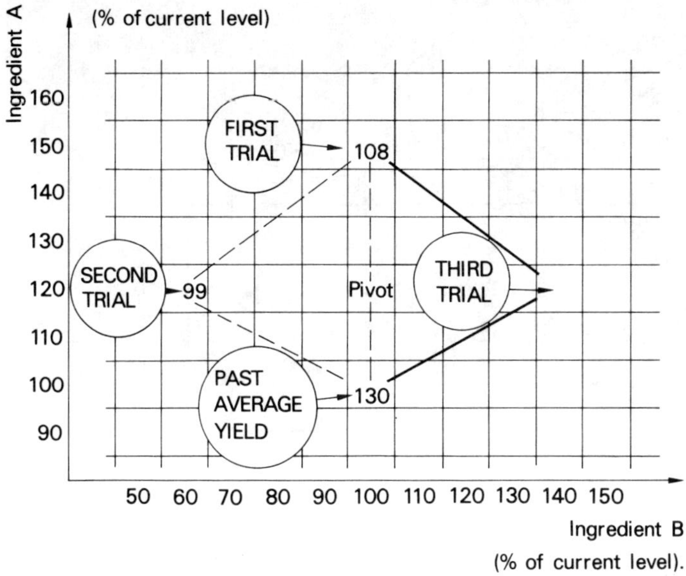

Figure 7.2 Trials at corners of equilateral triangles

yield for the current level of A and B to form an equilateral triangle. The values of A and B for the third trial are selected by using the edge formed by the two corners with the highest results as a pivot, and rotating the triangle away from the lowest of the three results, (the second trial).

Table 7.5. Log of trials

Trial	Amount of ingredient A	Amount of ingredient B	Profit	Gain over standard
1	150	100	108	− 22
2	120	60	99	− 31
3	120	140	128	− 2
4	70	140	164	+ 34
5	50	100	154	+ 24
6	20	140	116	− 14
7	70	120	151	+ 21
8	50	130	141	+ 11
9	90	130	138	+ 8
10	50	130	142	+ 12

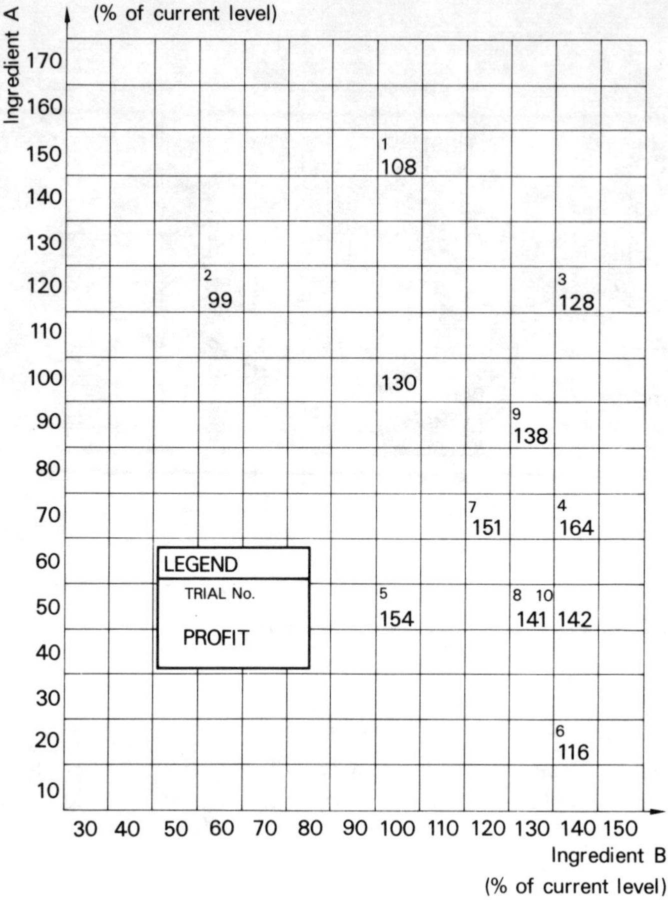

Figure 7.3 Chart showing results of trials

The results for the third and subsequent trials are shown in Table 7.5 and Fig. 7.3. Applying the simple rule of making the triangle pivot away from the lowest result after the sixth trial would have meant repeating a previous trial. It was decided instead to place trials 7 and 8 at the vertices of a smaller equilateral triangle, with the highest result as the third vertex in order to explore the region around this result. This led to trial 9 and repetition of trial 8.

These ten trials have quickly identified a region of operating which is more profitable than the current standard. If it is feasible and economic, this method of operating the plant would be continued indefinitely to search out and maintain the most profitable operating conditions.

7.4. Role and nature of network analysis

Network analysis provides a discipline through which management can plan and control non-repetitive projects, particularly projects involving a complex inter-relationship of activities in fields such as research and development, maintenance work and construction. There are two well known, almost branded, approaches: P.E.R.T. (Programme Evaluation and Review Technique) and C.P.M. (Critical Path Method). The title 'network analysis' has been adopted to embrace this group of closely similar techniques.

C.P.M. originated in the internal consultancy group of Dupont in U.S.A. in 1958. They wanted to supplement their production planning procedures in order to be able to plan one-off projects. In particular they wanted to plan and schedule large maintenance tasks which involved the dismantling, renovating and rebuilding of large chemical plants. P.E.R.T. was developed by the Special Projects Office of the U.S. Navy, assisted by consultants and members of the missile industry. It is best known through its application to the Polaris project. This project was completed two to three years ahead of the original schedules, and it is claimed that this was largely due to the planning and control achieved through P.E.R.T. The U.S. Government insists that all large U.S. Government contracts must be planned by P.E.R.T.

In spite of the proliferation of titles found in the literature on the use of networks in planning, there is only one basic technique. This is an analytical approach which plans one step at a time:

1. *Sequence*
   Use a flow chart to show the way in which the start of one job or activity depends on the completion of another.
2. *Activity duration*
   Use estimates of the men and equipment likely to be employed, together with details of the activity, to assess the time needed on each activity.
3. *Timetable of start times*
   Use simple arithmetical rules to calculate when each activity can start. This can be done by a clerk or a computer.
4. *Pinpoint critical activities*
   Use similar arithmetical rules to pinpoint activities which must be finished on time if the project is to be completed on time.
5. *Isolate and measure spare time*
   These simple rules also pinpoint the spare time in the

network. This is valuable information since it can often be used to obtain benefits.

6. *Revise initial plan*
By concentrating on the critical activities the project can often be speeded up by: switching resources from non-critical activities; doing critical activities in parallel; and, reducing the work content on some critical activities.

Although network analysis has been most widely used in construction and in research and development, it is applicable to all areas of management. Since it is a planning tool, in fact a planning discipline, it is suitable for such projects as:

planning the marketing responsibilities in launching a new product;
scheduling the tasks to be done in preparing statements of accounts;
co-ordinating all the diverse management responsibilities incurred in closing down a factory and opening it up in another location;
planning shut-down of plant, such as a glass furnace, followed by rebuilding or maintenance, and recommissioning.

7.5. Step by step approach

7.5.1. Draw a sequence diagram

The first step is to draw a sequence diagram to ensure that a correct, or at least a feasible, sequence of activities is planned. At this stage the length of time needed to complete each activity is completely ignored.

The need to think out and place all the activities in a project in the correct sequence, in order to draw a valid diagram removes much of the haziness and ambiguity of the plans produced by traditional methods. The sequence diagram takes the form of a network, from which the term 'network analysis' was derived.

The flow chart form of network in which an activity is denoted by a rectangle and the precedence of one activity before another is denoted by an arrow, has considerable practical advantages over the 'traditional' arrow diagram. To readers familiar with method study, the flow chart form of network will be clearly recognizable as a simplified version of the flow process chart.

The simplicity of the flow chart notation can be seen from Fig. 7.4. In this figure the training of salesmen must follow both their recruitment and the design of the sales strategy, whereas the preparation of advertising copy only depends on the design of the sales strategy. This method of representation is extremely simple to use in practice, and moreover, the flow chart diagram can be modified at any stage without having to check whether or not the modification is completely free from ambiguity.

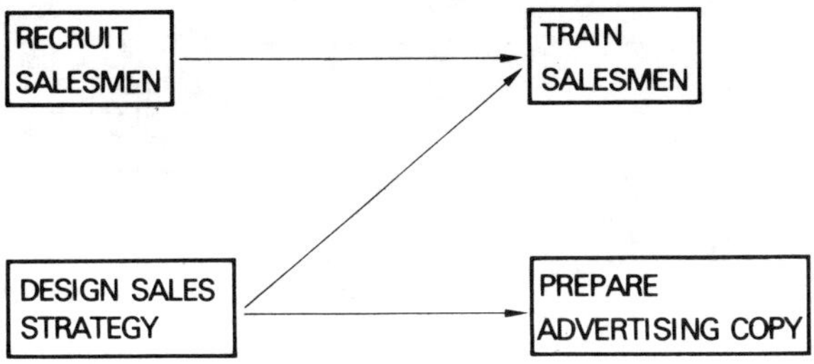

Figure 7.4 Sequence diagram for flow chart form of network

7.5.2. Estimate duration of each activity and determine timetable of activity start times

The accuracy of the plan depends on the accuracy of the facts used to prepare it. The best possible estimate should be made of how long each activity should take under normal conditions, assuming the normal level of resources for that activity. What is wanted is the average time if the activity could be repeated a large number of times under the same identical conditions, with no speeding up as a result of an acquisition of skills. Where appropriate, time standards, either predetermined or specially established, should be used. Comparative estimating methods can also help to provide a more systematic estimating procedure. In many instances, where this degree of refinement is not possible, it has been found best if the estimate of the duration of the activity is made by the foreman, section leader or manager responsible for it.

Once the time estimates have been made they are marked up on the network diagram.

Fig. 7.5 on page 156 shows a flow chart network of seven activities whose durations have been entered on the network and this will be used to demonstrate how to determine a timetable of

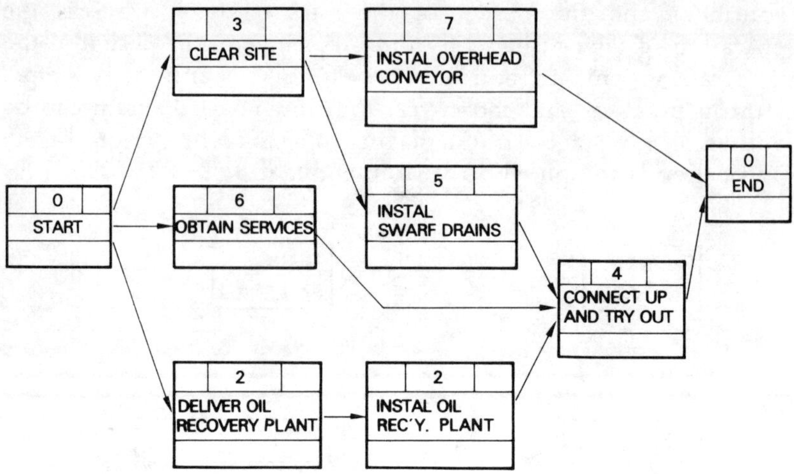

Figure 7.5 Flow chart network of specimen project

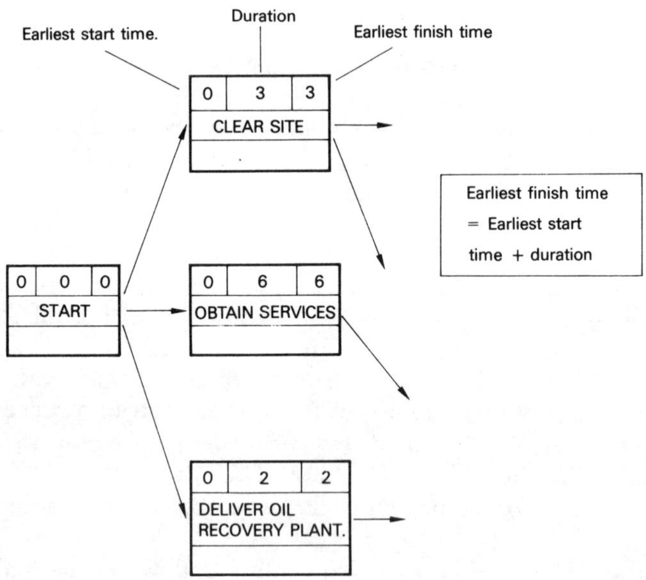

Figure 7.6 Earliest start and finish dates

activity times. In order to simplify the scheduling calculation procedures two artificial activities, START and END, have been introduced to ensure that the network has a single starting point and a single finishing point.

(a) *Earliest times.* The earliest start time and the earliest finish time for each activity are calculated and shown respectively in the top left and right hand corner of each rectangle. This is illustrated in Fig. 7.6.

The earliest start time of the initial activity START is taken as 0, and since its duration is 0, the earliest finish time is also 0. Fig. 7.6 shows that the earliest finish time of START is the earliest start time of the three activities, CLEAR SITE; OBTAIN SERVICES, and DELIVER PLANT. The duration of each activity is added to its earliest start time to determine its earliest finish time.

Applying the same principles the earliest start and finish times for the activities INSTAL PLANT; INSTAL SWARF DRAINS and INSTAL CONVEYOR can be calculated.

These are shown in Fig. 7.7 from which it can also be seen that

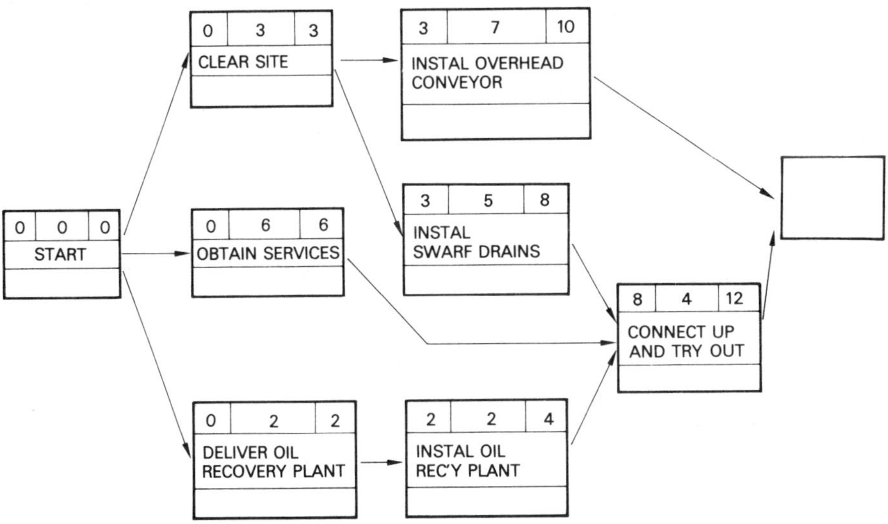

Figure 7.7 Activity 'connect up and try out' must wait until all three preceding activities are completed

the earliest time at which the activity CONNECT UP AND TRY OUT can start is the earliest time at which all of the *three* activities INSTAL PLANT: INSTAL SWARF DRAINS, and OBTAIN SERVICES are complete, namely 8. The activity CONNECT UP AND TRY OUT consequently has an earliest finish time of 12.

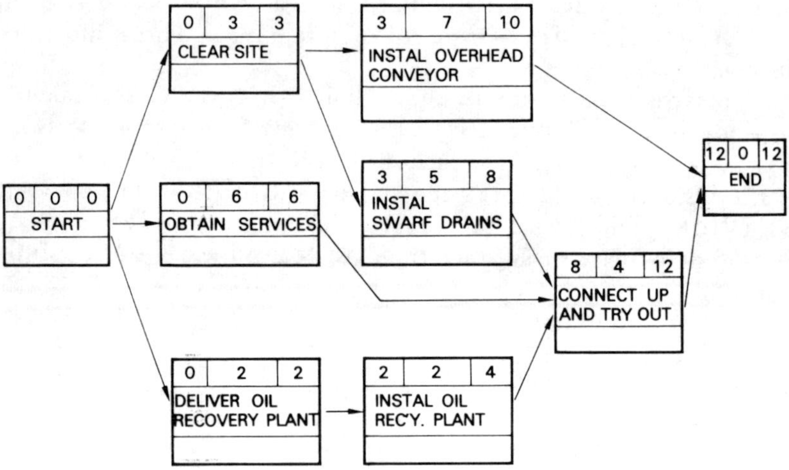

Figure 7.8 Earliest start and finish times for all activities in project

In a similar manner Fig. 7.8 shows how the activity END can only start at the earliest time at which both the activities INSTAL CONVEYOR and CONNECT UP AND TRY OUT are complete, namely the later of the two earliest finish times, 12. Its earliest finish time is also 12. The earliest start and finish times for each activity can be read directly from Fig. 7.8 and these are tabulated in Table 7.6.

Table 7.6. Earliest start and finish times

Activity	Duration	Earliest time	
		Start	Finish
Clear site	3	0	3
Obtain services	6	0	6
Deliver plant	2	0	2
Instal plant	2	2	4
Instal swarf drains	5	3	8
Instal conveyor	7	3	10
Connect and try out	4	8	12

(b) *Latest times.* The latest finish and start time for each activity are calculated in a similar manner. They are placed respectively in the bottom right and left hand corner of each rectangle. This is illustrated in Fig. 7.9. It is assumed that the

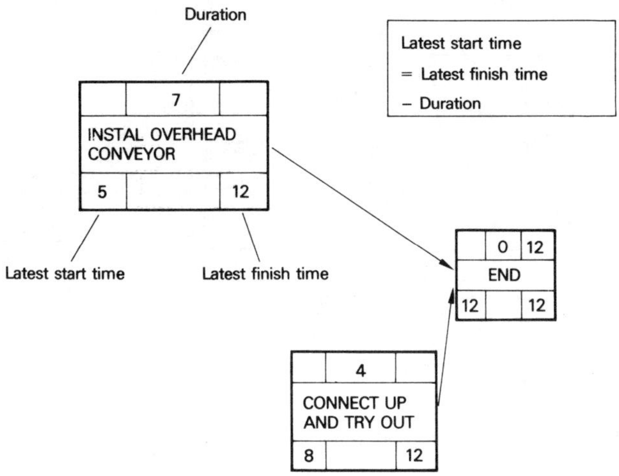

Figure 7.9 Latest start and finish times

earliest finish time of the activity END, namely 12, is the required latest finish time and since its duration is 0, the latest start time is also 12. The latest time at which each activity can finish without holding up the completion of the project can now be determined. The latest finish times for the activities INSTAL CONVEYOR and CONNECT UP AND TRY OUT are taken to be the same as the latest start time of the activity END. The latest start time of each activity is obtained by subtracting its duration from its latest finish time.

The latest start and finish times of the activities INSTAL SWARF DRAINS: OBTAIN SERVICES, and INSTAL PLANT are obtained directly from their durations and the latest start time for the activity CONNECT UP AND TRY OUT. The latest start and finish times of the activity DELIVER PLANT are obtained from its duration and the latest start time of the activity INSTAL PLANT. These are shown overleaf in Fig. 7.10 from which it can be seen that the latest time by which the activity CLEAR SITE must be completed without holding up either of the two following activities, INSTAL CONVEYOR and INSTAL SWARF DRAINS is the earlier of the two latest start times, namely 3.

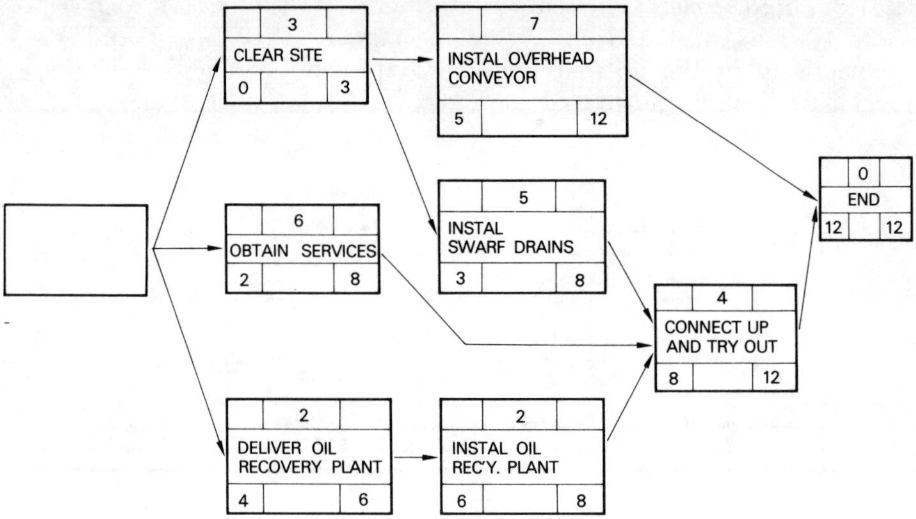

Figure 7.10 Activity 'clear site' must not delay latest start of either of two following activities

Finally, the latest finish and start times for the initial activity START are determined from the latest start times of the activities CLEAR SITE; OBTAIN SERVICES and DELIVER PLANT, and its duration.

The latest start and finish times for each activity, read directly from Fig. 7.11 are tabulated in Table 7.7.

Table 7.7. Latest start and finish times

Activity	Duration	Latest time	
		Start	Finish
Clear site	3	0	3
Obtain services	6	2	8
Deliver plant	2	4	6
Instal plant	2	6	8
Instal swarf drains	5	3	8
Instal conveyor	7	5	12
Connect and try out	4	8	12

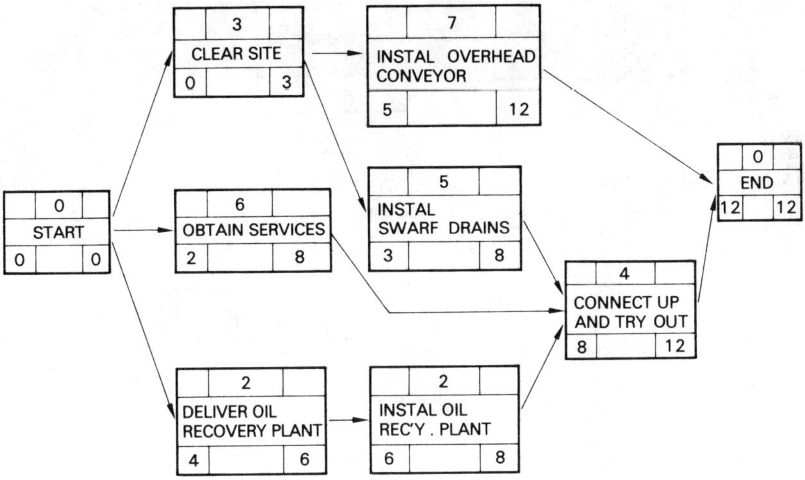

Figure 7.11 Latest start and finish times for all activities in project

7.5.3. Pinpoint critical activities and measure float

The network containing the earliest and latest start and finish times for each activity is shown in Fig. 7.12 on page 162. Activities with the same earliest and latest start times cannot be delayed otherwise the completion of the project could be delayed. These activities are called *critical activities*. They form a chain, or a path through the network, a chain called the *critical path*. The sequence arrows linking the critical activities in Fig. 7.12 have been marked by two short crossing lines.

In practice only a small percentage of activities are critical and it is on expediting these activities that management should attach first priority.

The spare time available on the non-critical activities has been called *float*, and it has been found useful in practice to evaluate two types of float. These are total float and free float. Total float can be described as the total amount of spare time on an activity, and if the delay on the activity exceeds the total float on the activity the project completion date will be delayed. It can be calculated readily from the difference

(Latest start time – Earliest start time).

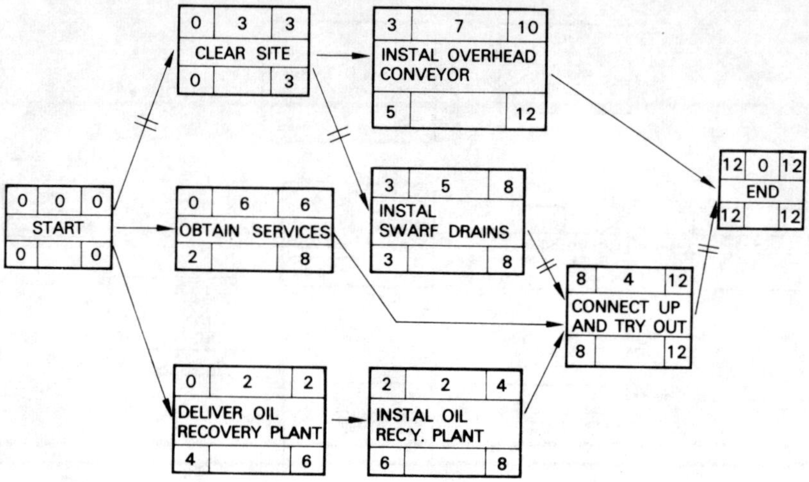

Figure 7.12 Earliest and latest start and finish times for all activities in project

Activities with zero total float are of course critical activities. The total float for each of the activities in the specimen project is shown in Table 7.8 and illustrated in Fig. 7.13.

Table 7.8. Total float

Activity	Start time		Total float
	Latest	Earliest	
Clear site	0	0	0
Obtain services	2	0	2
Deliver plant	4	0	4
Instal plant	6	2	4
Instal swarf drains	3	3	0
Instal conveyor	5	3	2
Connect and try out	8	8	0

The critical path is a chain of activities each of which has zero total float. The non-critical activities also fall into chains, and the total float calculated for an activity belongs not to a single activity but to a chain of activities. For instance, the total float on the activity DELIVER PLANT has the same value as the total float on

INSTAL PLANT. It is in fact the same time—if it is used up on DELIVER PLANT then the activity INSTAL PLANT would become critical.

Free float is the amount of float which allows all subsequent activities to start at their earliest times. The free float on an activity is the difference between the earliest of the earliest start times for all the activities which follow the activity in question, and its own earliest finish time. Fig. 7.12 on page 162 shows that free float only occurs on three activities in the specimen

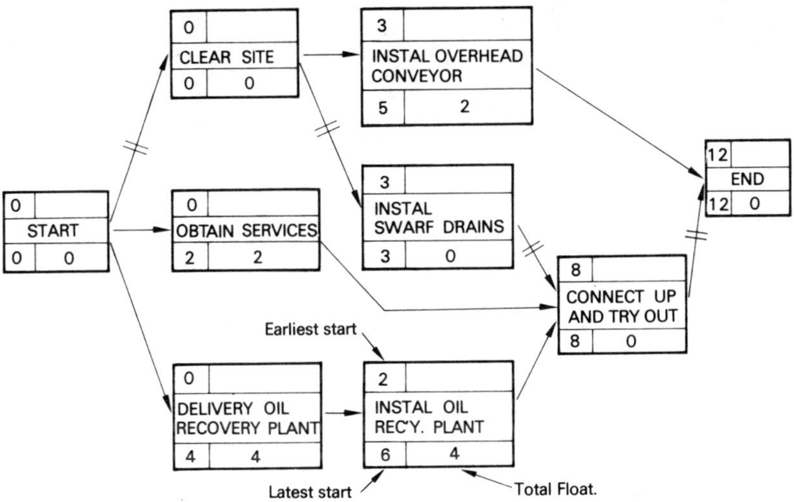

Figure 7.13 Total float belongs to chains of activities

project INSTAL CONVEYOR; OBTAIN SERVICES, and INSTAL PLANT, and the respective values are shown in Table 7.9. Free

Table 7.9. Free float

Activity	Earliest finish time	Earliest start time of all following activities	Free float
Obtain services	6	8	2
Instal conveyor	10	12	2
Instal plant	4	8	4

float must be absorbed on activities in the chain terminated by the activity under consideration. It cannot be passed on to subsequent activities. The total planning information relating to the specimen project is shown in Table 7.10.

Table 7.10. Total project information

Activity	Duration	Start times		Finish times		Float		Critical activity
		Earliest	Latest	Earliest	Latest	Total	Free	
Start	0	0	0	0	0	0	0	*
Clear site	3	0	0	3	3	0	0	*
Obtain services	6	0	2	6	8	2	2	
Deliver plant	2	0	4	2	6	4	0	
Instal plant	2	2	6	4	8	4	4	
Instal swarf drains	5	3	3	8	8	0	0	*
Instal conveyor	7	3	5	10	12	2	2	
Connect and try out	4	8	8	12	12	0	0	*
End	0	12	12	12	12	0	0	*

A list such as this can be prepared separately for each section or area of a complex project, showing the manager in charge of that section the activities for which he is responsible. It may be decided to suppress information on the latest start and finish times and float, to ensure that float is properly used and not squandered by an activity at the beginning of a float chain.

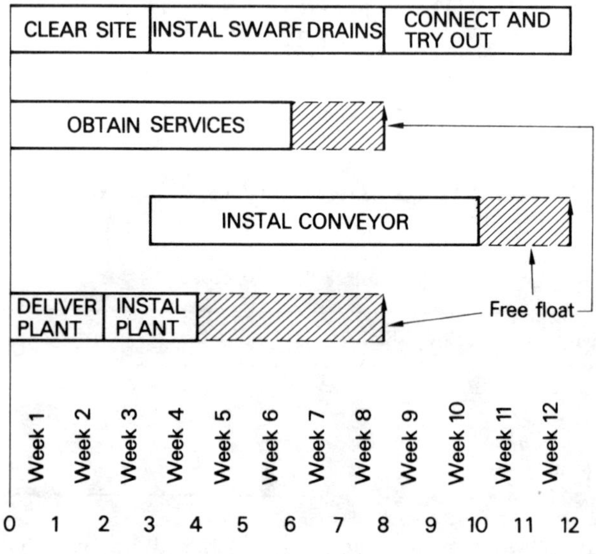

Figure 7.14 Bar chart showing project plan

From these calculations it is quite straightforward to prepare a bar chart for the project in those companies where it is customary to use this means of communication project plans. A bar chart for the specimen project is shown in Fig. 7.14. In this figure the links between the activities are shown by a vertical arrow and the free float by shading.

7.5.4. Revise the plan

One of the principal reasons for revising a project plan is to reduce the duration of the project. This can only be achieved by shortening the critical path. Consequently, all effort to reduce the project duration must be concentrated on critical activities.

Is it possible to switch resources from a non-critical activity to speed up a critical activity? Switching manpower from INSTAL PLANT to INSTAL SWARF DRAINS may perhaps save a week at the expense of taking a fortnight extra on the installation of the oil recovery plant.

Is it possible to overlap two critical activities? Could not the activity CLEAR SITE be split into two parts, so allowing the work on the swarf drains to start before the site for them was fully cleared? This is illustrated in Fig. 7.15 and shows a saving of one week.

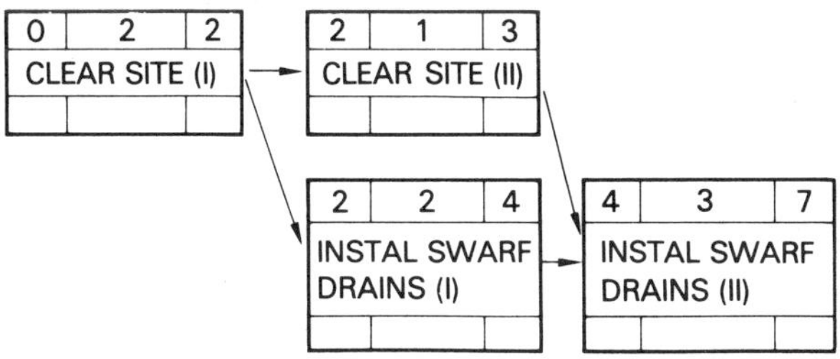

Figure 7.15 Overlap critical activities

Finally, *is it possible to reduce the work content on any of the critical activities*? Doesn't four weeks seem excessive to connect up and try out the oil recovery system? Will it not be possible to delay some of the proposed checks until the first shutdown period and so save at least one week?

If all these three steps were taken the network would be changed both in the inter-relationship of the activities and also in their durations. The revised network is shown in Fig. 7.16 from which it

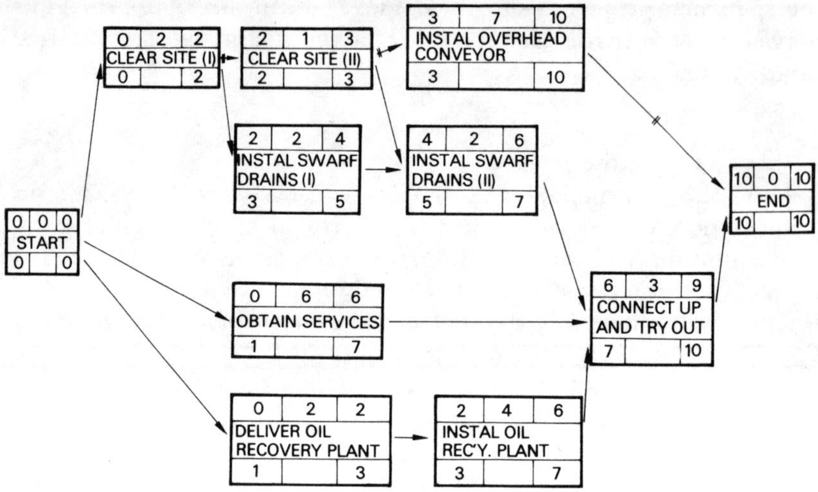

Figure 7.16 Shortening the critical path introduces a new critical path

can be seen that the three weeks have not been saved. A new critical path has been introduced by shortening the existing critical path by more than the float on the longest non-critical path. There is in fact only one week's float on all the non-critical activities and a project as tight as this would need careful supervision to ensure that no slippage occurred.

7.6. Resource planning

One of the major problems which is quickly encountered when applying network planning is the scheduling of existing resources. In some instances there is a limit on the resources available, for example only *two* design engineers able to do specialized design calculations. This means that activities which logically could be done simultaneously have to be done in sequence because there is insufficient men or plant to do them all at the same time. In other instances, although the resources may not be limited, it is desirable to keep them at a steady level. If all activities are planned for their earliest start dates, it is quite likely that the resource requirements will fluctuate throughout the different stages of the project. In practice, it is desirable to build up the resources at a steady rate, hold them reasonably constant through most of the project and run them down at a steady rate.

The first stage in planning the use of resources such as manpower, plant and finance, is to determine the resource requirements. The next stage is to match these requirements against the available resources as closely as possible. Float provides a margin of flexibility within which activities can be adjusted both to take account of limitations on resources and also to level out fluctuations in the rate of resource absorption. However, occasions will arise on the one hand when limited resources will have to be supplemented by overtime, by contracting out, and by hiring extra plant and manpower; or otherwise the completion date for the project will have to be delayed. On the other hand, short-time working, cancellation of sub-contracts, off loading of plant and manpower, may have to be introduced during periods of under utilization.

The degree of detail in which resource planning can be carried out depends on the uncertainty both in the specification of the activity, the plant and skills needed to carry it out, and also in the estimate of the time taken to carry it out. One of the skills of management is the detailed matching of resource requirements with resource availability. However, to be able to make a reasonable match, the availability and requirements should be compatible and the activity timetable should still contain sufficient float to enable management to accommodate the inevitable changes.

7.6.1. Resources required

The simplest form of resource statement is obtained by assuming that all activities can start at their earliest start date. It can be obtained manually by drawing a bar chart, stating the resources assumed when estimating the duration of the activity, and summing the amount of each resource needed in each time period. The length of the time period chosen depends both on the necessity to balance requirements against resource availability and also on the amount of flexibility both in the resources and the juxtaposition of the activities.

Fig. 7.17 shows a simple bar chart together with a statement of the resources needed if all activities are to start at their earliest start times.

It was prepared by ignoring the limitations on resources and drawing a network based solely on the logical sequence of working. Limitations on resource availability will be taken into account at a later stage. The bar chart shows the activities in the project plotted at their earliest times, in order of increasing total float, with each activity chain on a separate line. A vertical arrow has been used to link the chains of activities. The space between the arrow and the end of the activity chain represents the free float on that chain. The number of men of different trades and the equipment needed has been indicated on each of the bars on the chart.

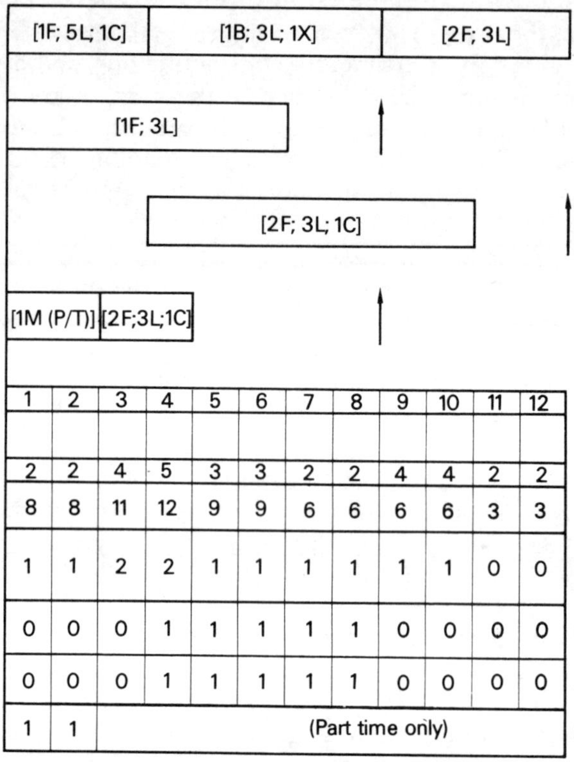

1	2	3	4	5	6	7	8	9	10	11	12	Week No.
2	2	4	5	3	3	2	2	4	4	2	2	F
8	8	11	12	9	9	6	6	6	6	3	3	L
1	1	2	2	1	1	1	1	1	1	0	0	C
0	0	0	1	1	1	1	1	0	0	0	0	B
0	0	0	1	1	1	1	1	0	0	0	0	X
1	1	(Part time only)										M

Legend F–Fitter L–Labourer C–Crane
B–Bricklayer X–Excavator M–Manager

Figure 7.17 Resources needed to start all activities at earliest time

The total number of men of each trade and the total equipment needed to begin each activity at its earliest start time has been determined, week by week, from the bar diagram. These requirements are shown in Fig. 7.17 below the bar chart. If these demands for resources do not exceed the resources available and do not fluctuate unduly from week to week and if the project completion date is satisfactory, then the bar chart shows a feasible schedule for the project.

If, however, the demands on the resources exceed the resources available, then some of the activities have to be delayed. The method of plotting the bar chart, in which activity chains are shown on one line, and are keyed into other more critical activity chains by vertical arrows, ensures that if an activity is delayed, then activities affected by the delay can be readily identified.

There are a large number of alternative plans, the most extreme of which would be to delay all the activities in the project to their latest start date. This instance is shown in Fig. 7.18 at the bottom

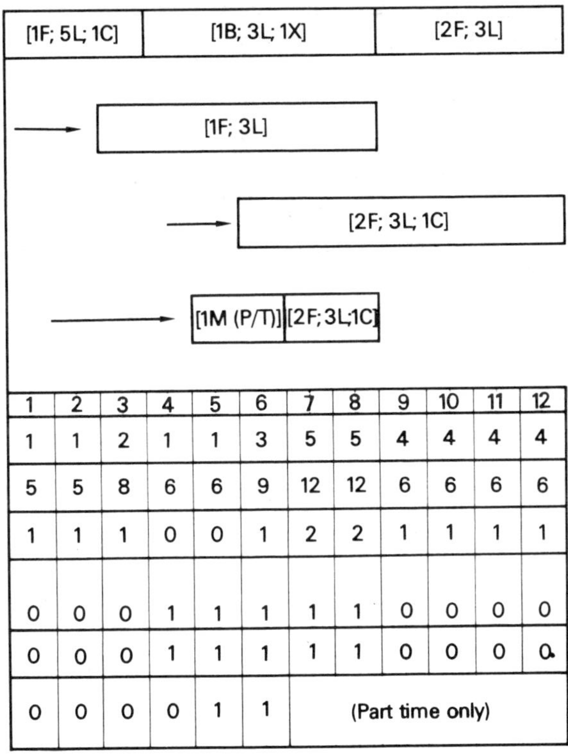

Week No.	1	2	3	4	5	6	7	8	9	10	11	12
F	1	1	2	1	1	3	5	5	4	4	4	4
L	5	5	8	6	6	9	12	12	6	6	6	6
C	1	1	1	0	0	1	2	2	1	1	1	1
B	0	0	0	1	1	1	1	1	0	0	0	0
X	0	0	0	1	1	1	1	1	0	0	0	0
M	0	0	0	0	1	1	(Part time only)					

Legend F–Fitter L–Labourer C–Crane
B–Bricklayer X–Excavator M–Manager

Figure 7.18 Resources needed to start all activities at latest time

of which the appropriate resource requirements have been tabulated. It is clear from Figs. 7.17 and 7.18 that the only resource requirements likely to be difficult to meet are fitters, labourers and cranes. A broad assessment of the requirements of these latter resources can be obtained if the cumulative requirements needed to start all activities at their earliest start time and to start all activities at their latest start time, are calculated and shown on a chart. The chart for each resource inevitably takes the form of an envelope and any plan with resource requirements within the envelope is feasible for the resource considered.

Table 7.11. Cumulative resource requirements

Week No.	1	2	3	4	5	6	7	8	9	10	11	12
Fitters	2	4	8	13	16	19	21	23	27	31	33	35
Labourers	8	16	27	39	48	57	63	69	75	81	84	87
Cranes	1	2	4	6	7	8	9	10	11	12	12	12

At earliest start times. This table shows the cumulative man-weeks and crane-weeks needed through the project if each activity is to start at its earliest time. It was obtained by accumulating the weekly requirements shown in Fig. 7.17.

Week No.	1	2	3	4	5	6	7	8	9	10	11	12
Fitters	1	2	4	5	6	9	14	19	23	27	31	35
Labourers	5	10	18	24	30	39	51	63	69	75	81	87
Cranes	1	2	3	3	3	4	6	8	9	10	11	12

At latest start times. This table shows the cumulative resource requirements if each activity is to start at its latest time, and was derived from Fig. 7.18.

The cumulative requirements for earliest and latest start times for fitters, labourers and cranes are shown in Table 7.11, and the envelope showing the cumulative requirements for labourers is shown in Fig. 7.19.

7.6.2. Taking account of resources available

The cumulative man weeks available to the project if there are eight labourers and alternatively if there are nine labourers, are shown in Fig. 7.19. From the resource envelope it would appear that the project could be completed on time with only eight labourers, but a careful examination shows that this is only possible if the number of labourers allocated to several activities

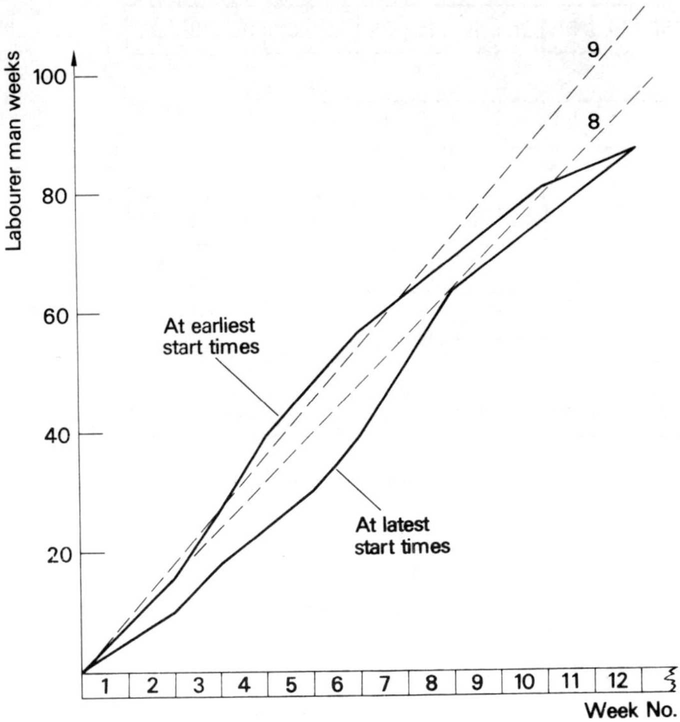

Figure 7.19 Envelope showing labourer requirements

can be modified. Fig. 7.20 on page 172 shows the re-allocation of resources to activities and indicates that this solution is only possible if work can be carried out on a number of activities by either one labourer or three labourers. A restriction to eight labourers means that the start of some activities must be delayed and the duration of others extended, and as a result almost all the float on the project has been absorbed.

It can be readily seen from Fig. 7.19 that if nine labourers could be made available to the project the majority of the activities should start at their earliest times. In this instance the resource restrictions could be met by delaying one activity by two days and another by one day, as is shown in Fig. 7.21. The requirements for fitters and cranes have been shown at the bottom of this figure, in addition to the requirements for labourers. The project can be completed on time with only four fitters and only one crane.

In practice, there will be inevitable changes in plan due to the uncertainties both in the nature and work content of the job and

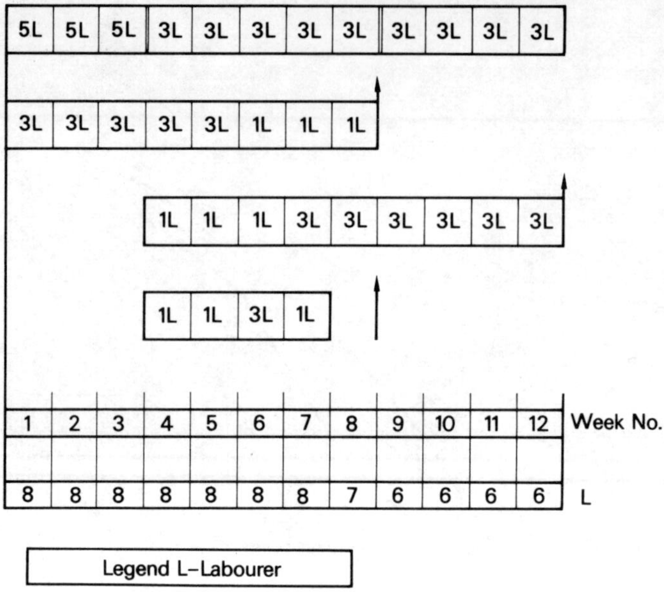

Figure 7.20 Resource planning—8 labourers

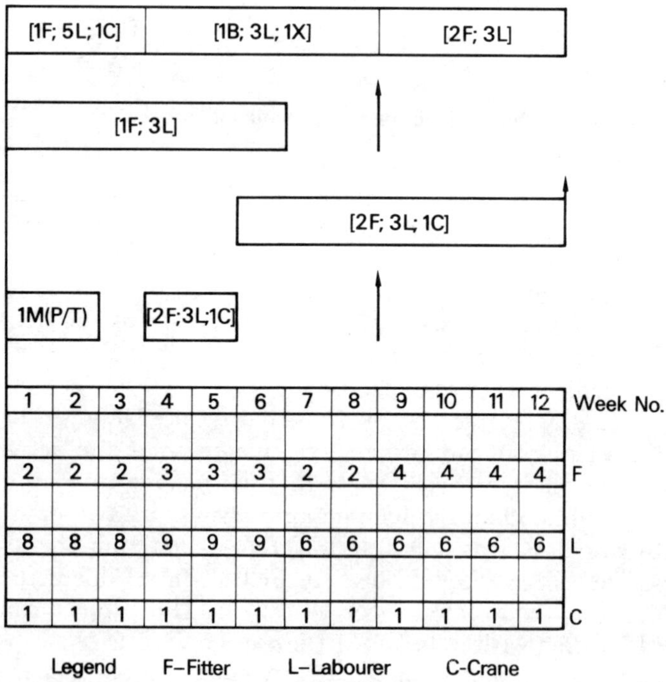

Figure 7.21 Resource planning—9 labourers

also in the available resources. These changes make it undesirable to expend more effort at the planning stage than is needed to remove the major fluctuations. The day to day smoothing will have to be made on a short term basis by the project management.

7.7. The potential of figures in planning

Where is the profit in planning? It comes from the avoidance of losses, losses from employing men or machines which are standing idle; loss of production or sales, particularly arising from delay in going into production. It comes from avoiding the need to pay overtime rates or a premium to subcontract labour. Planning allows the manager to foresee the problems attendant on change or in providing a service and to take steps to anticipate these problems. Figures and the statistical approach where it is relevant can help to do a better job of planning.

The potential field for planning is wide and a few selected topics have been listed in Table 7.12. The key question to ask is 'Can we do anything about this uncertain event when it has

Table 7.12. Selected fields for planning

Function	Buffers	Networks
Development	Recruitment and training of staff, e.g. apprentices	Research and development projects
Manufacturing	1. Raw material stocks 2. Seasonal build up of finished stocks. 3. Labour requirements 4. Equipment capacity 5. Delivery times Routine production planning	1. Installation of new machines 2. New systems 3. Relay-out of production facilities 4. Maintenance of large equipment
Sales/service	1. Finished stocks 2. Planning of sales calls: salesmen's time	1. Launch of new product 2. Re-planning sales areas
Control	1. Staffing of clerical jobs 2. Availability of liquid capital	1. Computerization of accounts, records 2. O & M projects 3. Preparation of annual budget, and of long term company plans
Personnel	Succession planning	Negotiation of agreements with unions

happened?'. If not, then the only answer is to provide a buffer as cheaply as possible. If there is sufficient time to correct for the effect of the uncertain event then adaptive planning techniques such as network analysis can be brought to bear.

Planning, in all these fields, enables management to know what is going on and to concentrate effort where it is needed. The routine responsibilities are planned and then delegated. Only the exceptions and the important few need disturb the accustomed routine. Management can concentrate on identifying and strengthening the profit making areas.

List of terms used

Forecasting
Planning
Mathematical model
Simulation
Project
Buffer stocks
Uncertainty
Average
Variability
Systematic changes
Random fluctuations
Adaptive methods
Network analysis
Standard deviation
Activity
P.E.R.T.
C.P.M.
Critical activity
Sequence diagram
Flow chart form of network
Arrow diagram
Comparative estimating
Earliest start time
Earliest finish time
Latest start time
Latest finish time
Critical path
Float
Total float
Free float
Bar chart
Resource planning
Activity chain
Resource envelope

Italicized terms are defined in the glossary (page 262) as well as in the text where it is appropriate.

8. Finding a better way

How do we assess the ideal performance of a company? Is it to manufacture or buy at lowest cost, to produce at maximum output, with least losses and with maximum machine utilization? Is it to achieve a maximum sales revenue and most profit? Does any one of these characteristics dominate and form the natural measure of your company's performance? Which characteristic is important depends where you stand. The production manager's ideal performance is related to measures of productive efficiency; the sales manager's to measures of sales efficiency; the managing director's to return on invested capital, to the company's dividend on ordinary shares, to the assessment by his peers of the quality of the company's products, and to the skill and expected length of service of his staff and work people.

There have been a number of theoretical studies on how to achieve the optimum performance but these are not always easy to implement in practice. The figures used as a basis for the calculations are subject to uncertainty, (for instance in forecasting demand); to change, (for instance the prices of raw materials); and to incorrect assumptions (as may occur in establishing costs). By the time the 'correct' information has been collected, if this is possible, and the decisions implemented the ideal operating conditions may well have changed. The practical approach is not to throw these theoretical approaches overboard but to realize their limitations, and to use the figures collected to get an improvement: to ensure that an opportunity is not being missed to increase profit, output or sales revenue, or to decrease costs, or losses due to such factors as unsatisfactory quality, idle machines or manpower. It may not be the optimum, but it could well be a significant step forward.

This chapter deals with several instances illustrating some of the different techniques which have been adopted in theoretical studies to find the optimum. These instances should be viewed not as subtle approaches to finding ideal operating conditions which will be true for an impractically short space of time, but as a guide to a better way of operating. All of these studies assume certain restrictions, such as limited supply or availablity of materials, manpower, machines or money, and determine the optimum way of working subject to these restrictions. Management action to remove these restrictions can provide an opportunity to do even better than the 'optimum'.

8.1. Making the best out of a situation

8.1.1. Balancing out alternative losses

When a process is too variable to be able to meet the tolerances required by the product it is inevitable that some of the product will fall outside one or other, or possibly both, of the tolerances.

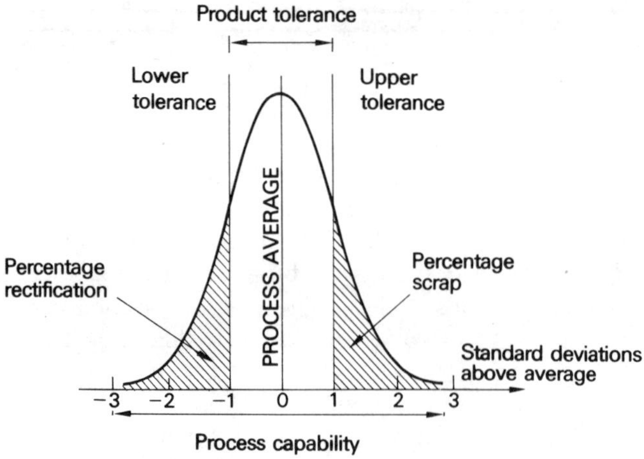

Figure 8.1 Choosing the process average to minimize the cost of scrap and rectification

It often happens that product outside one tolerance is either scrap or very expensive to rectify and that product outside the other tolerance is far less expensive to rectify. First reactions are to ensure that the average of the process is set so that no product falls outside the unfavourable tolerance. If the cost of 'rectification' is much smaller than the cost of 'scrapping' then this is the correct policy. However, as the relative costs become closer together the optimum policy is to make more and more product outside the 'scrap' tolerance.

Fig. 8.1 shows an example in which the product tolerance is only two standard deviations of the process capability. The percentage above the upper tolerance and the percentage below the lower tolerance can be readily determined from tables of the normal distribution. If the relative costs of scrapping or rectifying product above the upper tolerance, and of rectifying product below the lower tolerance are known, then the setting which minimizes the total cost of 'scrap' and 'rectification' can be calculated. Table 8.1 shows two alternative cases, the first when it

Table 8.1. Calculations to determine optimum level of rectification when tolerance is only two standard deviations

Upper tolerance (Standard deviations above average)	Percentage scrap (Percentage above upper tolerance)	Lower tolerance (Standard deviations below average)	Percentage rectification (Percentage below lower tolerance)	10 x (Percent scrap) + percentage rectification	100 x (Percent scrap) + percentage rectification
1.0	16	1.0	16	176	1616
1.5	6.7	0.5	31	98	701
2.0	2.3	0	50	73	280
2.1	1.8	– 0.1	54	72	234
2.2	1.4	– 0.2	58	72	212
2.3	1.1	– 0.3	62	73	172
2.5	0.6	– 0.5	69	75	135
3.0	0.14	– 1.0	84	85	98
3.5	0.02	– 1.5	93	93	95
4.0	0.00	– 2.0	97	97	97
Col. 1 chosen arbitrarily	Col. 2 from table of normal distribution	Col. 3 two standard deviations below Col. 1	Col. 4 from table of normal distribution	Col. 5 10 x Col. 2 + Col. 3	Col. 6 100 x Col. 2 + Col. 3

* N.B. All the subsequent values of the lower tolerance are *above* the average.

costs ten times as much to deal with a unit of product above the 'scrap' tolerance than to deal with a unit below the 'rectification' tolerance, and the second when this ratio is a hundred. When the cost ratio is ten, the policy which minimizes the total cost is to produce 1 per cent to 2 per cent above the 'scrap' tolerance and 50 per cent to 60 per cent below the 'rectification' tolerance. On the other hand, when the cost ratio is a hundred, the optimum policy is to produce only 0.02 per cent above the 'scrap' tolerance. To achieve this 93 per cent of the product would need to be rectified, and it would be best to develop a less variable process.

This approach has been applied to a variety of alternative conditions to determine the optimum percentage rectification and scrap for different widths of tolerance and different ratios of the cost of dealing with a unit above the 'scrap' tolerance to the cost of dealing with a unit below the 'rectification' tolerance. The results of these calculations are shown in Table 8.2. These values

Table 8.2. Optimum rectification and scrap percentages when it costs more to scrap than to rectify (in situations where product outside one tolerance is scrapped and outside the other is rectified)

	Tolerance (Standard deviations)									
	2.0		3.0		4.0		5.0		6.0	
Cost* Ratio	Rec-tify %	Scrap %	Rec-tify %	Scrap %	Rec-tify %	Scrap %	Rec-tify %	Scrap %	Rec-tify %	Scrap %
1	16	16	8	8	2.3	2.3	0.6	0.6	0.2	0.2
2	25	9	11.5	3.6	3.9	1.6	0.8	0.5	0.26	0.07
3	34.5	5.5	11.5	3.6	5.5	0.8	0.8	0.5	0.26	0.07
4	34.5	5.5	11.5	3.6	5.5	0.8	1.6	0.3	0.26	0.07
5	44.8	3.4	18	2.1	5.5	0.8	1.8	0.25	0.54	0.05
6	50	2.3	21	1.4	5.5	0.8	1.8	0.25	0.54	0.05
8	55	1.8	21	1.4	7.5	0.6	1.8	0.25	0.54	0.05
10	56	1.6	21	1.4	7.5	0.6	2.3	0.14	0.54	0.05

$$\text{* Cost Ratio} = \frac{\text{Cost of scrap or repair item outside one tolerance}}{\text{Cost to rectify item outside other tolerance.}}$$

are of course only a guide but they provide target values for scrap or rectification under a wide variety of conditions. The maxims which this table demonstrates clearly are:

1. Either widen the tolerance if this is practicable or reduce the process variation when there are less than six standard deviations in the tolerance, and
2. When there are six standard deviations in the tolerance, the ratio of the two costs is not very important.

In another instance it is not the percentage in each of the categories which determines the total loss, but the average value of two parts of the frequency distribution. Such a situation occurs when a product which is to be supplied from stock has a limited shelf life. If the stock level is chosen too high then some of the stocked items will be held beyond their shelf life and will have to be scrapped. The amount scrapped will depend on the actual sales during the shelf life period and the amount of lost sales on the actual demand during the replenishment time. This is illustrated in Fig. 8.2. To calculate the optimum stockholding level the average

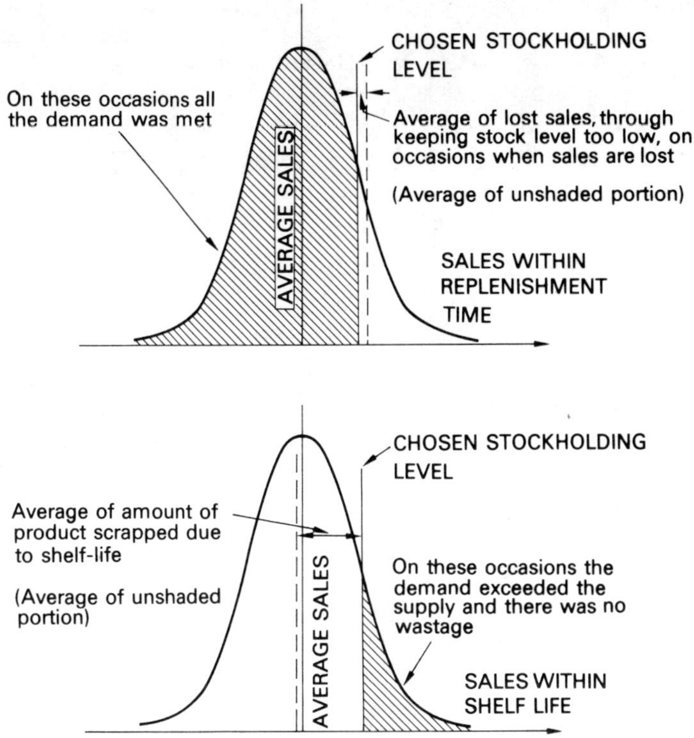

Figure 8.2 Choosing stockholding level to minimize the cost of lost sales and scrapped product. (In this example, the replenishment time and the shelf life are equal.)

amount of lost sales and the average amount scrapped must first be determined and the relative costs taken into account. The basic data needed for this calculation is shown in Fig. 8.3 overleaf.

Fig. 8.2 illustrates the special case when the replenishment time and the shelf life have the same value and this is examined in Table 8.3 on page 181. This would arise if all the old product is withdrawn and replaced by the new delivery. The same two alternative cost ratios as were used in the previous study, namely ten and a hundred, have been taken.

Table 8.3 shows that when the cost ratio is ten, a stockholding level 1.3 standard deviations above the average minimizes the total losses. When the cost of a lost sale is a hundred times the cost of scrapping the product, the optimum stockholding level is 2.3 standard deviations above the average.

A typical example would be a bakery with a forecast day's sale of 1000 loaves with a standard deviation of the forecasting error

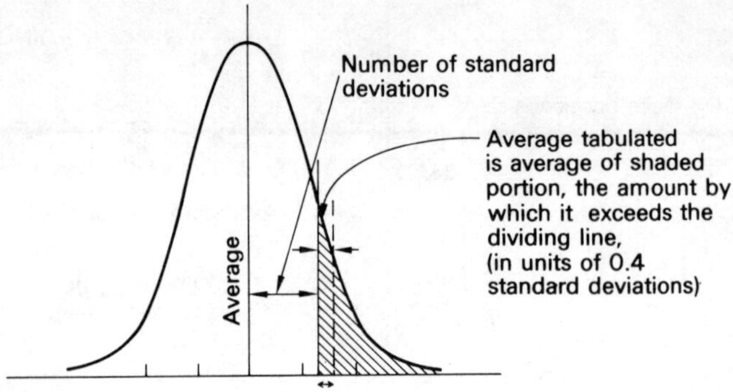

Standard deviations	Average	Standard deviations	Average	Standard deviations	Average
– 3.0	7.521	– 1.2	3.149	1.3	0.114
– 2.9	7.271	– 1.0	2.715	1.4	0.0919
– 2.8	7.020	– 0.8	2.307	1.6	0.0583
– 2.7	6.771	– 0.6	1.927	1.8	0.0358
– 2.6	6.521	– 0.5	1.749	2.0	0.0213
– 2.5	6.272	– 0.4	1.580	2.1	0.0162
– 2.4	6.023	– 0.2	1.271	2.2	0.0122
– 2.3	5.774	0	1.000	2.3	0.0092
– 2.2	5.527	0.2	0.769	2.4	0.0068
– 2.1	5.280	0.4	0.578	2.5	0.0050
– 2.0	5.035	0.5	0.496	2.6	0.0037
– 1.8	4.548	0.6	0.423	2.7	0.0027
– 1.6	4.069	0.8	0.301	2.8	0.0019
– 1.4	3.601	1.0	0.209	2.9	0.0014
– 1.3	3.373	1.2	0.141	3.0	0.0010

Figure 8.3 Average of part of normal distribution lying to right of specified number of standard deviations above average

of 100 loaves. If the profit on a sale were ten times the loss incurred by scrapping the stale bread, Table 8.3 can be used to determine the quantity to make, namely the forecast 1000 loaves plus a safety stock of 1.3 standard deviations, making 1130 loaves in all. If, on the other hand, the loss incurred by scrapping were ten times the profit on a sale, the quantity to make would be the forecast 1000 loaves less 1.3 standard deviations, that is only 870 loaves.

8.1.2. Putting in the right bid

Basic statistical ideas have been found valuable in the area of contract tendering–provided that sufficient historical data on

Table 8.3. Calculations to determine optimum level of stockholding when product has limited shelf life

Shelf life equal to replenishment period

Stockholding level (Standard deviations above average)	Average lost sales (Arbitrary units)	Average scrapped (Arbitrary units)	10 (Average lost sales) + average scrapped	100 (Average lost sales) + average scrapped
0.0	1.00	1.00	11.00	101.0
1.0	0.209	2.72	4.81	23.6
1.2	0.141	3.15	4.56	17.3
1.3	0.114	3.37	4.51	14.8
1.4	0.092	3.60	4.52	12.8
1.6	0.058	4.07	4.65	9.9
2.0	0.021	5.03	5.24	7.1
2.1	0.016	5.28	5.44	6.9
2.2	0.012	5.53	5.65	6.7
2.3	0.009	5.77	5.86	6.7
2.4	0.007	6.02	6.09	6.7
2.5	0.005	6.27	6.32	6.8
Col. 1 chosen arbitrarily	Col. 2 read from Fig. 8.3 corresponding to Col. 1	Col. 3 read from Fig. 8.3 corresponding to Col. 1	Col. 4 = 10 x Col. 2 + Col. 3	Col. 5 = 100 x Col. 2 + Col. 3

contracts is available. The approach which has been adopted is to analyse the bidding pattern of all competitors on past contracts and to use this information to maximize the company's profit.

(a) *Information needed.* Once again a frequency diagram is used, this time to describe the bidding pattern of competitors. The following information is required for a number of past contracts:

(i) The company's own price, excluding profit.
(ii) The price submitted by every competitor (ignoring the prices submitted by competitors when it was known that they were not trying to win the contract).

Since the tender prices submitted will range from very low prices, on small contracts, to very high prices, on large contracts, it is necessary to standardize them. This is done by dividing each bid by the company's own cost estimate for the contract. The resulting ratio has been called the bid ratio. The calculation of the bid ratio is illustrated in Table 8.4 on page 182. A bid ratio of 1.05, for example, represents a price 5 per cent over the cost estimate and should yield a 5 per cent margin.

Table 8.4. Bids and bid ratios on specimen contract

Company's cost estimate:		£50 000
	Bid (£)	*Bid ratio*
Competitor A	49 000	0.98
Competitor B	52 500	1.05
Competitor C	52 000	1.04

(b) *Chance of winning.* Suppose that there was sufficient information over a number of contracts to determine twenty-five bid ratios and the results were those shown in Table 8.5 and Fig. 8.4. If this pattern of bidding remains the same for future contracts we can predict that in the future the chance of a competitor bidding

higher than 1.05 is 4 per cent (one in twenty-five);
higher than 1.04 is 8 per cent (two in twenty-five);
higher than 1.03 is 20 per cent (five in twenty-five);

and so on. The outcome, whatever our bid, will vary from contract to contract due to the inherent variability. However, the chance of our bid winning the contract is the chance that the competitor's bid is higher than ours. In fact the frequency diagram of past bids may be used to calculate the chance of our winning a contract,

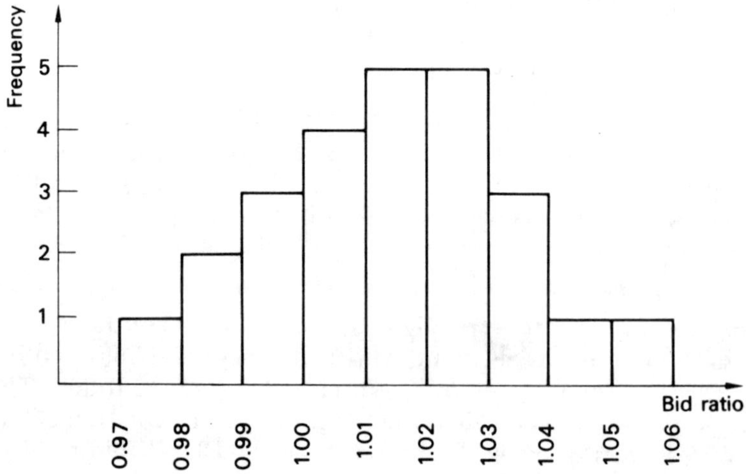

Figure 8.4 Frequency distribution of bid ratios

Table 8.5. **Summary of bid ratios (25 bids)**

Bid ratio	Frequency
0.971-0.980	1
0.981-0.990	2
0.991-1.000	3
0.001-1.010	4
1.011-1.020	5
1.021-1.030	5
1.031-1.040	3
1.041-1.050	1
1.051-1.060	1

against only one competitor, with any particular bid. This analysis is shown pictorially in Fig. 8.5.

(c) *What profit.* Clearly our chance of winning the contract will increase as our bid ratio is dropped, but this will mean that the profit on the contract will drop. A bid ratio of 1.05, which yields a margin of 5 per cent, has a 4 per cent chance of success; a bid ratio of 1.02, which yields only 2 per cent margin, has a 40 per cent chance of success.

Suppose there were 100 contracts, each worth £10 000. If we consistently bid with a bid ratio of 1.02, then we would expect to win forty of these contracts giving us an expected turnover of £400 000. A margin of 2 per cent on this turnover would amount to £8000. If, however, we bid with a bid ratio of 1.05, then we

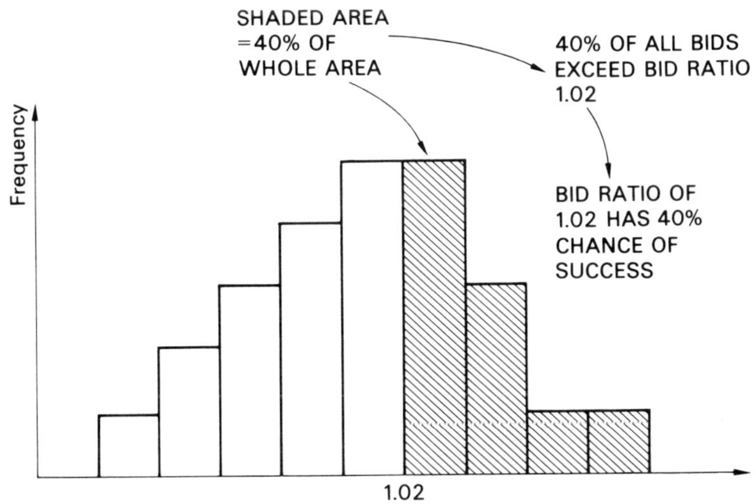

Figure 8.5 Chance of winning derived from frequency distribution

would expect to win only four of the contracts, giving a turnover of only £40 000. A margin of 5 per cent on this turnover would amount to only £2000.

(d) *What is the best bid.* The basic ideas just outlined are now applied to calculate the optimum bid, the bid which will bring the biggest expected profit to the company. It is assumed that there is only one competitor and the past history of bidding shown in Fig. 8.4 is directly relevant to the current situation. This is done by comparing the outcome for different bid ratios when bidding on 100 contracts, each of £10 000 value. The results of this comparison are shown in Table 8.6.

Table 8.6. Calculations to identify best bid

Bid ratio	Margin (% of cost)	Expected No. of contracts won (out of 100)	Expected turnover at cost (£)	Expected margin (£)
0.97	3% loss	100	1 000 000	30 000 loss
0.98	2% loss	96	960 000	19 200 loss
0.99	1% loss	88	880 000	8 800 loss
1.00	nil	76	760 000	nil
1.01	1% profit	60	600 000	6 000
1.02	2%	40	400 000	8 000
1.03	3%	20	200 000	6 000
1.04	4%	8	80 000	3 200
1.05	5%	4	40 000	2 000
1.06	6%	0	nil	nil

The maximum expected margin is £8000, for a bid of 1.02, on a turnover of £400 000. The bid of 1.02 is therefore the optimum bid in this very simple example. Such a bid would be successful on 40 per cent of contracts on the average and yield a 2 per cent margin.

(e) *Other factors in the bidding situation.* The previous example has been over-simplified deliberately in order to describe the basic principles of the approach. In a realistic tendering situation other factors must be taken into account, the most important of which are:

1. *The number of competitors.* An increase in the number of competitors decreases the chance of winning the contract with a given bid, but this can be calculated if the number of real competitors is known.

2. *The different types of contract and competitor.* The frequency distribution of the bid ratio for different types of contract (governmental, industrial, commercial development, etc.) and for different types of contractor (national or local, large or small, and so on) cannot be expected to be the same. Systematic differences must be established and taken into account if they are relevant.
3. *Turnover requirements.* It may prove necessary in the short term to change the chance of winning a contract in order to match the company's turnover to its planned capacity. Demand in excess of available staff and equipment can be reduced by increasing the bid ratio, and a slackening in demand countered by lowering the bid ratio.
4. *Bidding trends.* The average level of the bid ratio may well be affected by the economic climate of the industry. If this is so there will be significant systematic changes over a time scale. Monitoring of the average level of the bid ratio will detect such changes. The optimum bid will need to be adjusted accordingly.

8.2. Better order quantities

8.2.1. How to calculate the optimum order quantity

Choosing the best quantity to order is also determined by balancing out two alternative costs. Placing a large number of small orders will produce high ordering costs. Reducing the number of orders will reduce the ordering costs but the quantity ordered at each order will increase. In consequence, the average stock level will increase and this will mean more working capital tied up in stock, greater losses due to deterioration and obsolescence, and probably increased storage costs. Do the savings on less frequent ordering outweigh the cost of holding additional stock? Just where is the balance, what is the optimum quantity?

Consider the following example:

The purchase price of an item is £0.01 each, and in all 25 000 of this item are sold each year. The cost of ordering and delivery from the supplier amounts to £10 each order. The annual cost of storage, including interest on capital tied up is £2 for 1000 items. If twenty-five orders, each of 10 000 are placed each year, the total cost of ordering, at £10 an order, is £250. When the order is delivered the stock will rise by 10 000 and will gradually fall down to its previous level. The average amount by which the stock will rise because of the size of the quantity ordered is halfway between these values, namely 5000. Since the cost of holding 1000 items for a year is £2, the stockholding cost of 5000 is £10. Consequently the combined cost of ordering and stockholding is £260. This total cost, which depends on the number of orders placed, has been evaluated for a range of ordering policies in Table 8.7. The manner in which the cost of holding stock, the cost of ordering and the total cost depend on the order size is illustrated in Fig. 8.6.

Table 8.7. Calculation of total cost of ordering and holding stock

Order size (1000)	Orders each year	Annual order cost (£)	Average stock (1000)	Annual stock cost (£)	Total cost (£)
10	25	250	5	10	260
20	$12\frac{1}{2}$	125	10	20	145
30	$8\frac{1}{3}$	83.3	15	30	113.3
40	$6\frac{1}{4}$	62.5	20	40	102.5
50	5	50.0	25	50	100
60	$4\frac{1}{6}$	41.7	30	60	101.7
70	$3\frac{4}{7}$	35.7	35	70	105.7
80	$3\frac{1}{8}$	31.2	40	80	111.2
90	$2\frac{7}{9}$	27.8	45	90	117.8
100	$2\frac{1}{2}$	25.0	50	100	125

Fig. 8.6 and Table 8.7 show that the optimum order size occurs when the annual order cost equals the annual stockholding cost. This fact can be used to determine a formula for calculating the economic order quantity.

Suppose that: Annual sales rate = A units each year,
Cost of ordering and delivery = £B each order,
Order size = N units.

Then the number of orders placed each year = A/N and
the annual cost of ordering = £ (AB/N)

If the cost of holding an item in stock for a year = £S, then
the annual cost of holding stock = £S (N/2).

The optimum order size occurs when

$$AB/N = NS/2,$$
$$\text{namely when } N = \sqrt{2AB/S}$$

This formula is contrary to the common notion that order or batch sizes should be proportional to sales, as when ordering or manufacturing two weeks' or three months' stock at a time. It can provide a good guide to economic order or batch quantities provided that it is used with care.

The costs involved in the calculations are only those which vary as the order size is varied. Warehousing charges are usually a legitimate stockholding cost, but if no changes take place in warehouse rents, light, heat, wages and so on, then warehousing costs must be excluded.

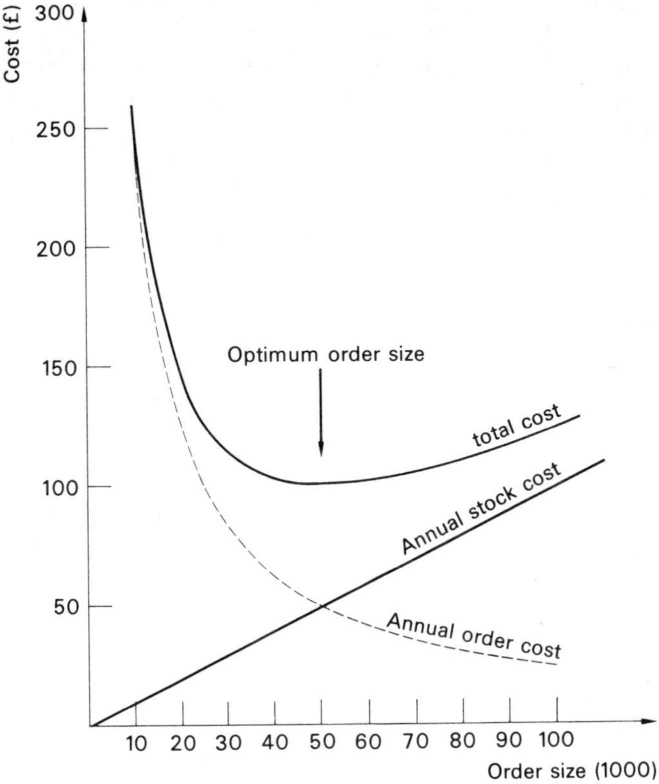

Figure 8.6 How the costs of ordering and stockholding depend on order size

In determining economic batch quantities in manufacturing there are no apparent variable set-up costs, except for the loss of profit on the production lost during the change-over time. In such cases, optimum batch quantities are determined by the level of demand. If the extra production could not be sold, there is no loss of profit and so the batch sizes can be reduced until the production lost during change-overs equals the spare capacity available.

These two instances illustrate the clear thinking which must precede the application of the simple economic order formula. Furthermore, if by O and M or work study the cost of placing an order or setting up a machine can be significantly reduced, considerably greater savings can accrue than if the optimum order quantity is out by 20 per cent.

The optimum order quantities calculated by the formula will be for varying amounts some of which are impractical. Fig. 8.6 shows that it is better to adjust these amounts upwards, rather than downwards, to more appropriate values. Moreover, in establishing manufacturing batches, it is often desirable to standardize the order quantities and to arrange for them to follow a range of preferred numbers. Table 8.8 illustrates this idea for three alternative lists of preferred batch sizes.

Table 8.8. Rounding off to preferred batch sizes

Standard batch sizes

All economic batch quantities must be rounded off upwards into the following batch sizes

Scheme A	Scheme B	Scheme C
100	100	100
200	175	150
500	325	250
1000	550	400
2000	1000	650
5000	1750	1000
10000	3250	1500
	5500	2500
	10000	4000
		6500
		10000

8.2.2. Tackling a large range of stock items

The basic principles of the economic order quantity calculation have been known since 1922, but practical application involves detailed item by item calculation to choose the economic order quantity. Recent developments have evolved a technique which provides a quick means of improving the ordering policy over a large range of stock items. It is possible, furthermore, by this approach to make a quantitative estimate of the potential reduction in stockholding costs arising from the adoption of the optimum ordering policy.

This technique, called coverage analysis, minimizes stockholding costs when the total number of orders placed in a year remains unaltered. It is based on the assumption that the cost of placing an order and the variable cost of holding stock, expressed as a percentage of the item's unit value, are both constant: or alternatively, the ratio of these two costs is constant for all items. The basic principle of this technique is to redistribute the total number of orders placed each year for the range of stock items in a manner which will minimize stockholding.

Coverage analysis is particularly applicable to large inventories of bought-out items, but it should not be applied to made-in items where production phasing and plant capacity considerations arise. Nor is it suitable for highly seasonal items or fashion goods. Ideally, very slow moving items should be treated separately also, but this is not always practical.

(a) *Method of applying coverage analysis.* The method is based on a sample of stock item records, which is then analysed to estimate:

(i) the value of the average stockholding costs arising from the present order quantities;
(ii) the value of the average stockholding costs if the total number of orders placed in a year is redistributed according to an optimum ordering policy; and
(iii) the potential saving of excess capital currently tied up in stocks.

Following this analysis the turnover of each item is used to prepare a schedule of economic order quantities.

(b) *Sample of stock item records.* It has been pointed out in chapter 3, that the selection of a sample must be done with care. It is best if the sample is divided into several sub-samples, firstly to eliminate as far as possible the biases which may occur and secondly to provide a realistic measure of the reliability of the inferences to be drawn from the sample.

For every item selected for the survey the following information is required:

(i) The number of orders placed on suppliers in the last year;
(ii) The quantity, in units, issued during the last year;
(iii) The item cost, or alternatively its retail price; and
(iv) The value of annual issues, computed from the last two entries.

This information has been summarized in Table 8.9 for a specimen sample. For ease of computation it has been grouped into classes

Table 8.9. Summary of information collected by sample survey

Value of annual usage (£)	Mid-point (of Col. 1)	Square root of mid-point	Total number in group of: Items	Orders	Total value of year's issues (£)	Average order size (£)
0	0	0	64	19	0	—
1	1	1	58	94	58	0.62
2-6	4	2	25	109	100	0.92
7-25	16	4	6	93	96	1.03
26-50	38	6	3	57	114	2.00
51-150	100	10	2	21	200	9.5
151-300	225	15	2	7	450	64.3
	Totals:		160	400	1018	

or turnover value, each class being chosen so that its midpoint has a square root equal to a convenient whole number.

(c) *Calculation of Economic Order Quantity for a Stock Item*. It was shown in the previous section (page 186) that the optimum order size N occurs when

$$N = \sqrt{2AB/S}$$

where A represents the annual sales rate in units;
B represents the cost of ordering and delivering an order; and
S represents the cost of holding an item in stock for a year.

Now if the optimum order in value is denoted by Q, then it can be shown that

$$Q = \sqrt{2YB/R}$$

where Y represents the year's sales in value;
B (as before) the cost of ordering and delivering an order; and
R the rate chargeable for holding stock for a year, expressed as a fraction of one. (For example, 20 per cent would be expressed 0.2).

If the cost of ordering, B, and the rate chargeable for holding stock, R, are both constant (or approximately so) or if the ratio B/R is roughly constant from one stock item to another then the optimum order quantity Q becomes

$$Q = k\sqrt{Y}$$

where $k = \sqrt{2B/R}$ is the same for all stock items. The optimum number of orders, T, placed each year for a stock item is its yearly usage Y, divided by the optimum order Q. This becomes

$$T = (1/k)\sqrt{Y}.$$

In other words, the optimum number of orders placed for a stock item is directly proportional to the square root of the year's sales in value for that item. The basic approach of coverage analysis is to redistribute the total number of orders placed in a year for a range of stock items so that the number of

Table 8.10. Determining optimum number of orders for each stock item

Square root of mid-point	Total number of items in group	Sum of square root of mid-points in each group	Optimum number of orders for each item	Value of annual usage (£)	Optimum order size (£)
Col. 1	Col. 2	Col. 3	Col. 4	Col. 5	Col. 6
0	64	0	0	0	—
1	58	58	2	1	0.5
2	25	50	4	2-6	1.0
4	6	24	8	7-25	2.0
6	3	18	12	26-50	3.0
10	2	20	20	51-150	5.0
15	2	30	30	151-300	7.5
	from survey	Col. 1 x Col. 2	$\frac{400}{200}$ x Col. 1		Midpoint Col. 4
	Total	200			

Total number of orders to be allocated (from Col. 5 of Table 8.9) = 400
Total of sums of square roots of midpoints for all groups = 200
Multiply square root of midpoint (Column 1) by 400/200, namely 2, to determine optimum number of orders for each item in group

orders placed on each stock item is proportional to the square root of the year's sales in value for that item. Table 8.10 illustrates how this is done in practice. The total number of orders to be placed, namely 400, is divided by the sum of the square roots of the midpoints of each group, namely 200, to determine a multiplying factor, two. Then the optimum number of orders for each item in a group is obtained by multiplying the square root of the midpoint of that group by the multiplying factor. For instance, the group with annual usage seven to twenty-five has a midpoint of sixteen, the square root of which is four. Each of the stock items in this group should be ordered 2 x 4, namely eight times a year.

Table 8.11. Calculation of saving in average stock arising solely from using optimum order size

Optimum order size (£)	Average order stock (£)	Number of items in group	Average stock held due to order size (£)
Col. 1	Col. 2	Col. 3	Col. 4
—	—	64	0
0.5	0.25	58	14.5
1.0	0.5	25	12.5
2.0	1.0	6	6
3.0	1.5	3	4.5
5.0	2.5	2	5.0
7.5	3.75	2	7.5
(From Table 8.10)			

Optimum Policy: Total average stockholding: £50

Average order size (£)	Average order stock (£)	Number of items in group	Average stock held due to order size (£)
—	—	64	—
0.62	0.31	58	17.98
0.92	0.46	25	11.50
1.03	0.515	6	3.09
2.00	1.00	3	3.00
9.5	4.75	2	9.50
64.3	32.15	2	64.30
(From Table 8.9)	½ x Col. 1	(from survey)	Col. 2 x Col. 3

Previous policy: Total average stockholding: £109

(d) *Potential stock saving arising from use of economic order quantities.* Table 8.11 shows how the average stock needed to service the optimum order sizes can be calculated. First the optimum order size for each group is determined (from Table 8.10). Since the stock will rise by this quantity and then fall to its original value, the average stock arising from the order is half the order. The final column of Table 8.11 shows the average stock for each group, and the total which amounts to £50.

A similar procedure can be adopted as shown in the bottom half of Table 8.11 to calculate the stock arising from the previous ordering policy, and this amounts to £109.

In this hypothetical case, choosing the correct economic order quantities reduces the stock arising from ordering alone by £59 which amounts to about three weeks' stock.

The effect of varying the total number of orders placed each year can be readily examined. Doubling the order rate would halve the average optimum stock, a further saving of £25; halving the order rate would double it–giving a value of £100. So potential alternative ordering policies can be examined, their effects reconciled against practical operating limitations, and a suitable choice made.

(e) *The advantages and limitations of coverage analysis.* Coverage analysis is a practical tool which can be applied by non-mathematical staff. The use of samples allows rules for economic quantity ordering to be established rapidly. It avoids the tricky problems of evaluating the cost of ordering and the cost of holding stock and, moreover, it provides a definite estimate of potential savings. In summary, it is a useful first step in reducing total stockholding costs where the number of stock items is high.

On the other hand, it does not take into account the effects of discounts for quantity and limitations on order size because of obsolescence. It is only a first step, in that it gives no guidance on the size of buffer stock needed to cover fluctuations in usage and supply. Furthermore, with small samples the errors in estimating the potential savings may be large. However, by dividing the sample into several sub-samples the size of the error in estimating the savings can be readily measured as was shown on page 63.

8.3. Better service from stock

Effective control of stocks is a major factor in the profitability of any enterprise concerned with physical goods. It is not unusual for half the capital employed in a business to be tied up in stocks of raw material, work in progress and finished goods. Moreover, surveys of industrial companies indicate that the annual cost of holding stock is of the order of 20-25 per cent of the stock value.

Quite apart from the financial aspects, stocks have an important influence on an enterprise. Unbalanced stocks can ruin service to customers and generate a permanent state of crisis in production departments.

8.3.1. The purpose of holding stocks

Making money is the only valid reason for holding any stock. In other words, stock should only be held if the benefits which result outweigh the cost of holding it. There are four basic areas where stock can earn money:

(a) *Batch Stock.* Stocks are created whenever materials are purchased, manufactured, or transported in bulk quantities. In all such cases goods are acquired more quickly than they are sold or used and temporary stocks arise naturally. Batch stocks earn money since manufacturing economies arise from longer production runs and distribution economies from a reduction in the number of orders to be delivered. These economies are often reflected in quantity discounts on the purchase price. The previous section (page 185) has discussed the choice of an optimum order quantity and an optimum batch size.

(b) *Anticipation Stock.* Stock is also created whenever, as a deliberate policy, goods are purchased or manufactured in advance of expected demand or in anticipation of a predicted increase in costs.

In a highly seasonal industry, stocks can be accumulated prior to the peak season. These stocks earn money by allowing the peak demand to be met by a smaller production capacity than would otherwise be necessary.

(c) *Process Stock.* Work in progress and stocks in transit arise whenever manufacturing and distribution processes take time to complete. If, for example, the manufacturing time from raw material to finished product is four weeks, then inevitably there will be four weeks' work in progress.

It can be argued that process stock earns money by allowing a slow cheap process to be used instead of a fast expensive one. However, a detailed study coupled with effective production planning and control can pay handsome dividends when work in progress has got out of control.

(d) *Safety Stock.* In almost all stock situations there is a significant time lag between initiating an order for stock replenishment and receiving the goods into stock, a time lag which has been called the delivery time or the lead time. Having placed the replenishment order, deliveries to customers must be maintained throughout the lead time from existing stocks. Customer demand is usually variable and impossible to predict and there is, therefore, an inevitable risk that existing stocks may be exhausted before the replenishment arrives.

In these circumstances, the quality of customer service can be maintained only by creating a buffer stock which absorbs any fluctuation in the demand made during the lead time. Such stock provides a safety against running out and so earns money by securing business and profit which would otherwise be lost.

If stocks are to be held, they must serve one of these four roles and consequently stock control must not be solely concerned with reducing stock levels. The objective should be to establish the 'right' stock levels, namely those which maximize the return on capital invested in stock.

8.3.2. The role of safety stock

Safety stock, by definition, exists to cover fluctuations in demand which cannot be predicted. An intuitive choice of safety stocks usually leads to excessively high levels ('when in doubt, play safe'), coupled with an uneven distribution of these stocks. At any point in time, some items are likely to be overstocked and others understocked, and in these circumstances high stocks are no guarantee of a uniformly high level of customer service. In fact one can get the worst of both worlds.

These problems can be resolved by applying the statistical approach to measure the average and variability of past records of

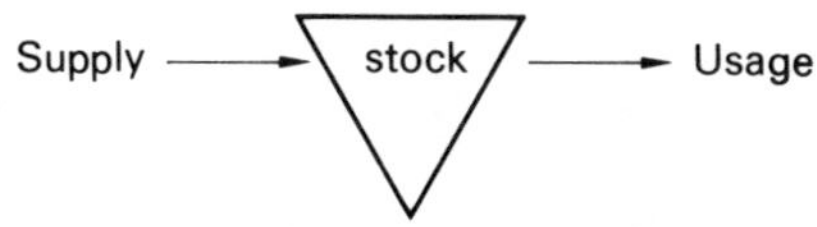

Figure 8.7 Stock is the buffer between supply and usage

sales and delivery times and to predict from this evidence the pattern of future demand. From this pattern it is possible to choose appropriate safety stock levels.

A schematic representation of the role of stocks as a buffer between supply and usage is shown in Fig. 8.7.

It is of course necessary to clothe this with more detail to take account of the variability in lead times and the variability in usage rates. This is done, as shown in Fig. 8.8 on page 196, by expressing the pattern of supply as a frequency diagram of delivery times and the pattern of usage as a frequency diagram of usage rates. An important point to notice is that the unit of time for the lead times and the unit of time over which the usage is totalled are the same. In Fig. 8.8 the lead times are expressed in weeks and the usage rates as quantity per week. From these two frequency diagrams a further frequency diagram is derived, namely the frequency diagram of the usage during the lead time. One method of doing this is explained in the next section.

As an illustration of how this latter diagram is used, consider the instance where the usage in the lead time of a stock item

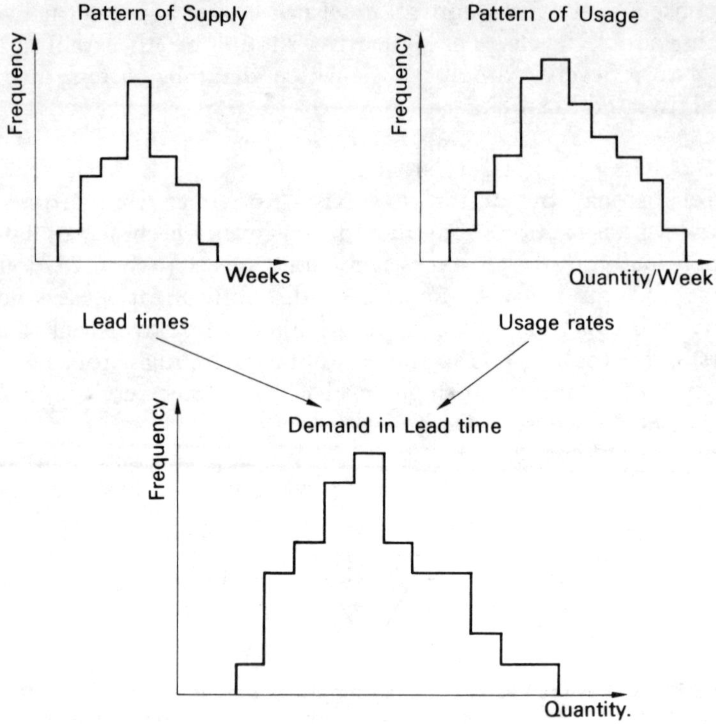

Figure 8.8 Statistical approach to determine pattern of demand in lead time for a particular stock item

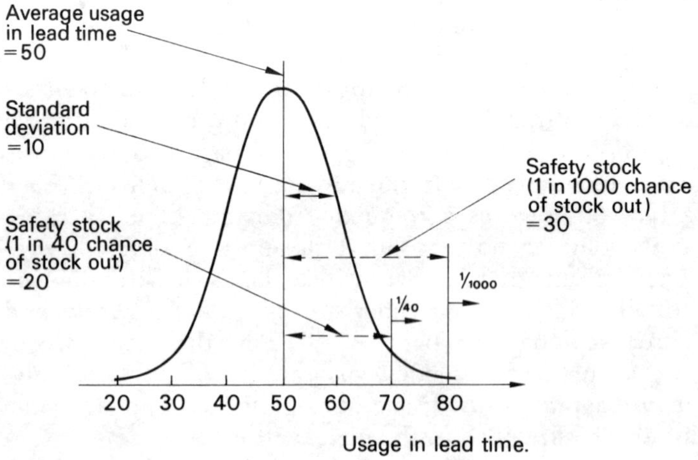

Figure 8.9 Determining the amount of safety stock needed

approximates to the normal distribution, with an average of fifty and a standard deviation of ten, as shown in Fig. 8.9.

Now if the company's policy is to run out on only one in 1000 replenishment orders, a safety stock of thirty will be needed in addition to the average usage of fifty. Consequently, a replenishment order would need to be placed whenever the stock fell to eighty. If three months' stock is ordered at a time, this would mean a stock out once in 250 years. Moreover, even when a stock out situation occurred, the bulk of the demand in the lead time would be met. For example, if the demand in the lead time was eighty-one, the stock would be sufficient to supply eighty and only a single unit would be outstanding, and this once in 250 years.

A saving in safety stock of ten units could be made if the risk of running out of stock could be increased from one in 1000 to one in forty. Theoretically, this should be done if the cost of holding this stock is less than the losses which occur through running out of stock. In practice, it is extremely difficult to put a figure on the loss which occurs through running out of stock and a choice is made on commercial judgment. To aid this judgment it is possible to estimate the average stock holding needed to provide different levels of protection against running out of stock. Two typical instances of estimated company stock holdings needed to provide different levels of protection are shown in Table 8.12.

Table 8.12. Estimated company stockholdings needed to provide different levels of protection against running out of stock

Company A—Estimated value of stocks			
	Risk of stock out during replenishment		
	1 in 40	1 in 200	1 in 1000
Product 1	£37 000	£48 000	£59 000
Product 2	£52 000	£69 000	£84 000

Company B—Estimated value of stocks			
	Risk of stock out during replenishment		
Average Lead time	1 in 10	1 in 40	1 in 1000
3 months	£22 000	£35 000	£63 000
2 months	£19 000	£31 000	£57 000

It is important to differentiate between the calculated levels of protection against running out of stock when the stock is being replenished, and the availability of stock on demand. The demand will always be met in full when the stock level is too high to justify a replenishment order, and on the bulk of the occasions when a replenishment order has been placed. Consequently, the level of availability of stock on demand is going to be much higher than the level of protection against running out of stock on replenishment. For instance, a level of 98 per cent to 99 per cent availability of stock on demand is being achieved in a warehouse, by a system designed to give a 90 per cent level of protection against running out of stock when the stock is being replenished.

8.3.3. Calculation of safety stocks

There is, needless to say, a major problem to solve—how to turn the frequency diagrams of lead times and usage rates into the frequency diagram of usage in lead time. One way of doing this is to determine:

The average usage in a week, D;
The standard deviation of the weekly usage, S_D;
The average lead time in weeks, L; and
The standard deviation of the lead time, S_L.

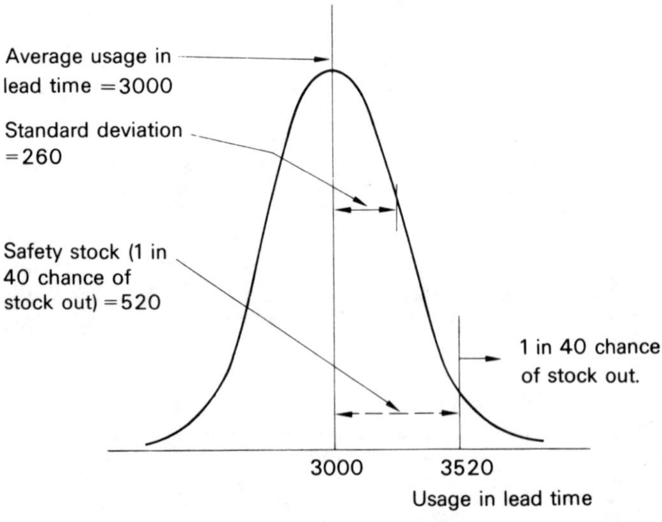

Figure 8.10 Derived frequency diagram of usage in lead time

From these values two simple formulae are used to determine:

1. The average usage in the lead time = L x D, and
2. The standard deviation of the usage in the lead time,

$$=\sqrt{L(S_D)^2 + D^2\ (S_L)^2}$$

For example if:

Average lead time = 25 days;
Standard deviation of lead time = 2 days;
Average daily demand = 120; and
Standard deviation of daily demand = 20,

then the average usage in the lead time = 25 x 120, namely 3000 and the standard deviation of the usage in the lead time

$$=\sqrt{(25 \times 400) + (14\,400 \times 4)}$$
$$= 260.$$

The derived frequency diagram, assumed to be a normal distribution is shown in Fig. 8.10.

8.3.4. Simple system of stock regulation

The preceding sections have dealt with the purposes of holding stock and a method of calculating safety stock levels. These levels are applied in practice through a systematic stock control procedure which monitors the current stock level and arranges for stock to be replenished whenever it is appropriate. Many different systems of regulating stocks have been developed to meet particular situations and there is no single answer to all such problems. Nevertheless, it is useful to outline the basis of one of the most simple yet effective procedures for controlling stock levels, which is often called the 'two bin' system. In this system, the rule is to order a fixed quantity (the economic order quantity) whenever current stocks fall to a pre-defined re-order level. If the demand or usage is varying considerably, the system responds by varying the interval between placing orders. This procedure reduces stock control to simple formal rules which allow the routine replenishment of stock to be carried out by stock clerks.

To operate the two-bin system, up to date records of current stock are required for each item, as well as the formal calculation of the re-order quantity and the re-order level. Even this simple system will be inappropriate in those instances where the items concerned are difficult to count in and out of stock, and accurate records of past usage and lead times are not available. Provided records of usage and lead times can be collected, the system can be run effectively without continuous and accurate stock records. This is done by holding the stock of each item in two separate 'bins', the second of which is the reserve. When the first bin is empty, the second bin is breached and at the same time a replenishment batch is ordered. The second bin contains a quantity equal to the re-order level and so provides protection against stock out during the delivery of the replenishment batch. When the new stocks arrive an amount equal to the re-order level is set aside in the reserve bin, and the rest of the delivery brought into current use.

When the items being controlled are very inexpensive the system can be simplified still further by making the reserve in the second bin equal to the quantity ordered. Now, whenever the last delivery has to be breached, the same amount is ordered again. With normal procedures the economic order quantity on such items will almost certainly be greater than the re-order level. The penalty for the simple approach is paid in excessive stocks and so it should be limited to very low cost items.

8.4. Making better use of limited resources

Linear programming is a tool, based on mathematics, for making the best allocation of limited resources. It is possible to use linear programming to choose operating conditions which will result in minimum cost, or maximum output or maximum profit (whichever criterion of success is appropriate), when the operating conditions are subject to limiting restrictions. There is always the proviso that the quality of the solution depends on the accuracy of the data which form the basis of the calculations. However, although the analysis may not identify the true optimum, significant profits have arisen from finding a better way. Consider, for example, a company which makes two kinds of a consumer product, Type A and Type B, subject to the following restrictions:

	Type A	Type B
Unit man-hours	2.0	1.0
Sales capacity	450/day	700/day
Materials capacity	A & B combined: 800 yds/day	
Materials needed	1 yd./unit	2 yds./unit
Unit Profit	£4	£3
Production capacity	1000 man-hours/day	

The company wished to maximize their profit, subject to the restrictions on sales, materials and production capacity. Linear programming has shown that it is necessary to choose *only one* criterion to optimize: restrictions can be placed on the permissible values of other criteria, provided that these restrictions are consistent. In this instance it is necessary to determine how many of each type should be made. Usually we are satisfied when we achieve a feasible solution to such problems; the linear programming approach turns feasible solutions into optimum solutions. Of course the value of the optimum solution and also its practical usefulness depend on the accuracy with which the problem has been defined.

8.4.1. Graphical solution

When there are only two alternative products for which the production level has to be chosen, this type of problem can be solved graphically. In practice, there are almost always more than two alternative products whose levels have to be chosen, and more sophisticated mathematics and extensive calculations are needed. However, the type of problem tackled by linear programming and the method of solution can be illustrated by the simplest case.

In Fig. 8.11 overleaf, the horizontal axis denotes the number of items of Type A scheduled for production, and the vertical axis the number of items of Type B scheduled for production. Any point on the chart will denote an allocation of production and materials capacity to make a specific number of items of Type A and a specific number of Type B. The point shown on Fig. 8.11 denotes a decision to make 400 units of Type A and 600 units of Type B.

The area in which an allocation can be made, compatible with the restrictions imposed by limited resources, is called the *area of feasible solutions.*

The first restrictions are that a negative number of Type A and Type B cannot be made, consequently OY and OX are boundaries of the feasible area.

Similarly, since the sales capacity of Type A is 450 and the sales capacity of Type B is 700, the feasible area, as shown on Fig. 8.12 on page 203, is bounded by the lines S1 to S2 and S3 to S4.

The next restriction is based on the production capacity. If only Type A are produced, then the production capacity is 500. If, on the other hand, only Type B are produced, then the production capacity is 1000. The straight line P1 to P2 provides an upper limit on the feasible area, and cuts off the top right hand corner of the previous feasible region.

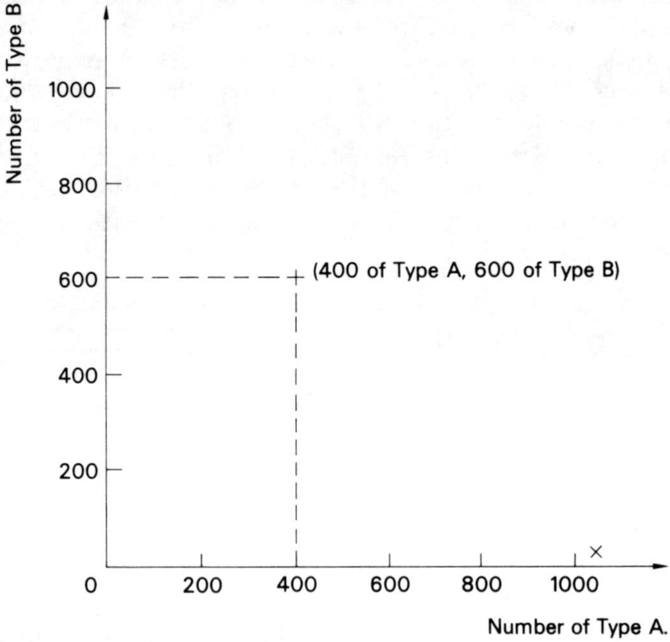

Figure 8.11 Any point on the chart denotes a decision to make a specific number of type A and a specific number of type B

In a similar manner, the restriction based on the material's capacity represented by the straight line joining M1 to M2 reduces the feasible area still further.

One of the feasible solutions is to make only 150 of Type A (each at a profit of £4) and none of Type B, at a total profit of £600. If instead it were decided to make only 200 of Type B and none of Type A, the profit would remain at £600. In fact, all the solutions represented by the points on the line p3 to p4 on Fig. 8.13 will have the same profit, namely, £600. If it were decided to work at double this scale, namely, to make either 300 of Type A or 400 of Type B, the profit would be £1200. All the solutions represented by the points on the line p5 to p6 would have the same profit, namely, £1200.

Now the line p5 to p6 is parallel to the line p3 to p4 but displaced in a north-easterly direction. If this line is moved as far as possible in this direction and yet kept in the area of feasible solutions, it will end up at the optimum solution. This occurs at

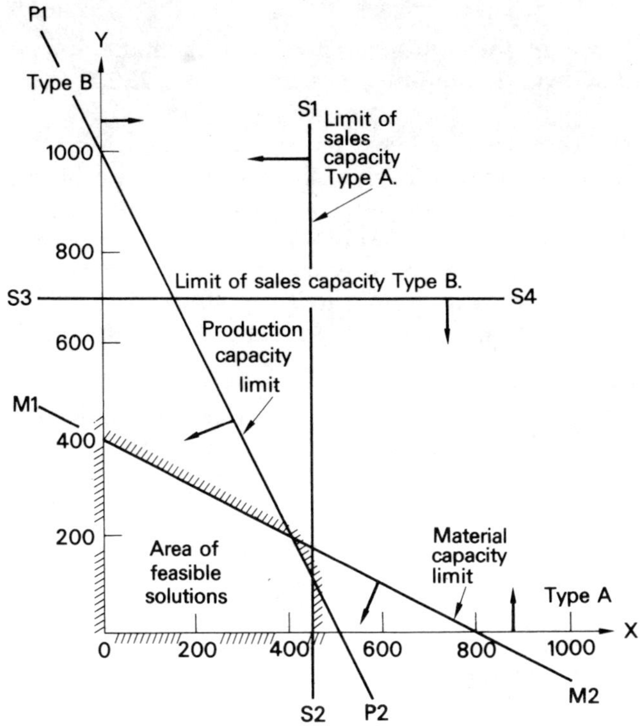

Figure 8.12 Taking account of limitations to fix area of feasible solutions

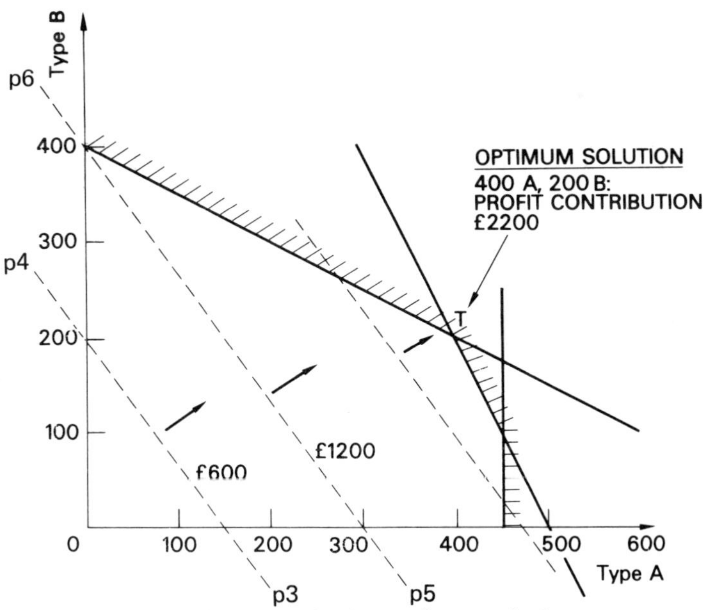

Figure 8.13 Contours of profit indicating optimum solution

point T, where the solution represented is 'make 400 of Type A and 200 of Type B' and this gives a profit of £2200.

8.4.2. Formulating a linear programming solution

Consider, as an illustration of how to frame a problem in a form suitable for linear programming calculation, a company with three products which are each sold in entirely separate markets. In addition to the records of sales and costs for each product, shown in the top half of Table 8.13, it is necessary to calculate the unit profit contribution (as shown in Table 8.13) and to define the restrictions on the resources available.

Table 8.13. Records of sales, costs and profit contribution

Operating data for products over past year

	Product code		
	Gleem	Torch	Star
Annual sales—units of product	32 400	49 350	152 800
Sales price per unit—£	1.5	2.0	1.0
Material costs—material X	11 800	—	34 800
£ —material Y	2 800	4 300	11 600
—material P	—	14 600	17 000
Labour costs £	8 600	27 200	22 700
Variable overhead cost incurred £	17 300	38 500	47 600

Estimated profit contribution

	Gleem	Torch	Star
Variable expense (£)	40 500	84 600	133 700
Sales (units)	32 400	49 350	152 800
Variable unit cost (£)	1.25	1.71	0.875
Price per unit (£)	1.50	2.00	1.00
Contribution per unit (£)	0.25	0.29	0.125

The restrictions on next year's activity have been tabulated in Table 8.14.

Within these restrictions, the planned production of the three products has to be chosen to maximize the total profit contribution.

In order to determine the effect of these restrictions on the choice of how many of each product to manufacture, it is first necessary to determine the amount of each material and the

Table 8.14. Restrictions on next year's activity

Characteristic	Next year's limit
Supply of material Y	£17 000
Supply of material P	£24 300
Labour force (wage bill)	£45 200
Maximum unit sales	
—Gleem	35 000
—Torch	100 000
—Star	200 000

amount of labour used on a unit of each product. This has been done in Table 8.15 and the amounts shown in monetary value. Since there is no limit on the availability of Material X there is no point in calculating the amount of Material X used on each product.

The linear programming formulation of this problem can now be drawn up as follows:

If G denotes the number of units of Gleem,
T denotes the number of units of Torch, and
S denotes the number of units of Star to be manufactured, the objective is to maximize
Profit Contribution = 0.25G + 0.29T + 0.125S.
(The unit values of profit contribution are taken from Table 8.13.)

The choice of G, T and S is subject to the restrictions on the use of materials Y and P; on the use of the labour force, and on maximum sales of Gleem, Torch and Star, shown in Table 8.16.

Table 8.15. Calculation of amount of material and labour used in a unit of each product

Total expense (£)	Gleem	Torch	Star
Material Y	2 800	4 300	11 600
Material P		14 600	17 000
Labour	8 600	27 200	22 700
Total sales (units)	32 400	49 350	152 800

Unit cost (£)	Gleem	Torch	Star
Material Y	0.086	0.087	0.076
Material P		0.296	0.111
Labour	0.265	0.551	0.149

The calculations required by linear programming are too complicated and lengthy to tackle any practical problem by hand and the calculations are carried out on a computer. A computer was in fact used to find the solution to this problem and the steps taken are outlined in chapter 10. The data fed into the computer and the form of answer it produced are shown on page 245. The solution is to make:

35 000 units of Gleem
22 335 units of Torch, and
158 511 units of Star.

This solution uses up all the available supplies of Material Y and all the available labour. In the case of Gleem it is set at the maximum sales forecast. Although it is not shown in chapter 10, linear programming identified that it would be more profitable to increase the availability of Material Y than labour. In other words, an extra £100 of material would produce more profit than an extra £100 of labour.

Table 8.16. Linear programming formulation of restrictions

Amount used		Total available
Material Y		
0.086 G + 0.087 T + 0.076 S	Does	17 000 (£)
Material P		
0.296 T + 0.111 S	not	24 300 (£)
Labour		
0.265 G + 0.551 T + 0.149 S	exceed	45 200 (£)
Sales G		35 000 (units)
T		100 000 (units)
S		200 000 (units)

8.4.3. Types of problem solved by linear programming

(a) *Distribution.* A number of power stations are supplied with coal from a number of collieries. How should the requirements of the power stations be met from the limited capacities of the different collieries to minimize transportation costs?

(b) *Blending.* A manufacturer of agricultural food stuffs mixes together ingredients each containing different amounts of vitamins. What proportions of the ingredients should be mixed together to meet the minimum vitamin requirements at minimum cost?

(c) *Product Mix.* A steel mill produces a number of types of strip each using the different processes of the steel mill. Given the process capacities, the rates of output, the profit per ton, and the sales potential of each type of strip, determine the amounts of each type of manufacture in order to maximize the profit.

(d) *Production Programming.* A manufacturer of children's assembly kit toys has a sales forecast for each of twelve months ahead. He has a capacity restriction of the monthly output on normal working hours, and a higher capacity restriction if overtime is worked. The cost of manufacture on overtime is higher than the cost of manufacture during normal working hours. Both costs are known. It is possible to manufacture in advance of peak requirements and store the completed kits. The cost of storing one kit for a month is also known. Determine the programme of monthly production which minimizes the annual cost of manufacture and storage.

8.4.4. Pros and cons

Linear programming is a practical mathematical tool for choosing optimum allocations of resources where these resources are limited. One major difficulty of applying the technique lies in the absence of the data needed to solve the problem after it has been formulated. This is why its present fields of application have been restricted. Where it has been applied to complex situations, considerable savings have occurred.

8.5. The routes to a better way

This chapter has been concerned with:

Balancing alternative losses, when a product outside one tolerance is rectified and outside the other is scrapped, to minimize the total losses;

Balancing the losses due to failing to meet customers' demand and the losses of having to scrap a product with a short shelf life, in order to minimize the total losses;

Balancing the chances of winning a contract and the percentage profit on the contract in order to maximize the expected profit;

Balancing the cost of placing many small orders against the cost of holding extra stock if the order size is increased in order to minimize the total cost of ordering and holding stock;

Balancing the cost of holding extra safety stock against the value to the company of a better service from stock; and

Choosing a set of optimum operating conditions in the face of restrictions which limit the company's range of choice.

There is a basic pattern to all of these problems and although the precise method of 'solving' them may vary from problem to problem there is also a basic approach. This approach is summarized in the following steps.

1. Build a framework for thinking. To do this, irrelevant detail will have to be stripped away and commonsense approximations adopted.
2. Decide what information is relevant, collect it and examine the nature and patterns in this information.
3. Decide whether or not it is necessary to take account of the variability and uncertainty in the information collected. Restructure the framework for thinking to take account of this variability if this is appropriate.
4. Carry out a mathematical analysis, and come up with an estimate of the best way.

Remember that the 'optimum' solution has to be tested for feasibility in the face of all the practical detail of the operating situation. Moreover, the 'optimum' solution is the answer to the immediate problem and the answer will certainly need to be revised when conditions change. Finally, one of the most profitable fields of investigation will lie in finding out how to get rid of those restrictions which have the greatest effect on limiting the company's profit growth.

List of terms used

Tolerances
Standard
Average
Normal distribution
Frequency distribution
Frequency diagram
Bid ratio
Expected profit
Systematic differences
Economic order quantity
Preferred numbers
Coverage analysis
Sample
Sub-sample
Batch stock
Anticipation stock
Process stock
Lead time
Buffer stock
Safety stock
Variability
Two bin system
Linear programming
Area of feasible solutions

Italicized terms are defined in the glossary (page 262) as well as in the text where it is appropriate.

9. Simulating reality

From time to time, intricate operating problems arise which cannot be solved by simple mathematical models. Such problems are usually handled intuitively, although one would often like to adopt the 'suck it and see' approach—if it were not too costly, or too risky, or perhaps too slow in providing a comparison. Simulation of complex operating problems by means of complex mathematical models provides a means of having a dry run in order to generate comparable facts on which to base a decision. This can be done without risk and ten years' experience can be collected in a matter of days.

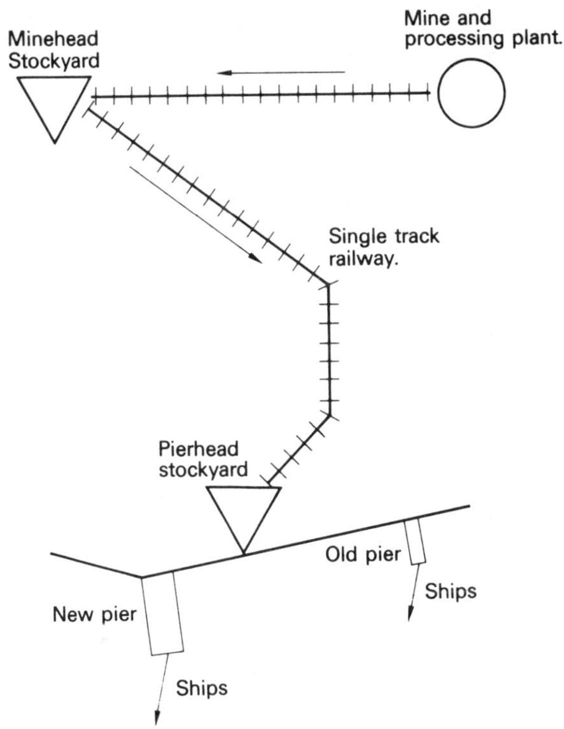

Figure 9.1 Schematic layout of mining facilities

The use of a mathematical model of a proposed system is analagous to the use of models of wing sections which are tested in a wind tunnel. Simulation of the system, usually by means of a computer, is equivalent to testing the model of the wing in a wind tunnel. Whereas the model of the wing may well be made of wood and glue, the mathematical model is built from logic and numerical information. In both instances, however, the simulation should consist of trials carefully planned both to give a closer understanding of underlying principles and also to develop prototype or modified systems.

The problem which arose when a mining company decided to increase the output of a mine from one million to four million tons over a period of five years will be used to illustrate the principles and practice of simulation. In anticipation of this new level of output a new pier had been built at the despatching port, and further pierhead stockyards were planned. Appropriate and expensive mechanical handling equipment had been ordered when the board had misgivings. A mathematical model of the system, concentrating on the stockyards, was built to estimate the additional stockyard capacity which would be needed as output increased from one million to four million tons. The layout of the physical facilities of the company is shown in Fig. 9.1 on page 209.

9.1. Building the model

The model is built firstly by chains of logical decisions, and secondly by numerical measurements of the factors in the model. This numerical data, together with the decision rules, forms a complete specification or model of the real system and may vary from a simple caricature to a detailed portrait. The factors fall into two categories:

1. *Controlled factors* which are deliberately held constant throughout one or more simulation run to assess what happens under specific conditions. They could then be changed to different levels and further simulation runs made to assess what would happen under different conditions. The controlled factors in the model of the stockyard operation are shown in Fig. 9.2. They are:

    the planned output of the mine,
    the tonnage delivered into the stockyard each day,
    the capacity of the stockyard, and
    the number of ships which can be loaded each day.

The appropriate levels of the controlled factors chosen to simulate a particular situation could be an annual output of four million tons; a daily throughput on the railway of 12 000 tons; a planned capacity in the stockyard of 300 000 tons, and only the new pier operating, capable of loading two vessels each day.

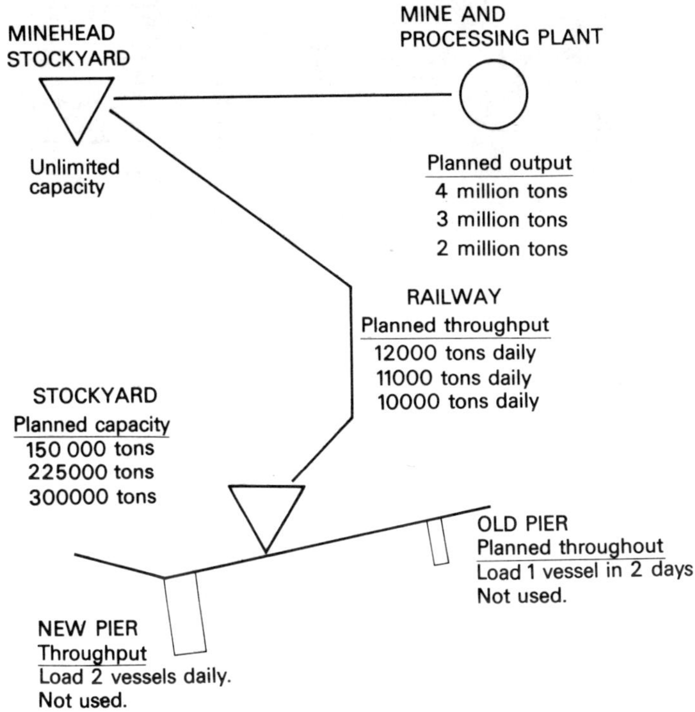

Figure 9.2 Controlled factors, showing alternative levels of activity

2. *Uncontrolled factors* which are allowed to vary randomly within the simulation run, subject to the random fluctuations similar to those which occur in real life situations. Uncontrolled factors in the stockyard model are:

   the number of ships arriving at the port each day;
   the size of each ship arriving.

   These factors are usually specified in terms of the relative frequency with which each level of each factor occurs, as in Table 9.1 on page 213.
   The levels of the uncontrolled factors are chosen, rather like drawing raffle tickets out of a hat. However, to choose the

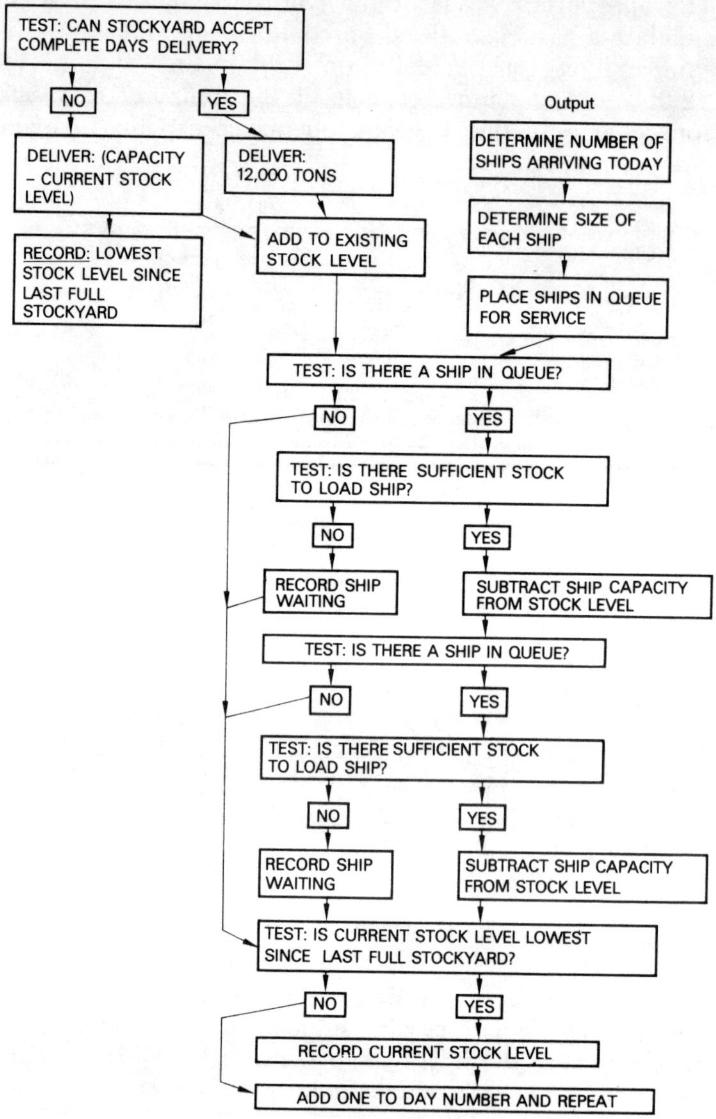

Figure 9.3 Framework of model of stockyard operation

daily number of arrivals there would be fifty-five tickets numbered 0, thirty-three numbered 1, eleven numbered 2 and one numbered 3, to ensure that the number of arrivals was distributed in the correct proportions. In practice, tables of random numbers are used in place of the hat and tickets

Table 9.1. Factors allowed to vary randomly in model of stockyard operation.

Relative number of arrivals each day

Number of arrivals	Proportion of days
0	55%
1	33%
2	11%
3	1%

The number of ships arriving each day is chosen at random, using the proportions in this table.

Relative size of arrivals

Capacity (Tons)	Number of arrivals each year
13 000	46
16 000	96
19 000	38
23 000	28

The size of each arrival is chosen at random, using the proportions in this table.

and if a computer is used the computer generates its own 'random' numbers.

The chains of logical decisions which link together the specific values of the controlled and uncontrolled factors and form the framework of the model of this particular system are shown in Fig. 9.3.

9.2. Establishing and using measures of effectiveness

An investigation of this kind involves a series of trials simulating different operating conditions or strategies. To make a fair comparison, measures are needed of the effectiveness of the alternative conditions or strategies and appropriate measures will depend on the objective and the form of the simulation. Moreover, because of the variability inherent in the uncontrolled factors, the results will almost inevitably vary from trial to trial. It may well be necessary to use the results of the trials to establish frequency distributions of the measure or measures of effectiveness.

In some instances it is important to apply the principles described in chapter 4 to assess the reliability of the estimates and to ensure that the trials are planned and analysed efficiently. By this means the simulation can avoid the errors either of repeating the runs far more than is needed or of stopping before a satisfactory level of precision has been achieved.

In the mining stockyard case the input into the pierhead stockyard was chosen to be marginally higher than the output into vessels alongside the pier and consequently there were occasions when the stockyard was full and rail deliveries had to be temporarily suspended. The simulation calculated the stock level at the end of each day's operation, taking account of the regular delivery and the uncertain output. The figure which put the stocks

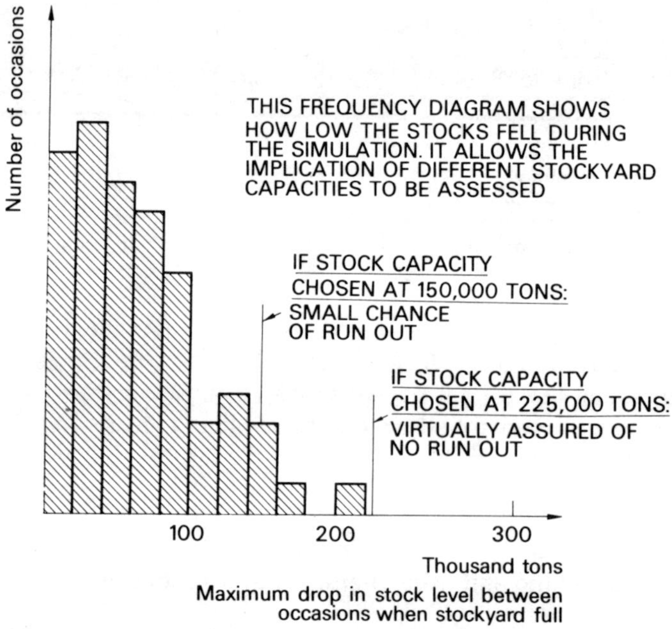

Figure 9.4 Frequency diagram of maximum drop in stock level over the equivalent of 5 years' operation

at greatest risk was the lowest stock level between the successive occasions when the stockyard was full. The amount by which stock had fallen below the level of the full stockyard, namely the maximum drop in stock, was calculated. A frequency diagram of this maximum drop in stock on successive trials is shown in Fig. 9.4. This frequency diagram represents the pattern of the measure of effectiveness when successive trials are made with the controlled factors held constant at certain chosen values. It shows that for these conditions a stockyard capacity of about 200 000 tons is needed to ensure that the chance of being out of stock during a five year period is at an acceptably low level.

9.3. A simple simulation

One of the most difficult problem areas for a manager to handle effectively is the provision and control of service facilities. There is an almost inevitable conflict between the department providing these services and the people using them. For example, should a manufacturer install two or three loading bays for lorries being used to distribute his goods? If only two bays are installed there could be considerable delays to lorries waiting to be loaded although the loading bays are working at a high level of efficiency. If three bays are installed the delays to the lorries would be considerably reduced, but the level of efficiency of the work force on the loading bays would fall. The simple simulation described in this section is used to examine this problem.

In this example lorries arrive, on average, once every seventeen minutes and the time taken for loading is for all practical purposes the same on all occasions, namely thirty minutes. An apparently logical calculation says that two bays should be ample since on average two lorries arrive in thirty-four minutes and on average two bays can each load one of the lorries in thirty minutes. The bays should therefore be able to load these lorries with time to spare (two minutes on each bay every thirty minutes to be precise). Why is it then that past experience says that it cannot be done? How can a convincing argument be put forward that not only are there going to be delays to the lorries if only two bays are provided, but also that it could be more profitable to have three bays?

This situation is an ideal one for simulation. The full details of the loading system are as follows:

Controlled factor
Number of loading bays: two, three or four.

Uncontrolled factor
Interval between lorry arrivals. Lorries arrive on average every seventeen minutes but the frequency distribution of lorry arrival times (collected with the aid of a stopwatch) is most unsymmetrical. It is shown in Fig. 9.5.

Measures of effectiveness
In this example, all the lorries are hired and the cost of keeping a lorry waiting can be readily estimated. In addition, the cost of

providing an extra loading bay has been estimated. A measure of effectiveness of the system appropriate to this example is the total cost of hiring the lorries and providing the loading facilities.

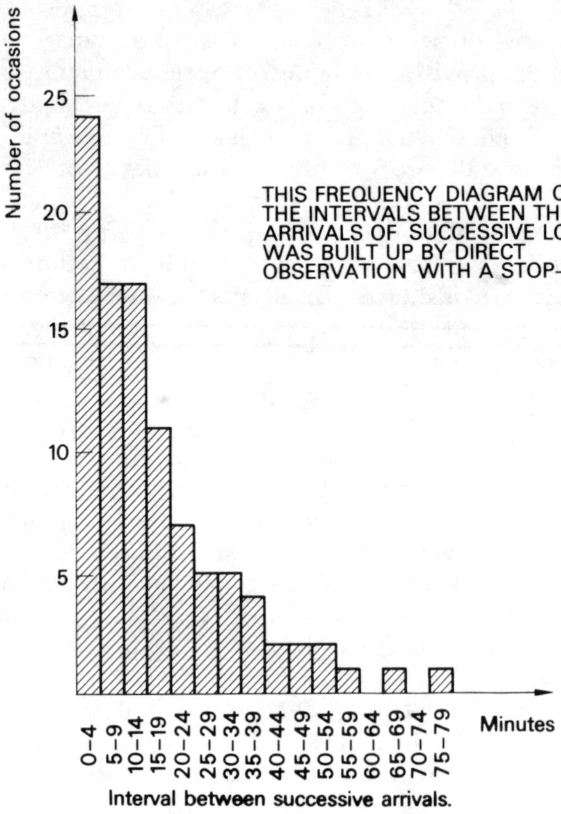

Figure 9.5 Frequency diagram of intervals between arrivals

In other instances a composite measure of effectiveness would be to provide an acceptable level of service to the owners of the transport fleet and minimize the cost of the loading facilities.

Method of operating and other related facts

1. The rule is 'first come, first served'.
2. The time to drive in, load the lorry and drive out again is thirty minutes.
3. Lorries are hired at a cost, including the driver, of £2 an hour.
4. The bays are empty at the beginning of each day.

5. If a lorry arrives before time 500 it is loaded that day. No lorries are held over to the following day. If it arrives at time 500 or later it is turned away empty.
6. The cost, including labour, of providing a third bay is estimated as £12.50 for each working day.

A flow chart showing the basic logic of this system is shown in Fig. 9.6.

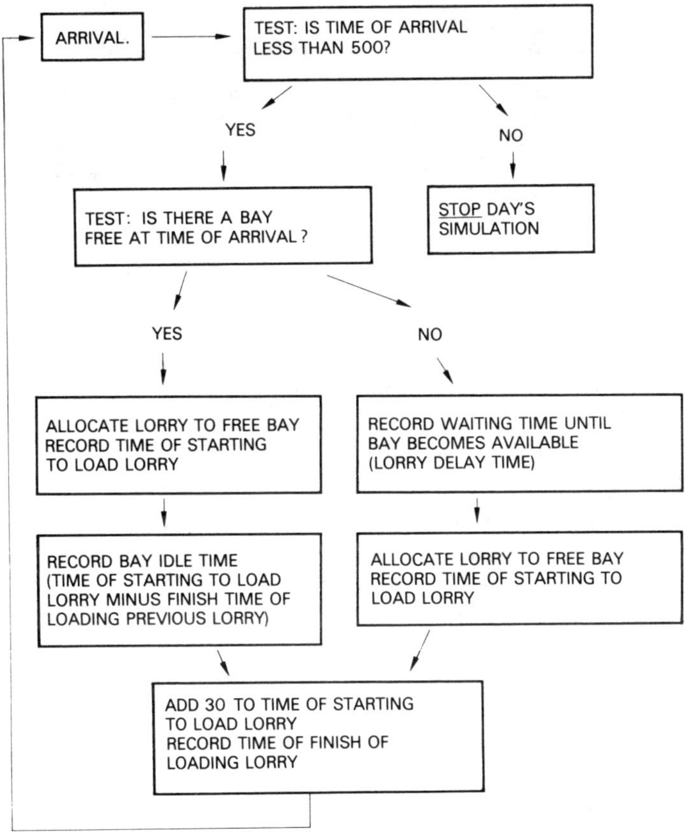

Figure 9.6 Framework of model of warehouse and lorry operation

Method of simulation

In order to introduce the randomness typical of the arrival intervals, the arrival intervals shown in Fig. 9.5 are selected one at a time in a random manner. The most efficient way of doing this is to use specially prepared tables of random numbers, such as those shown in Table 9.2 overleaf.

Table 9.2. Specimen table of random numbers

78	61	12	39	63	76	74	18	69	29
59	92	27	29	28	97	30	35	21	39
71	99	76	90	64	76	66	14	52	84
63	25	81	70	30	98	85	20	18	85
04	90	42	23	37	40	42	74	77	53
06	00	50	03	97	29	56	29	84	17
41	51	04	63	35	94	03	39	52	49
33	67	53	43	10	48	03	09	97	42
52	83	94	20	33	04	40	98	54	35
87	76	09	35	00	45	06	61	14	31
12	13	18	26	21	12	96	88	01	15
00	84	71	68	07	95	71	88	31	72
18	36	80	94	87	41	42	16	87	40
16	64	33	06	19	31	91	55	66	12
83	81	30	51	43	63	89	08	98	66

Example of use: Start at any arbitrary point, for example the number 97 in the middle of the table and use the natural sequence of numbers 97, 29, 56, 29, - - - -

A sequence of numbers is selected from Table 9.2 and a simple conversion table used to convert each random number into a time interval (Table 9.3). The time intervals in the conversion table are merely the values contained in Fig. 9.5 and the random numbers are making a random selection of time intervals from these values.

As an illustration of the method of using the table of random numbers, ten arrivals have been selected from Table 9.2 and are shown in Table 9.4. Once the arrival intervals have been determined from Table 9.3, it is straightforward to calculate the arrival time of each lorry.

The first lorry arrives fifty-nine minutes after the start of the

Table 9.4. Turning random numbers into lorry arrival times

Random number	Arrival interval	Arrival time
97	59	59
29	6	65
56	14	79
29	6	85
84	32	117
17	3	120
41	9	129
51	12	141
04	1	142
63	17	159

Table 9.3. Table for converting random number into time interval between arrivals

Random number	Time interval (mins)	Random number	Time interval (mins)	Random number	Time interval (mins)
00	0	34	7	68	19
01	0	35	8	69	19
02	0	36	8	70	20
03	0	37	8	71	21
04	1	38	8	72	22
05	1	39	9	73	23
06	1	40	9	74	23
07	1	41	9	75	24
08	1	42	10	76	24
09	2	43	10	77	25
10	2	44	10	78	26
11	2	45	10	79	27
12	2	46	11	80	28
13	2	47	11	81	29
14	3	48	11	82	30
15	3	49	11	83	31
16	3	50	12	84	32
17	3	51	12	85	33
18	3	52	12	86	34
19	4	53	13	87	35
20	4	54	13	88	36
21	4	55	13	89	37
22	4	56	14	90	39
23	4	57	14	91	41
24	5	58	14	92	43
25	5	59	15	93	45
26	5	60	15	94	48
27	5	61	16	95	51
28	6	62	16	96	54
29	6	63	17	97	59
30	6	64	17	98	67
31	6	65	17	99	78
32	7	66	18		
33	7	67	18		

Example of use: If the random 97 was selected, the time interval before the arrival of the next lorry would be chosen as 59 minutes.

day at time fifty-nine, the next lorry six minutes later at time sixty-five and so on.

As the arrival time of each lorry is determined it is allocated to one or other of the two bays to be loaded. This is done by calculating the start and end of loading and any delay on the lorry or idle time in the bay. The form of the calculation is illustrated in Table 9.5 on page 220. Even this short spell of simulation shows that there is likely to be considerable delay to lorries if only two bays are used.

Table 9.5. Calculation of start and end of loading, delay to lorries, and idle time on bays.

Arrivals				Allocation to service					
				Bay 1			Bay 2		
Random no.	Arrival intvl.	Time of arrival	Delay on lorry	Start loading	End loading	Bay idle	Start loading	End loading	Bay idle
97	59	59	–	59	89	59			
29	6	65	–				65	95	65
56	14	79	10	89	119	–			
29	6	85	10				95	125	–
84	32	117	2	119	149	–			
17	3	120	5				125	155	–
41	9	129	20	149	179	–			
51	12	141	14				155	185	–
04	1	142	37	179	209	–			
63	17	159	26				185	215	–

Example of allocation to service: The third lorry arrives at time 79. Since Bay 1 is busy until 89, and Bay 2 is busy until 95, this lorry has to wait 10 minutes. It can start loading at time 89, takes 30 minutes to load and so loading ends at time 119. Bay 1 is not idle at this juncture since it starts to load this lorry as soon as the previous lorry loading is ended.

Summary of performance and decision

Since the basic decision was whether to have two or three loading bays, the simulation was run over a period of five days under both conditions. The total delay to the lorries was reduced by the introduction of the third loading bay from 5576 minutes to 958 minutes a saving of 4618 minutes which is approximately seventy-seven hours.

At £2 an hour, this is a saving of £154 a week which is well in excess of the weekly cost of providing a third bay, £62.50. Consequently a decision to go for three bays, rather than two, would produce a profit of £91.50 a week.

It is worth noting that the total delay of 958 minutes with three bays incurs a cost of approximately £32 each week. If the cost of providing a fourth bay were the same as for the third bay, namely £62.50 each week, the fourth bay would not be justified.

Needless to say, there are a lot of other questions to ask. Are we really going to be able to get more working hours out of the lorries, or will they be dissipated at the end of the day? Can we improve the traffic conditions or reduce the bunching of lorry arrivals in some other way? Perhaps a better answer would be to move the warehouse into a less congested area and so eliminate the effect of urban traffic. Can we switch to articulated vehicles with a stock of rear halves for these vehicles and use this to buffer out the randomness and irregular pattern of arrivals? If so, how big a stock of rear halves is needed?

9.4. Problems tackled by simulation

Whenever intricate operating problems arise, the feasibility of simulating the situation should be examined. Facts and figures will need to be collected, and a model devised and tested before the pertinent questions are posed. This requires a lot of effort but the ability to try out alternative strategies without risk and at little cost can produce benefits many times greater than the total cost of the effort involved.

9.4.1. Problems of corporate strategy

One company had three factories, all manufacturing the same product, all operating well below capacity, and all serving a single market. What would be the effect of closing one or two of the existing factories? Which factories should be the ones to be closed?

Another company had several distribution depots throughout the United Kingdom. What would be the effect of operating with only one, or two, or even three centralized warehouses?

A third company had a combination of these two problems. It had started to erect a large new factory when the question of holding stock at a single central warehouse was raised. Two models were built in this instance, the first to study the potential benefits in reduced distribution costs, and the second to study what should be made where and in what quantity. It was found that a central warehouse would produce greater benefits through improvements in production than through the improvements in distribution costs. A further unquantifiable benefit was that the general manager of the new plant was able to study the operation of manufacture and distribution before the plant was actually built.

9.4.2. Tactical operating problems

What are tactical problems in some companies, are strategic problems in others and could therefore be tackled either at board level or at the level of a departmental manager. All the following problems have been the subject of a simulation:

Which of a number of alternative sets of rules is the best for scheduling work through a jobbing shop?
Which is the best of a number of alternative methods of handling materials through a factory? Needless to say, after experience with the model, several other alternative methods were devised and examined.
What are the consequences of adopting one of a number of alternative inventory control policies?
What should be the size of a retail sales force in a departmental store? What are the consequences of several alternative forms of organization?
What should be the size of the staff needed to maintain complex equipment? What are the consequences of several alternative strategies for using this work force?

9.4.3. Problems in non-manufacturing situations

Transport problems can be very complex and they have been examined by simulation over widely different conditions:

What is the most effective way of operating a fleet of cargo ships?
What are the consequences of alternative ways of controlling traffic in a city?
Which of a number of alternative ways of reclassifying waggons in a railway marshalling yard will keep delays to an acceptably low level?
What are the consequences of alternative systems of railway signalling?
What are the consequences of increased density of aircraft, increased times between take offs and between landings, on the efficient use of an airport?

National, municipal and city authorities have been concerned with some of the simulations of traffic problems. At least two further problems with which they are concerned have been simulated:

What are the consequences of alternative methods of staffing and operating ambulances on the cost and effectiveness of the ambulance service?
What are the cost and effectiveness of alternative firefighting methods?

9.4.4. Business games

Another application of simulation is the business game. Here controlled and uncontrolled factors operate on a 'business' and the sales of the company are made to depend in part on fixed laws and in part on chance laws. The objective of these games is to give experience of running a business without the risks attached to the real thing, experience which should result in the development of management skills.

The mathematical models which have been developed can differ to a marked degree from the individual's own business. It is argued that because of this weakness they have little value. However, if a model is constructed of the individual's business then such a business game has tremendous possibilities, not only for training but also for exploratory trials of operating strategies.

9.5. Use of computers in simulation

The simple simulation of the warehouse and the lorries which was used to illustrate the principles and the mechanics of simulation also illustrates that it involves a lot of simple logic and arithmetic. Moreover, the logic and arithmetic are repeated many times within a single simulation run, and many times more as alternative levels of the controlled factors are chosen in turn. This is just the sort of thing a computer does well and it would be inconceivable to carry out a large scale simulation without the assistance of a computer to do the routine donkey work.

The logic of the simulation, such as that embodied in Figs. 9.3 and 9.6; the values of the controlled factors; the frequency diagrams of the uncontrolled factors; a random mechanism for choosing the values of the uncontrolled factors; and a procedure for evaluating the effectiveness are all incorporated into a computer program.

Constructing a mathematical model of an operating system in a form suitable for simulation on a computer is not a simple task. A manager will need technical assistance in formulating the model; in collecting and analysing the relevant facts and figures; in planning the simulation trials; in writing and running the program on the computer. On the other hand he must be willing to absorb the detail of the mathematical model and of the trials, to ensure that the correct simulation is being made. Moreover, he needs to check with the specialist the logic of every step in the computer program. The cost of setting up a large scale simulation can be high, for example £20 000 to £30 000, but the prize can also be high. Annual savings in production and distribution expenses of £500 000 to £700 000 have been achieved.

9.6. Basic principles

Simulation of management problems is used:

1. To develop principles;
2. To try out prototype systems or modified systems; and
3. To make estimates on the basis of which fundamental decisions can be made.

The model of the system used in the simulation can either be very simple or very refined. In practice it should be based on broad assumptions and only as each assumption is challenged should the model of the system become more complicated. To satisfy the needs of a four year old boy, two pieces of wood and a nail can represent an aeroplane. A complete replica of the aircraft control system, coupled to a computer, is needed to satisfy a test pilot.

The basic principle of building a mathematical model of a management problem area is to keep it as simple as possible, compatible with a realistic representation of the system. What is a realistic representation? One which allows the objective of the investigation to be achieved in a reasonable time (with an appreciable improvement in profit contribution).

List of terms used

Mathematical model
Simulation
Controlled factors
Simulation run
Uncontrolled factors
Random fluctuations
Relative frequency
Random numbers
Computer
Frequency distribution
Reliability of estimate
Level of precision
Business game
Computer program

Italicized terms are defined in the glossary (page 262) as well as in the text where it is appropriate.

10. The role of computers

The computer has a significant role to play in making profitable use of figures. Such techniques as exponential smoothing, simulation, linear programming and multiple regression analysis have become practical and straightforward to apply because the donkey work can be done by computer. On the other hand, the computer in its role of data processor has the capacity to swamp you with figures unless care is taken to make them meaningful. The management information it provides becomes valuable when the computer printout shows the current achievement against the target or better still when it shows only those performances which have gone either above or below the limits calling for management action. In this way the computer can be used to indicate the pressure points in the business to which immediate attention is needed if inefficiency and loss are to be avoided.

10.1. What a computer can do

This section of the book is not intended as a detailed description of how a computer works or how it should be managed. It is simply an outline explanation so that the role of the computer in making a profit from figures can be considered.

The kind of computer in general use is a digital computer. It works with figures and does calculations in a way similar to which you and I do calculations on pieces of paper. It is also a general purpose computer since it can do any sort of calculation, provided that you know what you want. The detailed instructions which have to be fed into the computer to make it do specific calculations are known as a computer program. Once the program has been fed into the computer, either through a paper tape, a magnetic tape, or a punched card reader, the computer is set up to go through the routine of calculations appropriate to all problems of a particular class. What it now needs is the basic data relevant to your specific problem and this must be prepared in the form and the order required by the computer program. When this data has been fed in through a reader into the computer, the calculations are carried out and the results form the output from the computer. The output can be on paper tape, magnetic tape or punched cards. Alternatively, or in addition it can be printed by a teleprinter unit or by a high speed printer which prints a whole line at a time. In addition to carrying out straightforward calculations the computer can make the simple test of comparing two numbers which it has either read or calculated. This enables several alternative forms of calculation, manipulation, or output to be used depending on the results of one or more such comparisons.

In commercial applications, such as invoicing and order processing, the computer usually has both to read in and to print out a large amount of data, but is asked to carry out very few calculations or manipulations of the data. On the other hand, in those instances where the computer should be used to make figures talk, to make a profit from figures, there will be relatively little data to be read in or to be printed out—it is the weight of the calculation and manipulation which will justify its use.

It is worth underlining that the computer cannot formulate the problem to which these mathematically based techniques may be applied. There will always be a need to select which technique is appropriate, to structure the problem so that it can be solved by this technique and to collect the figures which will be turned to economic advantage. The computer will neither spot the economic advantage, nor will it make sure that it has been secured.

10.2. The craft of using a computer

Without a program, a computer is a useless piece of 'hardware'. It is the 'software', the set of computer programs which allows the user to instruct the hardware in what it is to do, which is the most important feature.

10.2.1. High level programming languages

When a computer manufacturer puts a new computer on the market he provides basic software which is designed to simplify the use of the computer and to increase its efficiency. This software is written in 'machine language', a language which is directly linked to the logic built into the computer hardware. It is this software and this language which needs to be understood by the computer specialist whose job it is to exploit the limits of the computer's capabilities.

Program	Meaning
DIMENSION VALUE (12)	There are 12 observations denoted by VALUE.
READ,(VALUE(I),I=1,12)	Read and store the observations.
SUM = 0	Clear the stores to be used to accumulate:
SUMSQR = 0	i. Sum of observations. ii. Sum of squares of observations.
DO 2 I=1,12	This loop will be repeated 12 times and calculate the sum of the observations and the sum of the squares of the observations.
SUM = SUM + VALUE (I)	
SUMSQR = SUMSQR + VALUE (I) * VALUE (I)	
2 CONTINUE	
PRINT, SUM, SUMSQR	
AVRGE = SUM/12	Calculate average.
VARNCE = SUMSQR/12 - AVRGE*AVRGE	Calculate standard deviation.
STDEVN = SQRT (VARNCE)	
PRINT, AVRGE, VARNCE, STDEVN	
STOP	

Figure 10.1 A short computer program written in Fortran

Most users communicate with the computer through computer programs written in high level programming languages which are much simpler to understand. The computer itself then uses a special program, called a compiler, to turn the high level language into machine language. Two high level programming languages most suited to the calculations and manipulations appropriate to the techniques of this book are FORTRAN and ALGOL.

These two languages are based on the symbolism of arithmetic and algebra together with specific logical words or phrases. Fig. 10.1 which is a short program written to calculate the average and standard deviation of twelve observations illustrates the nature of the symbols used in FORTRAN.

10.2.2. Program packages

Program packages are computer programs which have been written to tackle a problem area such as network analysis or stock control and which can be hired or bought from their originators. The outline details of a program package in network analysis are shown in Table 10.1.

Table 10.1. Outline specification of package program

General Description
The program is designed to carry out the basic arithmetic of turning a network diagram into a schedule of activities together with:

1. The earliest and latest activity start times.
2. The earliest and latest activity finish times.
3. The total, free, and independent floats.

Limit on program size
About 10 500 activities.

Facilities available
Calendar dates in output.
Choice of 5, 5½, 6, 6½ day week.
Ability to specify schedule dates.
Output can be sorted 4 deep for any characteristic.
Output can be in bar charts.

Computer facilities
Program written for KDF-9 computer.
Service bureau guarantees 48 hour turn round on review runs: new networks require an extra day for each 1000 activities. Cost for 1000 activities, about £33. Minimum charge £10.

The program package is written in a generalized form so that a wide range of problems in the area considered can be handled. The user first has to choose which of the options available within the package he wishes to use, and perhaps to supply the values, such as the smoothing constant to be used in exponential smoothing, which specify his own particular problem The kind of information needed to specify a particular problem when using a multiple regression analysis package is shown in Table 10.2.

Table 10.2 does not list all the possible options, nor does it show all the information required to specify the problem. As is apparent from the table, this information is punched onto cards which are read into the computer immediately following the pack of cards specifying the program package. If you know sufficient about regression analysis to decide that it is the appropriate technique to use, you should be able to complete the problem and sub-problem cards without difficulty. A specimen computer printout from the originator of the package should enable you to decide just what to expect from the package and which options to choose.

Finally, the user has to supply the data relevant to his own problem and the package does the rest.

Program packages make certain basic assumptions and follow definite fixed rules for solving the problem. These assumptions and rules must be thoroughly understood before the package can be used safely. For instance, what assumptions does the stock

Table 10.2. Some of the basic information needed to specify a particular multiple regression analysis (BMDO2R stepwise regression)

Problem card

1. Problem name (six letters or figures)
2. Number of observations (up to 9999)
3. Number of variables (up to 80)
4. Number of sub-problems (up to 99)
5. YES if average and standard deviation of each variable is to be printed; otherwise leave blank.
6. YES if covariance matrix is to be printed; otherwise leave blank.
7. YES if correlation matrix is to be printed; otherwise leave blank.

Sub-problem card

1. Number of the dependent variable.
2. Maximum number of steps (in step by step solution). Standard value will be taken if left blank.
3. F-Level for inclusion in regression. Standard value will be taken if left blank.
4. F-Level for deletion from regression. Standard value will be taken if left blank.
5. YES if list of residuals is to be printed.
6. YES if summary table is to be printed.

control package make about the frequency diagrams of lead times and demand?

The usefulness of program packages depends very much on the skill and experience of the man concerned in solving problems in the relevant area as well as on the skill of writing the program to give flexibility. Also, certain problem areas such as network planning and linear programming are much more precisely defined than others and in consequence are more suited to program packages. At their best, program packages are an extremely powerful tool, eliminating most of the mathematical analysis and the programming. At their worst, they can be extremely misleading if the wrong tools and techniques are chosen.

Table 10.3 lists a selection of the program packages available from one computer bureau. Although there are no packages listed for sales forecasting, stock control and production control at this bureau, packages are available from other sources to cover these problem areas. Moreover since developments are continually taking place, this list will almost certainly be extended before this book is printed.

By and large a package program has to be accepted without change. If the assumptions are not relevant to your specific problem, or the package presents the results in a completely unacceptable manner then the task of modifying it to your own use is usually impossible. A program package is quick, it is cheap

Table 10.3. A selection of the program packages available from one computer bureau (University Computing Company (Gt. Britain) Ltd.)

Statistical analysis	Three sets each containing about forty different programs.
Network analysis	Four packages. One devoted to resource scheduling.
Linear programming	Two alternative packages.
Vehicle routing	Program produces vehicle routes which minimize the distance travelled when distributing goods from one or more depots.
Warehouse optimization	Program produces method of supplying a number of customers from a number of alternative supply points at minimum cost.
Statistical surveys	Selective analysis and tabulation of survey data.
Technical packages	1. Cut and fill calculation for roadworks, etc. 2. A package of five programs used to minimize road construction costs. 3. Hydraulic network analysis to determine water flows and pressures.

to use, but unless flexibility has been specifically designed into the package it is better to start afresh rather than try to modify it.

10.2.3. Programming languages for special purposes

The more difficult it is to define a problem area precisely the more difficult it is to use program packages. In order to handle situations in which a wide variety of problems have to be tackled, a number of special programming languages have been developed. These programming languages simplify the job of writing a computer program in a specific problem area. For instance, the language CSL allows programs to be written for problems to be solved by simulation, five times as quickly as would be the case if it were to be written in FORTRAN.

These special purpose languages relate to one specific problem area, and although very powerful within that area, are of little use in other areas. The number of these special languages is limited

Table 10.4. Special purpose languages available from one computer bureau (University Computing Company (Gt. Britain) Ltd).

APT–*Automatically Programmed Machine Tools.*
Special language for computer assisted programming of numerically controlled machine tools and similar equipment.

STRESS
Special language for structural engineering used to analyse structures in two or three dimensions.

Cross Tabulation Program for Survey Data.
Special language used for selective analysis and tabulation of survey data.

GASP–*General Activity Simulation Program*
GPSSII–*General Purpose Systems Simulator II*
Simula–*ALGOL Simulation Language*
These are three special languages designed to assist simulation studies of industrial and other systems.

and the number of computers with the special programs needed to turn them into machine language is also limited. However in those instances when they can be used they are an extremely valuable programming tool.

Six languages, covering four problem areas are available from one computer bureau. Some details of these languages are given in Table 10.4.

10.2.4. Simplifying the use of program packages

In order to simplify the use of program packages and to make them readily available to the computer user some of the packages have been written so that the computer is used to instruct the

Computer printout	Explanation
USER NUMBER -- <u>XYZ21</u>	My number is XYZ21.
SYSTEM -- <u>BASIC</u> NEW OR OLD -- <u>OLD</u>	The program I wish to use is written in the high-level language BASIC. It is a program stored at the time sharing computer.
OLD FILE NAME -- <u>LINPRO***</u>	Its name is LINPRO***.
WAIT	
READY	

Underlined values are typed in by the user, and are answers to the questions posed by the computer.

The message READY from the computer indicates that the program has been loaded onto it and that the user can now send the data relating the particular problem he has to solve.

Figure 10.2 Conversational mode used in time sharing

SIMPLE VARIABLE DEMAND AND FIXED LEAD TIME MODEL

1. Ring the statement DD = 2 if the Demand Distribution is Normal.

2. The standard lead times present in the program are 1, 2 and 4 periods, if lead times other than these are required this section must be completed.

   How many lead times are there? Enter the number and ring the statement 'NLT = '. (Maximum = 12.) NLT =

   What are they:

	L(1)	L(2)	L(3)	L(4)	L(5)	L(6)	L(7)	L(8)	L(9)	L(10)	L(11)	L(12)	
L =													*

3. The standard levels of service present in the program are 95, 97.5 and 99. If levels of service other than these are required, this section must be completed.

   How many levels of service are to be used? Enter the number and ring the statement 'NLS = '. NLS =

   Ring the codes of the levels of service to be used.

   K = 90 95 97.5 98 99 99.5 99.8 *

4. What output is required?

   Ring codes of the output formats required P =

   Print Item Description 1
   Print Expected Demands 2
   Print Safety Stocks 3
   Print Reorder Levels 4
   Print Reorder Quantity 5
   Print Average Stocks 6
   Print Stock Turns 7
   Print Average Stocks Value 8
   Plot Demand Data 9
   Print Total Average Stocks Value 11
   *
   Z

Figure 10.3 Part of questionnaire used to specify inventory package

user. Fig. 10.2 shows the question and answer approach adopted to select a linear programming package available through a computer terminal. In most instances the instructions for using the package would have to be read before the questions could be understood, but these instructions could be printed by the computer if it was so decided.

As an alternative to this procedure, which takes up time on the computer and can be expensive unless time sharing facilities are available, some packages are specified by means of a questionnaire. The questionnaire can be completed at leisure and then be punched onto cards or tape to be read into the computer to specify the parts of the package to be used. Fig. 10.3 shows the questionnaire which is used with the Urwick Group's General Inventory Program. Even with a questionnaire it is essential to know what the package does and to read the footnotes intended to make it easier to complete.

10.3. Applying the computer to make profit from figures

It is clearly possible to use a computer whenever a calculation has to be done, but it may not be economic although of course the computer can be quick, cheap and accurate under the right circumstances. Just how long will it take and what will it cost to write the program or to identify and be sure about the right package? Then, how long will it take before you can get access to either your own or a bureau computer, both of which are probably heavily booked? Don't forget either that you may well have a large amount of basic data to be punched and read into the computer before you can start. In spite of these difficulties the computer has played a significant part in making a profit out of figures, as the following illustrations show.

10.3.1. Multiple regression analysis

There is a clearly defined problem area in which one important characteristic has to be related to a number of other characteristics. This is done, firstly, to assess which of them is most strongly correlated with the important characteristic and, secondly, to provide an equation for estimating its value. There are many program packages covering this area and still more variations being developed. Consider as an illustration, a problem tackled by the package BMDO2R (used at a computer bureau) in which the branch profitability at each of 200 shops was related to the following eight characteristics:

X1 A measure of the population density at or near the shop.
X2 The number of employees at the shop.
X3 Turnover in sterling.
X4 Number of customers with monthly accounts.
X5 Rateable value of the shop.

X6 Turnover of automatic slot machines.
X7 A measure of the population affluence at or near the shop.
X8 Monthly mileage of delivery vehicles.

Data on all eight characteristics, and also on profitability, was collected for each of the 200 shops and punched onto each of 200 cards. The package was specified to give:

1. The average and standard deviation of each characteristic;
2. A table of correlation coefficients, the correlation matrix, showing their simple interrelationship;
3. A step by step build up of a multiple regression relationship; and,
4. The residuals (the actual profit minus the profit estimated by the relationship).

The averages and standard deviations are shown in Table 10.5 and the correlation matrix in Table 10.6.

Each figure in Table 10.6 is called a correlation coefficient and it measures the degree of correlation between a pair of variables. For instance, the correlation coefficient between the variables X2 (number of employees) and X3 (turnover) is 0.683. A zero correlation coefficient denotes a complete absence of an association, whereas a correlation coefficient of 1.0 (or – 1.0) denotes a

Table 10.5. Averages and standard deviations of characteristics

VARIABLE		MEAN	STANDARD DEVIATION
Y1	1	174.42499	125.29004
X1	2	0.80500	0.39719
X2	3	14.67000	21.82703
X3	4	13.36500	9.15260
X4	5	325.41992	366.05933
X5	6	39.95000	41.18745
X6	7	3.98500	18.68091
X7	8	32.75000	8.37777
X8	9	1.04500	0.62845

Notation	Characteristic	Unit
Y1	Shop profitability	(£10)
X1	Population density at shop	Arbitrary
X2	Number of employees	—
X3	Turnover	(£1000)
X4	Number of monthly accounts	—
X5	Rateable value	(£100)
X6	Turnover of slot machines	(£1000)
X7	Population affluence at shop	Arbitrary
X8	Monthly mileage of delivery vehicles	(10 000 miles)

perfect association between two variables. Even where there is no true association, the random pattern in the measurements can cause the correlation coefficient to be different from zero. However, since there are 200 shops, statistical tables show that a correlation coefficient in excess of 0.22 is highly unlikely to occur by chance. Table 10.6 shows that the correlation coefficient between X2 and X3 (0.683); between X2 and X4 (0.705); and between X2 and X5 (0.224) are all greater than 0.22. In fact, Table 10.6 shows that there is a high intercorrelation between the

Table 10.6. Table of correlation coefficients (correlation matrix)

Table of correlation coefficients showing the degree of inter-correlation between the variables (correlation matrix)

Variable	Y1	X1	X2	X3	X4
Y1	1.000	0.257	0.168	0.612	0.230
X1		1.000	– 0.073	0.170	– 0.024
X2			1.000	0.683	0.705
X3				1.000	0.549
X4					1.000

Variable	X5	X6	X7	X8
Y1	0.412	0.138	0.115	– 0.094
X1	0.224	0.108	0.163	– 0.085
X2	0.260	0.149	0.086	0.078
X3	0.520	0.289	0.210	0.037
X4	0.433	0.373	0.020	0.100
X5	1.000	0.306	– 0.104	0.175
X6		1.000	0.048	0.029
X7			1.000	– 0.072
X8				1.000

Coefficients of 1.000 denote perfect correlation, zero coefficients denote absence of correlation. Underlined values, in excess of 0.22, could not reasonably have occurred by chance.

variables X2, X3, X4, X5 and X6, all of which measure some aspect of the size of the shop. Further analysis is carried out to decide which of these variables provides the best means of predicting profit and to determine the form of the appropriate relationship.

This is done by adding one variable at a time into the multiple regression relationship. The computer first selects X3 (turnover), the variable which is most closely linked with the profit, Y1 and calculates the best straight line linking profit with turnover. It then tries each of the other variables in turn and adds the one which gives the best estimating equation, the one for which the standard deviation of the estimating errors (the standard error of the estimates) is least. This procedure is continued until all the variables have been added.

In this case the calculation of the relationship stopped at the third step as none of the further steps significantly reduced the standard error of the estimate. The printout for step number 3 is shown in Table 10.7.

Table 10.7. Final significant step in calculations

```
STEP NUMBER        3
VARIABLE ENTERED      9

MULTIPLE R                 0.7069
STD. ERRORR OF EST.     89.2998
```
(Standard error = 89.3 in units of £10, i.e. £893)

VARIABLES IN EQUATION

VARIABLE		COEFFICIENT	STD. ERROR
(CONSTANT		62.50453)	
X2	3	-2.63255	0.39810
X3	4	12.71090	0.94716
X8	9	-18.50839	10.10587

In other words:

Y1 (Profit in units of £10)

= 62.50
− 2.63 X2 (Number of employees)
+ 12.71 X3 (Turnover in units of £1000)
− 18.51 X8 (Monthly mileage of delivery vehicles in units of 10 000 miles)

The relationship calculated has the form:

Shop profitability (£) = 625 + 127 × (Turnover in £000)
− 26.3 × (number of employees)
− 185 × (monthly mileage of delivery vehicles in units of 10 000 miles).

This estimate has a standard error of £893, showing that there is still a very large amount of variability unexplained by these three characteristics—and incidentally by the other five characteristics which could not justify a place in the equation.

The computer program tabulated the residual (the actual profit minus the profit estimated by this equation) for each of the 200 shops and this is shown as a frequency diagram in Fig. 10.4. There were two shops with exceptionally high residuals indicating that exceptional factors were operating at them. An investigation was carried out to identify these and two different factors affecting the profitable siting of shops were identified. The remaining

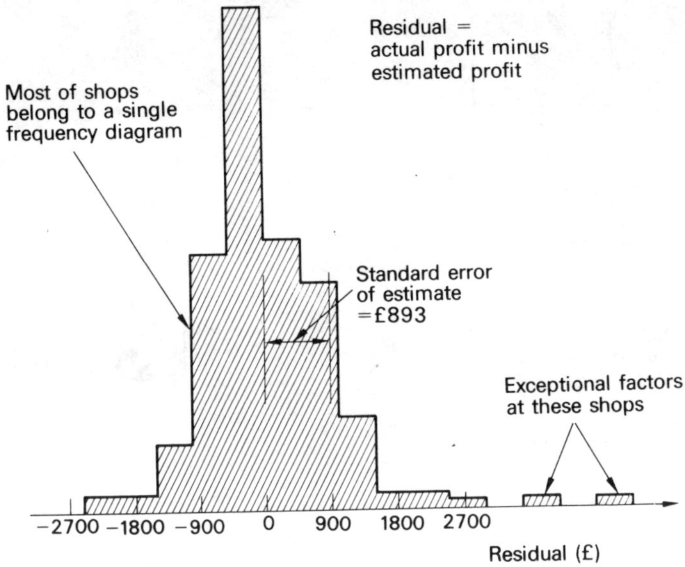

Figure 10.4 Frequency diagram of residuals. This shows the pattern of uncertainty remaining after the factors affecting profitability have been taken into account.

residuals were seen to belong to a single frequency diagram and no one shop could on this one analysis be separated from another.

The main conclusions coming from the above analysis are:

1. Profitability depends largely on turnover.
2. Efficient use of staff plays a significant role in increasing profitability.
3. The efficient use of delivery vehicles is also important, and,
4. After taking these three factors into account there was no shop with an exceptionally poor profitability record.

Although these figures were derived from a real-life situation, this situation has been heavily disguised to maintain anonymity, so these conclusions should not be taken at their face value.

10.3.2. Network analysis

The problem area tackled by network analysis is another well defined area in which package programs are very appropriate. The principal questions to ask are:

1. Which package is most suited by my particular needs?
2. Is it more economical to do the computation by hand, or by computer? and,
3. How long will I have to wait for the printout?

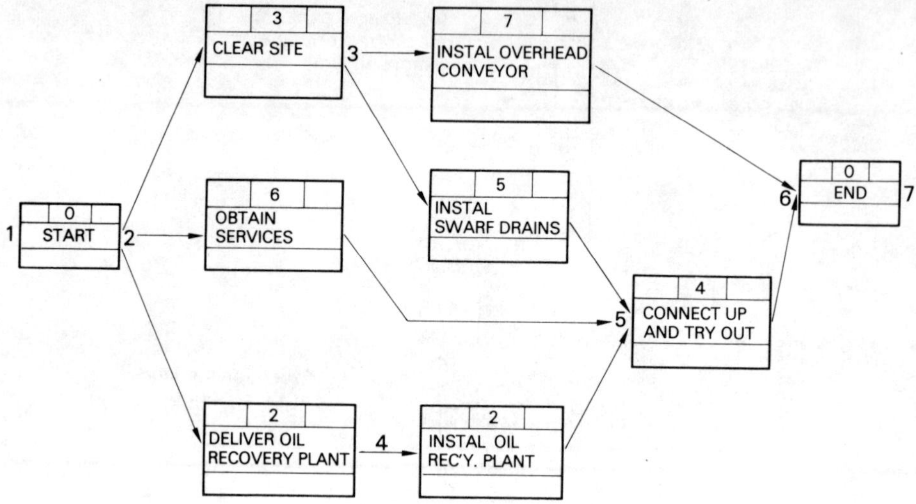

Figure 10.5 Numbering a flowchart network as a basis for computer calculation

Most package programs are able not only to calculate and print out the early and late start and finish dates for each activity together with total float and free float, but also they can print this information or any part of it. As a result, the project manager can have a complete picture of the project and yet supply each section foreman with a timetable of only those activities for which he is responsible. Provided that he is also told which activities are critical and which have an abundance of float, the section foreman has all the information he needs to plan the utilization of the resources at his disposal.

In order to feed a network into a computer, it must be broken down into individual activities and each activity labelled by two

Table 10.8. Form of computer input for simple network

Activity numbers	Description	Duration
1, 2	Start	0
2, 3	Clear site	3
2, 5	Obtain services	6
2, 4	Deliver or plant	2
3, 6	Instal conveyor	7
3, 5	Instal drains	5
4, 5	Instal or plant	2
5, 6	Connect and try	4
6, 7	End	0

Table 10.9. Systematic procedure for numbering flowchart networks for computer input

1. Place a number before the start and a number after the end of the network.
2. Number wherever there is more than one arrow leaving an activity.
3. Number wherever there is more than one arrow entering an activity.
4. Introduce a dummy activity (taking zero time) wherever an arrow is numbered both at its head and tail.
5. List the activities and dummy activities using two numbers to identify each activity, working in numerical order and observing where appropriate steps 6 and 7.
6. Wherever two activities would have the same identity introduce an additional number to remove the ambiguity.
7. Introduce additional numbers to identify activities within a chain, wherever necessary.
8. Identify and list dummy activities created by steps 6 and 7.

numbers. The first of these numbers comes before an activity and the second after it. Fig. 10.5 illustrates this form of numbering on the simple network used in chapter 7. The general form of the computer input is shown in Table 10.8. This list of activities tells the computer that the number 1 comes before the activity START and 2 after it. Consequently, all those activities which have 2 as the first of their activity numbers must wait until the activity (1, 2) is completed. The starting of (2, 3), CLEAR SITE; (2, 5), OBTAIN SERVICES; and (2, 4) DELIVER OIL RECOVERY PLANT depends on the completion of the activity (1, 2). It is in this way that the logic of the network diagram is developed within the computer program.

It was this problem of communicating the logic of the network to a computer which resulted in the arrow diagram notation, since an arrow diagram is extremely simple to number. In order to identify each activity in a flow chart form of network by a pair of numbers, a special procedure must be adopted. This systematic numbering procedure is shown in Table 10.9.

Part of the computer input data to a typical package program is shown overleaf in Table 10.10. In this program the department responsible for each activity is named and it is possible to accumulate resource requirements although the example used to illustrate this package does not make use of this capability.

The first form of output, shown in Table 10.11 on page 241, was a timetable printed in order of increasing total float, and within this in order of the early start time. This prints the critical activities first, identifying the critical path; then the semi-critical activities, and finally those well endowed with float.

Table 10.10. Computer input to typical package program for network analysis (part only)

NETWORK TITLE
PRODUCT LAUNCH

PREC EVENT	SUC EVENT	DESCRIPTION	TE	DEPT
6	40	PRODUCE ADVERTISING COPY	008	MRK
RESOURCES		MRK		
27	2	ADVERTISING CAMPAIGN "BUY"	012	MRK
RESOURCES		MRK		
29	3	PREPARE PRODUCT DESIGN	005	DES
RESOURCES		DES		
5	4	PREPARE DETAIL DRAWINGS	010	DES
RESOURCES		DES		
3	5	SALES APPROVAL OF PRODUCT DESIGN	001	MRK
RESOURCES		MRK		
5	6	ESTIMATE RATE OF SALES	001	MRK
RESOURCES		MRK		
14	7	PREPARE PROCESS PLANNING LAYOUT	005	PLN
RESOURCES		PLN		
15	8	MAKE PROTOTYPE	004	DES
RESOURCES		DES		
40	9	SALES APPROVAL OF ADVERTISING COPY	001	MRK
RESOURCES		MRK		
2	FINISH DUMMY		000	MFC
RESOURCES		MFC		

Table 10.11. Section of computer printout showing activities in 'critical path' order

REPORT SEQUENCE

TOTAL FLOAT/EARLY START

NETWORK TITLE

PRODUCT LAUNCH

PREC EVNT	SUCC EVNT	DESCRIPTION	DPT	TME EST	EARLY START	LATE START	EARLY FINISH	LATE FINISH	TOTAL FLOAT	FREE FLOAT
START	28	PREPARE INITIAL DEVELOPMENT SCHEME	DES	006	0	0	6	6	0	0
28	29	SALES APPROVAL OF INITIAL DEV. SCHEME	MRK	001	6	6	7	7	0	0
29	3	PREPARE PRODUCT DESIGN	DES	005	7	7	12	12	0	0
3	5	SALES APPROVAL OF PRODUCT DESIGN	MRK	001	12	12	13	13	0	0
5	4	PREPARE DETAIL DRAWINGS	DES	010	13	13	23	23	0	0
38	27	PRINT SERVICE MANUAL	PLN	008	35	44	43	52	9	9
10	24	SELECT AND TRAIN PRODUCTION MANPOWER	MFC	006	32	42	38	48	10	10
10	26	SELECT AND TRAIN INSPECTOR MANPOWER	MFC	008	32	42	40	50	10	10
6	16	SELECT SALESMEN	MRK	012	14	25	26	37	11	0
16	39	TRAIN SALESMEN	MRK	002	26	37	28	39	11	0
39	23	ESTABLISH DISTRIBUTION NETWORK	MRK	012	28	39	40	51	11	11

KEY
= ACTIVITY
- - - - = FLOAT

NETWORK TITLE
PRODUCT LAUNCH

SCHEDULED AT EARLIEST START

PREC EVNT	SUCC EVNT	ACTIVITY	DEPT RES
START	28	PREPARE INITIAL DEVELOPMENT SCHEME	DES
28	29	SALES APPROVAL OF INITIAL DEV. SCHEME	MRK
29	3	PREPARE PRODUCT DESIGN	DES
3	15	MAKE MODELS	DES
3	5	SALES APPROVAL OF PRODUCT DESIGN	MRK
5	4	PREPARE DETAIL DRAWINGS	DES
5	6	ESTIMATE RATE OF SALES	MRK
6	16	SELECT SALESMEN	MRK
6	40	PRODUCE ADVERTISING COPY	MRK
40	9	SALES APPROVAL OF ADVERTISING COPY	MRK
15	8	MAKE PROTOTYPE	DES
9	27	ADVERTISING CAMPAIGN "WATCH FOR"	MRK
14	7	PREPARE PROCESS PLANNING LAYOUT	PLN
16	39	TRAIN SALESMEN	MRK
8	36	DEVELOP AND TEST PROTOTYPE	DES
8	38	PREPARE SERVICE MANUAL	DES
39	23	ESTABLISH DISTRIBUTION NETWORK	MRK
7	30	PREPARE PURCHASE LIST	PLN
7	32	TOOL DRAWING	PLN
7	34	PREPARE ASSEMBLY LAYOUTS	PLN
7	35	PREPARE INSPECTION LAYOUTS	PLN
36	37	MODIFY DRAWINGS	DES
30	17	ORDER BOUGHT OUT PARTS	PLN
32	18	TOOL MANUFACTURE	PLN
34	19	OBTAIN ASSEMBLY TOOLING	PLN
35	20	OBTAIN INSPECTION TOOLING	PLN
37	10	MODIFY PROCESS PLANNING LAYOUT	PLN
10	26	SELECT AND TRAIN INSPECTOR MANPOWER	MFC

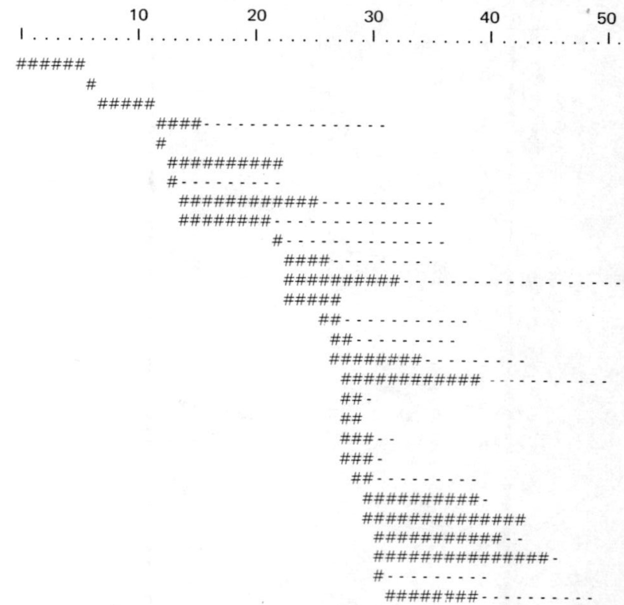

Figure 10.6 Bar chart form of printout for network analysis

A further option allows the timetable to be printed out in bar chart form, as illustrated in Fig. 10.6. Very many project teams are accustomed to working from these bar charts. Moreover, by specifying the resources used by each activity the manpower needed to start all activities at their early time can be evaluated. This particular package would carry out these calculations and prepare a list similar to that at the bottom of Fig. 7.17 (page 168), but as previously mentioned this option was not selected in this instance. Table 10.12 shows a further alternative, a list of the

Table 10.12. Timetable of early start times for manager of design department

DESCRIPTION	DEP	EARLY START	TIME EST
PREPARE INITIAL DEVELOPMENT SCHEME	DES	0	6
PREPARE PRODUCT DESIGN	DES	7	5
MAKE MODELS	DES	12	4
PREPARE DETAIL DRAWINGS	DES	13	10
DUMMY	DES	23	0
MAKE PROTOTYPE	DES	23	4
DUMMY	DES	23	0
DEVELOP AND TEST PROTOTYPE	DES	27	2
PREPARE SERVICE MANUAL	DES	27	8
MODIFY DRAWINGS	DES	29	2

activities for which the manager of the design department was responsible together with their early start times and time needed to complete each of them. A similar list was prepared for the managers of the other three departments involved.

Should the project be reviewed at regular intervals throughout its life, it is only necessary to prepare a list of the changes. These would principally be changes in time estimates, either for activities completed or activities still outstanding. Major changes in the structure of the network, needed to bring the project back onto schedule can also be made and these will require an alteration in the activity numbering. Extreme care is needed in preparing the activity list to ensure that the activities do form a viable network both on the initial run on the computer and also when the structure of the network is altered.

It should be obvious that there is a lot of work to be done before a computer can be used and in simple networks the best course is to carry out the calculations by hand. Furthermore, there will almost always be serious delay before the results are available from the computer, unless special arrangements can be made to book the computer facility in advance.

Various estimates have been given of the point at which it is necessary or economical to switch from clerical methods to a computer package. These can only be a guide since the ease of using a computer and the benefits of its use will vary in importance from project to project, even within a single company. The computer scores because it can print the results of the network calculations simply and clearly; it can provide alternative forms of output at little extra cost; it can provide each manager with a timetable for the activities for which he is responsible; and it makes the updating of project plans a very simple task indeed.

A further field in which computer packages have been developed is the preparation of project timetables which ensure that the resources needed do not exceed the resources available. In view of the uncertainty of resource availability throughout the project and of the uncertainty of when the resources will be needed, these programs should only be used to provide a broad brush check on the feasibility of the proposed programme.

Finally, in those instances where a large project is undertaken at very infrequent intervals, the use of a computer package can provide a means of augmenting the project staff for the limited period of the project.

10.3.3. Linear programming

The problem area in which the linear programming technique is appropriate is yet another well defined area. It is reasonably straightforward (as was shown in chapter 8) to structure a suitable problem so that the technique of linear programming can be applied. Consequently, the package programs available from computer bureaux and computer manufacturers are capable of handling the straightforward cases. The calculations associated with linear programming are sufficiently complicated and repetitive that the solution of any problem of worthwhile size is only feasible on a large computer.

A typical package will print out not only the solution to the problem, but also indicate both the range of cost or profit values

Phase 1 SET UP PROGRAM

```
USER NUMBER--XYZ21
SYSTEM--BASIC
NEW OR OLD--OLD
OLD FILE NAME--LINPRO***
WAIT

READY.
```

Set up computer to do linear programming calculations.

Phase 2 FEED IN DATA

```
10000 DATA .086,.087,.076
10001 DATA 0,     .296,.111
10002 DATA .265,.551,.149
10003 DATA 1,     0,     0
10004 DATA 0,     1,     0
10005 DATA 0,     0,     1
10006
10007 DATA 17000,24300,45200,35000,100000,200000
10008
10009 DATA .25, .28, .13
RUN
```

Feed in the data of particular problem:

i. Constants on left-hand side of six restrictions on resources.
ii. Constants on right-hand side of restrictions.
iii. Unit values of profit contribution.

(See pages 200 to 207 for the formulation of the problem)

Phase 3 SPECIFY DETAIL

```
LINPRO   9:47   LNDN C 23/10/68

TYPE '2' FOR OUTPUT OF TABLEAUS AND BASIS
AT EACH ITERATION, '1' FOR THE BASIS ONLY,
OR '0' FOR JUST THE SOLUTION. WHICH? 0

WHAT ARE M AND N OF THE DATA MATRIX? 6,3

HOW MANY 'LESS THANS','EQUALS','GREATER THANS'? 6,0,0
```

i. Choose either to printout detail of calculation or just the solution.
ii. How many restrictions? How many products (variables)?
iii. Type of restrictions?

Phase 4 SOLUTION

```
YOUR VARIABLES 1 THROUGH 3        (products)
SLACK VARIABLES 4 THROUGH 9       (spare capacity)

ANSWERS:
```

VARIABLE	VALUE	
3	158511.	– make 158511 units of Star
5	93.9852	– spare capacity of material P is £94
2	22335.6	– make 22335 units of Torch
1	35000	– make 35000 units of Gleem
8	77664.4	– spare sales capacity on Torch is 77664 units
9	41489.5	– spare sales capacity on Star is 41489 units

OBJECTIVE FUNCTION VALUE 35610.3 – estimated contribution is £35 610

Figure 10.7 Use of linear programming package

and the range of the limiting values of the restrictions over which the solution is valid.

Fig. 10.7 shows how a program package available on a time sharing computer was used to solve the problem specified in chapter 8 (pages 200 to 207).

Although linear programming is a field for experts, there is a significant role for management to play:

1. In ensuring that the logic of the constraints and the profit or cost equation is if not exact, at least a reasonable approximation to the truth.
2. In checking that the data compiled for the equations is free from serious error and,
3. In ensuring that what comes out of the computer is turned into a practical and profitable solution.

10.3.4. Production planning and control

The structure and form of production planning and control vary from company to company and are specifically related to the production facilities concerned. Because of the immense variety of production facilities and the way in which they are organized, they are difficult to classify, but at the very least the several categories shown in Table 10.13 exist. In fact, in many companies two or more of the above categories exist side by side. It is highly unlikely, therefore, that any package program can hope to meet the needs of all of these and the few companies who have moved in this direction have written their own computer programs.

Clearly linear programming has immediate potential for planning the use of limited resources in process industries such as an oil refinery, and network analysis potential for the control of one-off and very small batch manufacture. Other tools of production planning to which a computer can be profitably applied are:

(a) Short term forecasting;
(b) Explosion of the demand for finished products into demand for raw materials, components, machine hours and labour hours; and,
(c) Control of stocks of raw materials, components and finished goods.

(a) *Short term forecasting.* The calculations involved in short term forecasting by exponential smoothing are straightforward and can be learned and applied by any intelligent clerk. However, it is easy to make mistakes in the calculations particularly as plus and minus signs have to be watched carefully. Moreover, staff

Table 10.13. The varied nature of production planning and control

Type of manufacture	Example of application	Production planning and control problems
One-off	Shipbuilding, civil engineering	Co-ordination of many designers, suppliers, assembly and testing teams. Ensuring progress against plan.
Small production batches	Jobbing engineering, house building, fashion clothing	Estimating times for design and manufacture; train operators; estimate cost; purchase materials; allocate resources to competing jobs; deadlines; fixed sequence of working; capacity for unplanned work.
Assembly of standard products, either in batches or flowline	Machine tools, automobiles, mass produced clothing	Almost certainly manufacturing to supply from stock. Forecasting demand; batch sizes; ensuring supply of components; controlling work in progress and finished stock.
Processing industries, either operating in batches or continuously	Brewing, papermaking	Storage limitations of raw material, work in progress and finished stock; efficient use of limited production facilities.

leave and computation skills, although they may be straightforward, have to be learned by the new staff.

When more sophisticated forms of exponential smoothing are used and particularly if they are applied to forecasting the demand for a large number of items the use of a computer is desirable. When the demand for each of a thousand or more items is being forecast it becomes essential. This is a field of application in which the computer can be used to provide both the skills of computation and the capacity to carry them out.

When a company is using a computer to carry out order processing, it is a natural and logical step to extend this to make a short term forecast if a short term forecast is a reasonable basis for production planning. (A short term forecast is clearly redundant when orders are known with certainty sufficiently far in advance to plan the supply of raw materials, component manufacturing and assembly within the current delivery time).

As an illustration of the preparation and use of short term forecasting consider the procedures adopted in a textile manufacturing company, and shown in Fig. 10.8.

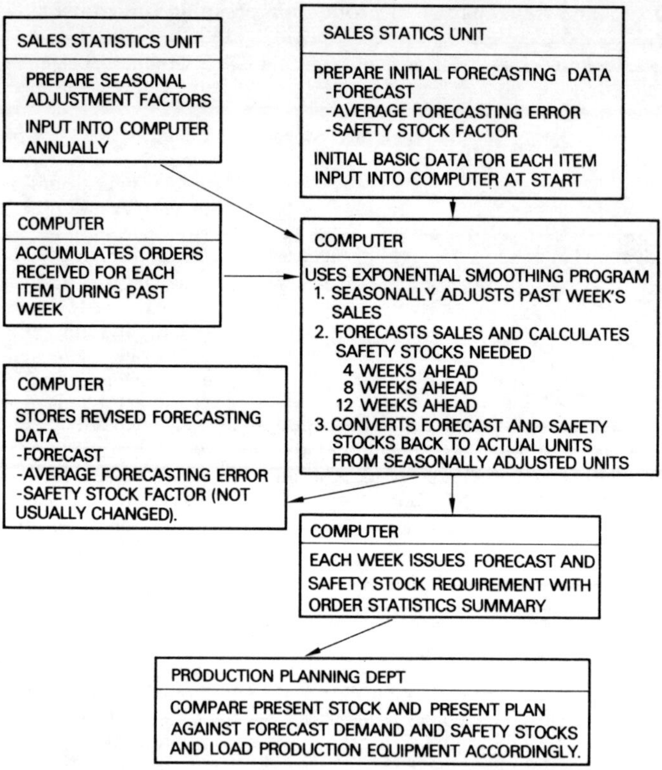

Figure 10.8 Outline of sales forecasting for production planning

To start exponential smoothing, initial forecasts and measures of the average forecasting error have to be provided and these are done manually for each item. The safety stock factor is chosen once only, although different levels of protection against stock run out are used for different product groups.

In this application the seasonality is reassessed annually by the sales statistics department, and revised seasonal adjustment factors introduced. A specially written computer program then takes over and uses the actual orders received week by week to prepare a forecast of demand and safety stocks over four, eight and twelve weeks into the future. This information is used by the production planning department to load production equipment so as to meet the demand of the customer as far as possible and as efficiently as possible with the resources at the company's disposal.

When the next week's order figures become available the same procedures are adopted to update once more the forecast and the safety stocks required. However, in this case there is no need for the sales statistics unit to provide the basic forecasting data. It was revised during the previous forecast and is already stored in the computer. On all subsequent occasions the forecasting data will be updated by the computer, unless there is a major change calling for manual revision.

(b) *Order explosion.* Translating an order for a product into the demand for components and raw material requirements is ideally suited to a computer application—provided that the effort of setting up the computer programs is justified by a sufficient degree of repetition. Technically, the computer is quite capable of breaking down orders into component detail, but the important questions to ask are 'How much will it cost?' and 'How big are the savings?' The most likely criteria for a successful application are:

(i) The existence of a properly structured part number code common to both design, production and service departments.
(ii) The manufacturing level at which each component is needed is clearly specified.
(iii) There are correct and up to date lists of where each part is used, particularly when parts are used in several products, assemblies or sub-assemblies.
(iv) Sound procedures exist for identifying and incorporating amendments.
(v) Spoilage records exist to ensure that adequate provision is made to replace defective work.

In practice, the major problem is not the computer program but the preparation of the above sets of data and keeping them up to date.

(c) *Stock control.* The example of forecasting and safety stock calculation in a textile manufacturing company (Fig. 10.8) showed how stock and production control are closely linked in most manufacturing companies. There are instances where production is controlled by the simple 'two bin' system in which a constant re-order quantity is issued as a works order when the finished stock level falls to a specific re-order level. In one such application a specially written computer program was used at a computer bureau to set the re-order levels for several hundred different stock items and to revise these every twelve months.

A slightly more sophisticated computer program is used to calculate re-order quantities and re-order levels for a distributor who has no production problems of his own. His suppliers'

Table 10.14. Data needed for each stock item to set re-order quantities and re-order levels

Supplier's identification code
Serial code number
Part number
Unit price
Carton quantity
Quantity sold for each of past twelve months
Delivery time in days of past six suppliers' deliveries

production problems are mirrored in their lead times, which can vary quite typically from one week to ten or twelve weeks with an average of three weeks; furthermore, the demand for each item varies to about the same extent as do the lead times. The distributor has about fifty branches each carrying about 6000 different stock items, the bulk of which are slow moving items. The re-order quantities and the re-order levels for the 'trivial many' were determined by a quick but appropriate set of ready reckoner type tables. The values for the 'important few', in this case about 15 per cent of the total number of items stocked, were calculated by computer. All re-order quantities and re-order levels are revised every six months to ensure that they are up to date. In the case of the important few, the computer program uses exponential smoothing to revise estimates of the average monthly

Table 10.15. Basic stock control data calculated by computer (left hand side of computer printout)

SUPPLIER CODE = 15

ANNUAL DEMAND £ RETL	ANNL DMND	RE-ORDER QTY	RE-ORDER LEVEL	CODE	PART NAME
983	358	15	50	10	XYZ1234
660	293	12	37	20	XYZ2345
568	252	11	23	30	XYZ3456

VALUE OF TOTAL AVERAGE STOCK £875.42

demand, the average lead time in months, and measures of the variability in demand and lead times.

The data needed by the computer to carry out these calculations, in addition to that built into the computer program is shown in Table 10.14. It includes a regular measurement of delivery lead times, an objective measurement of which is seldom made.

The result of the computer calculations (see Table 10.15), namely the information needed for control, is printed for each item on the left hand side of the computer printout.

The right hand side of the printout shown in Table 10.16 consists of the basic data which is needed to maintain a file of records. It also has space in which to enter new demand and lead time data at the next six monthly review. In other words the computer prints its own input documents.

In this company the stock records are kept on cards and the re-order quantities and re-order levels are written on the cards. When the stock balance falls to the re-order level, the re-order quantity is written onto the appropriate suppliers order pad and the accumulated orders are sent to the suppliers once a week.

Table 10.16. Computer output is source document for computer input (right hand side of computer printout)

Write last *six* monthly demands here

Write last *three* lead times here

```
             RETAIL           SUPP.      ORDER          CARTON
PART NAME    PRICE            CODE       FREQ.            QTY
             SHILL.

XYZ1234        55.0            15.        1.                1
                                            XXV     XXV    XXV
  XXXXA XXXXA XXXXA XXXXA XXXXA XXXXA
               29.8*         1127.5*     0.492*         0.328*
```

(Values followed by asterisk are summary measures of past demand and past lead times)

```
XYZ2345        45.0            15.        1.                1
                                            XXV     XXV    XXV
  XXXXA XXXXA XXXXA XXXXA XXXXA XXXXA
               24.5*          760.8*     0.327*         0.215*


XYZ3456        45.0            15.        1.                1
                                            XXV     XXV    XXV
  XXXXA XXXXA XXXXA XXXXA XXXXA XXXXA
               21.0*          753.4*     0.170*         0.042*
```

The last *six* monthly demands are written in space *above* XXXXA
The last *three* lead times (in days) are written in space *below* XXV

The level of mathematical skill is such that, without the computer to determine the re-order levels, this company could not hope to obtain adequate control of its stock investment and the service it is providing to its customers. The cost of punching cards for input and calculation by the computer amounts to only £30 for 1000 stock items.

10.4 Which computer to use

It is highly likely that in the management services department within large companies there exist all the skills needed to apply the company's own computer to tackle all but the most sophisticated problems. The medium sized and smaller companies have to find from one source or another, the skills of

(a) Formulating the problem so that mathematical or statistical techniques can be applied;

(b) Identifying suitable packages, modifying them if possible, or writing special computer programs;

(c) Collecting the basic data needed to solve the company's own particular problems; and,

(d) Interpreting the results contained in the computer output, and turning them into practical action plans.

Most computer bureaux provide advice about the packages which they supply, and are capable of modifying them, of writing additions to them, or of writing special programs for the user. However, once you start asking for individual treatment the costs of program writing and testing mount up rapidly.

A half-way house between owning your own computer, and using a bureau on infrequent occasions is the data terminal. The data terminal usually consists of a teleprinter typewriter which can be used to punch paper tape. The data and the programs can be fed into the computer either directly from the typewriter keyboard or by reading in prepared data tape. All you do is phone up a time-sharing computer and carry on from there as though the computer were your own. The rental of the terminal is reasonably modest, and you are only charged for the actual time for which you have used the computer.

Input and output through a teleprinter typewriter is relatively slow, but this is unimportant for program testing and for straightforward 'profit from figures' applications. Should you wish to carry out a large simulation or routine data processing the limitations of such a terminal are excessive and suitable facilities would need to be sought at a computer bureau.

The companies providing these 'time sharing facilities' have a number of package programs available and in addition the user can store his own programs so that they are ready to use on the time sharing facilities. Moreover, the telephone system allows you to connect the terminal to any time sharing facility and this provides a choice of several alternative sets of packages.

10.5. Unleashing the potential of the computer

It should be clear from the previous sections that whenever calculations have to be done, a computer can be used instead of pencil and paper or a calculating machine. It should also be clear that unless you can prepare instructions, that is write computer programs, the hardware of the computer is a useless and expensive piece of electronic equipment. We are reaching the stage now where everyone involved in complex calculation should be capable of writing simple computer programs in one or other of the high level languages. Any manager should be able to use a data terminal, or should have a secretary capable of writing in this particular form of shorthand. Moreover, it should be just as natural to find out the availability of computer packages as to refer to a management handbook. Only when this stage is reached will the true potential of the computer be realized.

The applications which have been described have tended to look inwards, at increasing the profitability of existing operations. How much more valuable could the computer be, if a manager could use it to simulate the many possible alternatives facing a company. Mathematical models of companies are few and far between, but where they have been built and explored by means of a computer the investment in time and money has paid off handsomely.

However, remember that a computer does not question the system embodied in the computer program, it just follows it. There is no point in having a management system designed from a distance; the manager who does not ensure that he has got what he wanted, does so at his peril.

Finally, investment in using a computer is just another form of capital investment. It should be examined in the same way that all other capital investment is examined and the following questions asked:

Is it cheaper?
It is quicker and more accurate and so produces savings by eliminating mistakes? and,
Is it sufficiently flexible?

List of terms used

Computer
Exponential smoothing
Simulation
Linear programming
Multiple regression analysis
Printout
Computer program
Paper tape
Magnetic tape
Punched cards
Reader
Teleprinter unit
Hardware
Software
Machine language
High level programming language
Compiler
Average
Standard deviation
Package, program package
Network analysis
Stock control
Smoothing constant
Frequency diagram
Programming
Computer terminal
Time sharing facilities
Computer bureau
Correlation coefficient
Correlation matrix
Residuals
Standard error
Total float
Free float
Computer input
Critical activity
Arrow diagram
Flow chart form of network
Critical path
Forecasting
Average *forecasting error*
Safety stock
Seasonality
Two bin system
Re-order quantities
Re-order levels
Lead time

Italicized terms are defined in the glossary (page 262) as well as in the text where it is appropriate.

11. A summary and an estimate

11.1. Management and people

Management means getting things done through people. What should be done, when it should be done and how, are the questions a manager has to answer. This book has been concerned with techniques designed to help him to do a better job in deciding 'what', 'when', and 'how'. However, since people are involved, the techniques of recruitment and selection, of organization and motivation are just as essential. Even in areas which seem inanimate such as sales forecasting, stock control, or quality control, people are involved, people who must be motivated to seek a better way, to accept change and to be fully involved in bringing it about. For make no mistake about it, increasing the profitability of a company means change, preferably of course change based on measurements, correctly chosen and analysed.

11.2. A summary

11.2.1. The basic tools

Measurement is essential to scientific management, but because it is measurement in an area of inevitable changes and fluctuations the resulting figures are almost always subject to considerable unpredictable variation. Under these circumstances the pattern of the measurements taken as a whole, in the form of a frequency diagram, becomes the basis for deciding policy. It is important to realize that the uncertainty in these measurements can be handled. The maxim is 'measure the variability and look for a way of making a profit from it'. The way will almost certainly mean ignoring the variation in the individual measurements and looking at them as a whole. Pareto's law of the 'important few and the trivial many' arises naturally when looking at measurements in some of the areas critical to a company's operating—provided you are willing to stand back, ignore the identity of the individual observations and study them as a group.

Because measurements play such an important role in modern management (they could and probably should play a part in every serious decision), it is highly desirable that the effort which goes into collecting them and into analysing them should be carried out as efficiently as possible. The use of samples can speed up and cheapen the cost of data collection: the main problem with their use lies in ensuring that the sample truly represents the 'population' from which it was taken. Methods of avoiding systematic bias exist, and the unrepresentativeness which could arise because of the size of the sample can be measured in the same way as the uncertainty or variability in any measurement. Careful use of sub-samples can give an answer and a measure of its reliability in all circumstances.

The analysis of figures to extract some profit from them is carried out by isolating and measuring the systematic variation in the figures. This systematic variation could mean, for example, that the sales in January are always lower than the sales in July. It could also mean that the sales are increasing systematically with time. Once the nature of the systematic variation is known it can be taken into account in decision making. The unpredictable variation, the random variation in the figures, will still remain to be measured and accommodated by means of a frequency diagram designed to show its effect not on individual measurements, but on them as a whole.

Another important role played by measurements is in the control of a company's performance. Control in this instance means measuring performance, comparing against a standard and taking action when the measure of performance is truly different from the standard set. Because of the inevitable fluctuations in the measurements, the standard should be set in the form of a frequency diagram, a frequency diagram which not only allows for the amount of variation to be reasonably expected but also shows up the exceptional circumstance calling for management action.

11.2.2. Putting the tools to work

Within every department there are problems of collecting and analysing measurements and also of monitoring performances against standards. There are also more general problem areas, typified by the tasks of forecasting and planning.

The tools of making a profit from figures are put to work in an analytical approach to forecasting demand. In this approach the pattern of seasonal demand is measured and an allowance made for the systematic differences through seasonal adjustment of the demand figures. Then the systematic pattern over a period of time in the seasonally adjusted figures is used as a basis for forecasting. Finally, since all forecasting is subject to some uncertainty, the amount of the uncertainty in the forecast is measured. This measure of uncertainty could be as important as the forecast itself since it can be used to indicate on the one hand the amount of safety stock needed, and on the other the amount of flexibility needed in the scale of the company's operation.

The analytical approach to planning differentiates between those instances where a quick response can be made once the performance against plan is known and those where such a response would be too late. In the latter instances the plan must be drawn up with a built in buffer against the uncertain outcomes. In the former, adaptive measures may be used and the plan is adapted as the results of current achievement against the plan become known, in order to meet the requirements of the project.

A large number of the problems of choice which face management have been tackled theoretically. There are theoretical solutions in such problem areas as:

(i) Putting in the right bid on contracts;
(ii) Making the right choice in balancing conflicting costs, for example in deciding how far to increase the size of the quantity ordered for stock and so reduce the cost of ordering stock, since fewer orders will inevitably cause the cost of holding stock to rise;
(iii) Ensuring a better balance from one stock item to another in the level of service provided from stock.

These solutions may well not produce the optimum benefits claimed by the specialist, however, there is a very good chance that they are better than the ad hoc solutions which have just 'growed like Topsy'.

There are some problems which do not fall simply to a theoretical approach but which may be examined by building a mathematical model and seeing what would happen in various circumstances by means of the technique of simulation. Provided the manager plays a significant role in developing the mathematical model of the situation, the results of a simulation are usually simple to understand both where they come from and what they mean.

11.2.3. The role of computers

Computers provide power to do the calculations involved in making a profit from figures, and in some instances they also provide speed. If the calculations are such that a program package can be used they can be done with very little effort. High level languages have simplified the job of writing computer programs and special languages and questionnaires developed to facilitate special applications. The choice between using a data terminal linked to time sharing computer facilities, using a computer bureau, or using the company's own computer must be made on economic and practical grounds. The principal question is how much technical assistance is needed to formulate the problem and programming assistance to get it onto the computer. Where time is of prime importance, the delay in writing and testing the program may mean that an existing program package has to be used. The availability of a suitable program package could well decide which specific computer bureau to choose.

Table 11.1. Queuing principles and management

Principle	Management implication
Service capacity must exceed arrival rate.	Plan to have spare time.
Control the number of arrivals in fixed time period.	Keep an appointment book. Plan work ahead, limit unscheduled work.
Schedule arrivals but avoid queues going underground.	Plan ahead to avoid rushed meetings. Deal with all callers—not everything falls inside the plan. Notify all concerned of your future programme.
Increase service channels and flexibility of server.	Develop subordinates. Let them make decisions, with guidance if needed. Check on their performance.
Make service time constant not variable and so reduce waiting time.	See people regularly before big problems arise. Avoid long committee meetings, delegate long jobs. Also avoid frequent short interruptions—save them up and deal with them in batches.
Reduce length of service time.	Evaluate and improve your own performance: reduce reliance on memory: check records are useful, available, and sufficient.
Do preparatory work before demand arises, but avoid wasted endeavour.	Be fully briefed on problems before the appropriate meeting. Avoid detailed thinking too far ahead, it inhibits concentration on current problems.
Break large queues before they form.	Do not overload yourself; avoid regular overtime; be ready to work late in an emergency.

11.3. Topics for another occasion

It is inevitable that some of the profitable areas for using the tools of making a profit from figures are omitted from this book. It is also inevitable that it has not covered all the potential tools. For instance, the mathematical theory of queues, which was originally applied to study the capacity of telephone systems, has resulted in standard tables of waiting times and of plant or operator utilization. These tables are of considerable value in the design and management of supermarkets; in judging the efficiency of machines when one operator looks after many machines; in the

Table 11.2. Cybernetic principles and management

Principle	Implication
1. Filter out faulty data.	Have several sources of information: When using samples, scrap the two extreme results, average the remainder.
2. Produce only information of significance and relevance.	Instead of a detailed status report, ask only for the exceptions.
3. Get reliable results by the use of redundant systems.	In areas of doubt, the consensus of a number of independent assessors improves the quality of the estimate. (Assessment teams in job evaluation).
4. Used damped corrections to eliminate 'hunting'.	Already applied in exponential smoothing. Avoid overcorrecting in all control situations.
5. The whole can be more than the sum of its parts.	Concentrate on company strategy and tactics. Don't be put off by departmental jealousies.
6. A system can be designed to improve itself.	The need for review and the setting of new targets.
7. A system can be designed to improve performance.	The use of adaptive techniques to seek more profitable operating conditions.

design of appointment systems for hospital consultants. The management implications of some of the principles of queuing theory, which are shown in Table 11.1, are an interesting and valuable aspect of this work.

A further topic which has been omitted is the impact of the theory and application of control engineering on the design of management control systems. Several of the simpler principles have been used in earlier chapters and a list of some seven principles and an assessment of their implication in management are given in Table 11.2.

A detailed study of the stability of control systems of the kind found in industry, commerce and government is obviously of considerable potential benefit particularly when parts of the control system are being operated, either independently of one another or possibly even in conflict.

11.4. Future development

This assessment of the future for the tools of making a profit from figures is a subjective one, and heavily biased by personal experience. There appear to be moves taking place to improve the quality of management information and to replace subjective assessments of performance by objective measurements in more and more fields of management activity.

There is an appreciation that managers require forecasts of what is likely to happen, rather than historical records however accurate they may be.

There is a gradual realization that having more and more figures available does not necessarily help. The Pareto principle of the 'important few' is soundly established but not the methods of identifying the true exception by comparing it against the pattern of a frequency diagram.

There is still an immense profit potential so far untapped and it is inconceivable that the thrusting manager in his search for more profitable methods of management is going to leave them undisturbed.

So far the automation of tactical decisions has been limited to a few areas, mainly stock control and resource scheduling. There are still a large number of companies who can move in this direction: there are still many areas of tactical decision which can be decided by general principles rather than a series of personal judgements.

Finally, the use of mathematical models to help companies to make strategic decisions is growing and growing. In my judgement, there will be a major development of this work and principles of management and of model building will intertwine like the honeysuckle and the ivy. All the techniques are available. Their greater use will lead to further simplification and this in turn will snowball into greater and greater use.

11.5. Getting the profit

The aim of this book has been to draw management's attention to some of the principles and some of the applications of the tools of making a profit from figures. The use of measurements to improve the quality of management, and the interpretation of these measurements is not an end in itself, although improving the quality of management should result in a company meeting the objectives for which it was established in a more profitable way.

There is an economic angle in all of the applications discussed, and experience has shown that the profit arising from the first applications of the tools of making a profit from figures can be very considerable. Clearly, there must be a potential for profit improvement, there must be losses either hidden or clearly visible before large savings can be achieved. One of the responsibilities of management is to ensure that these tools are applied in areas of greatest profit potential.

There are for the manager several by-products of using these tools: the satisfaction that the job is being done in the best possible way; the greater confidence which arises from using control systems based on fact, rather than on judgement alone; and a lowering of the tensions and pressures arising from putting management problems in perspective.

List of terms used

Sales *forecasting*
Stock control
Quality control
Variability
Pareto's law
Sample
Population
Systematic bias
Sub-sample
Reliability of estimate
Systematic variation
Random variation
Frequency diagram
Planning
Analytical approach
Safety stock
Adaptive methods (measures)
Level of service from stock
Mathematical *model*
Simulation
Computer
Program package
High level language programming
Computer program
Data terminal *(Time sharing)*
Time sharing facilities
Computer bureau
Resource scheduling

Italicized terms are defined in the glossary (page 262) as well as in the text where it is appropriate.

Glossary

This glossary covers only those terms which have been used in more than one chapter. Definitions of *italicized items* in the text of the glossary are contained within it.

ADAPTIVE METHODS—methods of controlling investigations or *projects* in which the results of the trials or the progress to date are taken into account in *planning* future work.

ARROW DIAGRAM—a graphical method of representing the sequence of the activities in a *project* in which an arrow is used to represent an activity; used in *network analysis*.

AVERAGE, ARITHMETIC AVERAGE, MEAN—the sum of a number of observations divided by the number of observations.

BUFFER STOCK—stock held with the specific purpose of damping out the fluctuations in either supply or usage.

CENTRAL VALUE—the value about which the observations in a *frequency diagram* are scattered.

COMPUTER BUREAU—an organization which offers for hire the services of a computer. It often provides a comprehensive advisory service and assistance with writing *computer programs* and the preparation of data in a form suitable for computer input.

COMPUTER PROGRAM—a set of instructions, written in a special code, which enables a computer to carry out specific calculations or manipulations.

CONFIDENCE LIMITS—the limits of *reliability of an estimate.* 90 per cent confidence limits determine the bracket within which the true value being estimated should fall 90 times in 100.

CONTROL LIMITS—the limits on a control chart within which the measure being monitored could reasonably be expected to vary.

CORRELATION COEFFICIENT—a measurement of the closeness of the relationship between a pair of variables. A zero correlation coefficient denotes a complete absence of an association, whereas a correlation coefficient of 1.0 (or −1.0) denotes a perfect relationship between the two variables.

CORRELATION MATRIX—a table of *correlation coefficients* (each showing the degree of closeness of relationship between a pair of variables), for all the possible pairs of variables.

COUNTING (DISCONTINUOUS SCALE)—the simplest form of assessing a performance in quantitative terms is to count the number of occasions the performance fails to meet a specific standard. The resulting observations fall on a discontinuous scale 0, 1, 2,. . . .

CRITICAL ACTIVITY—an activity in a *project* which must be started and finished without delay if the project is to be completed on time.

CRITICAL PATH—a chain throughout a *project* built up by the *critical activities.*

EXPONENTIAL SMOOTHING—a method of calculating an average value in which extra weight is given to more recent results; used in sales forecasting.

FLOW CHART FORM OF NETWORK—a graphical method in which a circle or a rectangle is used to represent an activity and an arrow to represent the sequence of the activities in a *project.*

FORECASTING—making an estimate of what is likely to happen in the future. A forecast should not be confused with a plan or a target.

FORECASTING ERROR—the difference between the forecast result and the actual result.

FREE FLOAT—the amount of spare time on a chain of activities in a *project* which must be used up on that chain.

FREQUENCY DIAGRAM—a method of visualizing a set of observations as a whole, based on the frequency with which specific observation values are repeated.

FREQUENCY DISTRIBUTION—the theoretical shape to which a *frequency diagram* would approximate if a very large number of observations were collected.

HIGH LEVEL PROGRAMMING LANGUAGE—a method of writing *computer programs* using straightforward phrases and mathematical symbols.

JOB EVALUATION—an analytical approach to comparing the relative worths of different jobs.

LEAD TIME—the time between deciding that an item needs to be ordered and its receipt into stock.

LINEAR PROGRAMMING—a mathematical method of determining optimum operating conditions in a situation constrained by several restrictions.

MEASUREMENT (CONTINUOUS SCALE)—a method of assessing a performance in quantitative terms in which the performance is compared against a continuous scale. Because the fineness of the division between alternative observations can be small, measurement provides a sensitive means of comparing performance.

MEDIAN—the value of the middle observation in a set of observations when the observations have been placed in order of increasing value.

MODEL, (MATHEMATICAL MODEL)—the representation of a management or operating situation by mathematical and logical rules coupled with measurements and other facts relevant to that situation.

MONITORING—the comparison of performance or of relevant data against standards.

MULTIPLE REGRESSION ANALYSIS—a statistical technique for calculating the best relationship between one characteristic and several other characteristics.

NETWORK ANALYSIS—a group of techniques for planning *projects* in which the sequence of the activities in the *project* is represented by a network. A principal feature is the identification of the *critical activities* in the project.

NORMAL DISTRIBUTION (NORMAL FREQUENCY DISTRIBUTION)—a symmetrical, bellshaped *frequency distribution.*

PACKAGE, PROGRAM PACKAGE—a *computer program* designed to carry out specific calculations or manipulations and which can be hired or purchased from its originator.

PARETO'S LAW—the law of the 'important few and the trivial many'. When dealing with figures relating to wealth, (or similar characteristics), a small percentage of the figures (10 per cent to 20 per cent) account for a large percentage of the wealth (80 per cent to 90 per cent).

PLANNING—the preparation of a plan to achieve objectives in the future.

POISSON DISTRIBUTION—a theoretical *frequency distribution* appropriate when information is collected by *counting* rather than by *measurement*.

POPULATION—the whole or the entirety from which a *sample* is drawn and which a *sample* should truly represent.

PRECISION, LEVEL OF—the degree of repeatability of an estimate. A high level of precision in an estimate does not necessarily mean that the estimate is accurate, but that a very similar estimate would be made on all subsequent occasions.

PROJECT—a group of activities linked together by a common objective, and a time at which the project is completed.

QUALITY CONTROL—methods used to ensure that a satisfactory level of quality is being achieved and to provide assurance that both raw materials and components and also the product shipped to the customer are of acceptable quality.

RANDOM—completely unpredictable. Random fluctuations and random variation are completely devoid of a predictable pattern other than that of a *frequency diagram* .

RANDOM NUMBERS—a series of numbers the value of any one of which cannot be exactly predicted from the remainder. Usually applied to random numbers in which each digit 0, 1, 2 . . . 9 has an equal chance of arising.

RANGE—the difference between the largest and the smallest values of a series of observations.

RELIABILITY OF ESTIMATE—synonymous with *precision*; the degree of repeatability of an estimate or the degree of confidence in the repeatability of an estimate.

RESOURCE PLANNING, SCHEDULING—matching the resources needed on a *project* with the resources available to it.

SAFETY STOCK—stock carried to cover for above the average demand and above the average length of delivery (or *lead*) time.

SAMPLE—a proportion or part of a whole. Ideally, should be selected to represent the whole as closely as possible.

SAMPLE PLAN, SAMPLING PLAN—a procedure for deciding whether or not to accept a batch of work on the basis of a sample.

SEASONALITY, SEASONAL PATTERN—*systematic variation* in sales or order figures arising when particular quarters or months have high or low results compared with other quarters or months and this is repeated year after year.

SEASONALLY ADJUSTED—sales or order figures from which the *seasonality* has been eliminated.

SIMULATION—a method in which a *mathematical model* is used to examine a particular situation under certain chosen conditions and in the face of *random* variation.

SMOOTHING CONSTANT—a constant between 0 and 1 used in *exponential smoothing*, the smaller the constant the more weight is given to the past and the less to the most recent result. Values between 0.1 and 0.3 are usually used in practice.

STANDARD DEVIATION—a standard measure of the variability of a set of observations, based on the difference of each observation from the *average*.

STANDARD ERROR—a standard measure of the uncertainty of an estimate, usually applied to an *average*. The equivalent of the *standard deviation* of the estimate, if this estimate were repeated on a number of occasions.

STOCK CONTROL—methods used to ensure that a satisfactory level of stock is carried, namely just sufficient to provide the desired level of service.

SUB-SAMPLE—a part of a *sample*. It is good practice separately to select and analyse several sub-samples since this not only ensures that the *sample* is representative but also provides a simple measure of the *reliability of the estimate* provided by the *sample.*

SUCCESSIVE DIFFERENCE—the numerical difference between two consecutive numbers in a sequence of such numbers.

SYSTEMATIC—completely predictable. Systematic *variation*, systematic differences follow a completely predictable pattern.

TIME SHARING FACILITIES—a specially designed computer system which allows several people to use a computer at the same time from their own offices. Data and *computer programs* can be fed into the computer over an ordinary telephone line using a teleprinter or similar terminal. The service is usually provided by a specialist *computer bureau.* Users only pay for the computer time they use plus telephone charges at usual rates.

TOLERANCES—limits applied on a characteristic of a product showing the maximum allowable deviation from the specification.

TOTAL FLOAT—the amount of spare time on an activity which if exceeded will result in the *project* being delayed.

TWO-BIN SYSTEM—a system of *stock control* in which two bins are used for each stock item The first bin is used to satisfy demand until it is empty. An order is then placed and the second bin is used to satisfy demand until the order is delivered.

VARIABILITY; VARIATION; SCATTER—these are three terms with the same meaning, used to describe the differences which occur in repeated observations. This variability may be *random* or *systematic*—in practice it is often a combination of both.

WORK SAMPLING—a method of assessing the nature of activities being carried out and of delays arising based on a *sample* of observations each made at a specific instant.

Reading list

This reading list is intended for those who wish to go to a greater depth than is possible in this book. Only a limited number of titles is given in each field: these are the books which the author has found most useful.

Sampling

Deming, W. E., *Sample Design in Business Research*, John Wiley and Sons, Inc., New York and London, 1960

Data analysis

Davies, O. L., (Editor), *Statistical Methods in Research and Production*, Third Edition, Oliver and Boyd, London, 1957

Cuming, H. G. and Anson, C. J., *Mathematics and Statistics for Technologists*, Heywood Books, London, 1966

Moroney, M. J., *Facts from Figures*, Penguin Books, Harmondsworth, 1951

Monitoring

Anson, C. J., *Quality Control as a Tool for Production*, Fourth Edition, British Productivity Council, London, 1969

Woodward, R. H. and Goldsmith, P. L., *Cumulative Sum Techniques*, Oliver and Boyd, London, 1964

Forecasting and stock control

Coutie, G. A., Davies, O. L., Hossell, C. H., Millar, D. W. G. P., and Morrell, A. J. H., *Short Term Forecasting*, Oliver and Boyd, London, 1964

Brown, R. G., *Statistical Forecasting for Inventory Control*, McGraw-Hill, New York, 1959

Magee, J. F., and Boodman, D. M., *Production Planning and Inventory Control*, Second Edition, McGraw-Hill, New York, 1967

Linear programming

Vajda, S., *The Theory of Games and Linear Programming*, Methuen, London, 1956

Network analysis

Lockyer, K. G., *An Introduction to Critical Path Analysis*, Third Edition, Pitman, London, 1969

Simulation

Tocher, K. D., *The Art of Simulation*, English Universities Press, London, 1963

Computers

Tatham, L., *The Use of Computers for Profit*, McGraw-Hill, London, 1969

Index

Printed in Great Britain by William Clowes & Sons Limited, London, Colchester and Beccles